Sir John Skelton

The Table-Talk of Shirley

Reminiscences of and Letters from Froude, Thackeray, Disraeli...etc.

Sir John Skelton

The Table-Talk of Shirley
Reminiscences of and Letters from Froude, Thackeray, Disraeli...etc.

ISBN/EAN: 9783744735032

Printed in Europe, USA, Canada, Australia, Japan

Cover: Foto ©Thomas Meinert / pixelio.de

More available books at **www.hansebooks.com**

The Table-Talk of Shirley

Reminiscences of and
Letters from Froude
Thackeray Disraeli
Browning Rossetti
Kingsley Baynes Hux-
ley Tyndall and Others
by John Skelton C.B.
LL.D.

"I have far more dead friends than living."

Dr JOHN BROWN.

William Blackwood & Sons
Edinburgh and London 1895

EXPLANATORY.

*T*HIS *little venture does not owe its genesis or its exodus to a public demand, or " the entreaties of friends."* A *spell of indifferent health last spring (1894) was the* origo mali. *Unfit for any exacting exercise of the brain during the evening (my only leisure for literature, other than blue-books), some half-dozen bulky bundles of old letters were taken from obscure pigeon-hole and secret drawer, and when the dust had been wiped off, and the cobwebs cleared, each bundle was untied and its contents drilled into some semblance of order—personal and chronological. Since Spring, Death has been busy—busy as on a battle-field; and here-after from more than one of the writers no more pleasant* *epistles will bring, as they were wont to bring (in these gloomy winter days), a glimpse of sunshine into our glen. But many of the letters (though yellow with age) are yet so fresh and animated, and so characteristic of the men who wrote them, in one or other of their many moods (moods pensive or whimsical it might be, but never unbecoming or unworthy), that it seemed a pity to put them back on their shelves. I may be mistaken in thinking that they disclose new traits of tenderness, fidelity, or generosity; but even if I am in error, the publication can do no harm to the living or to the dead; and I am happy to find occasion to say that some at least were life-long friends. So with such comment as is needful and such omissions as are fitting, with kindly greeting to Those who remain and a fair Goodnight*

To Those who have left us,

they are now in Mr Blackwood's most convincing and persuasive type presented to the more or less indulgent reader.

S.

CONTENTS.

TABLE-TALK OF SHIRLEY.

───◆───

I.

MAINLY ABOUT THE PROLOGUE.

A GOOD many of our friends, English as well as Scotch, know the Castle Hill. It is part and parcel of the famous ridge on which Edinburgh Castle stands. The castle from a military point of view has ceased to be of service; I suppose modern weapons of precision could pound it into a jelly in the course of a forenoon; though as an impregnable keep it played no mean part in our national history. From the artist's point of view, however, it is still intact, or nearly so. Rude hands have been laid upon it, no doubt; it is no longer reflected in the Nor' Loch, and huge barns have been built for barracks; but, somehow, it won't spoil. Even the barns, looming dimly through the smoke-cloud which still hangs over "Auld Reekie," become, if not too closely watched, august and venerable. The site impresses its own distinction upon them. But the outlook from the Castle Rock is quite as striking as the rock itself; and it is possibly for this that I mainly value it. The amateur architects of the War Office may build unsightly barracks, but they cannot vulgarise that spacious amphitheatre. The Lothian plain, and the Pentlands, and the blue Firth from Inchkeith to the Isle of May, and Arthur's Seat, and the Lomonds, and the Ochils, and far-off Ben Ledi, are to mortal weapon absolutely invulnerable. And then the busy city at our feet, and the murmur of its multitudinous life! There is no such coign of vantage elsewhere; no eminence where the past and present are so closely mated; or whence a wider bird's-eye view can be had. "He lives very high up in Gordon's Court," Sydney Smith said of the grave Francis Horner, "and thinks a good deal about mankind." But the Castle Hill is quite as commanding as Gordon's Court, and even better suited for the contemplation of mankind. Here, then, let us rest a bit—the modest tea-kettle meantime singing sedately on its hob—for such brief and occasional discourse as befits a rambler,—here, in the upper story of this old grey house, which has seen much famous company in its time, and round which the December twilight is closing in, as ages ago it closed in round Mary Stuart during that bitter and fateful December of 1566. "Ages ago;" but the primitive passions do not grow out of date; and indeed to those

who have counted their sixty winters, and seen them
fall away as softly and silently as the snow-flakes fall,
five times sixty is but the other day. "Thus we play
the fools with the time, and the spirits of the wise sit
in the clouds and mock us." But to-day they must
not mock. For to-day the marriage bells are clashing
merrily, and the fair young bride goes forth on the
well-trodden road with hope in her heart and a new
light in her eyes. There are flowers, and wedding
favours, and troops of friends, and the winter sun
shines kindly on old and young who have been bidden
to the feast.

> "Nor count me all to blame if I
> Conjecture of a stiller guest,
> Perchance, perchance, among the rest,
> And tho' in silence, wishing joy."

* *
*

I wonder sometimes if Mary Stuart, when within the
Castle walls, cared much, or at all, for the fair landscape which was spread out before her, as on a map.
The taste for the picturesque, we are now told, is
distinctively modern. Some highly artistic people
indeed appear to hold that it is not older than Mr
Ruskin, just as some political people appear to hold
that English history is not older than the Reform Bill.
It was the "Oxford Graduate," they tell us in effect,
who first opened our eyes to the fact that mountains,
and valleys, and waterfalls, and Swiss chalets, produce

a pleasant impression on the senses. While we may admit that the passion for mountaineering is of comparatively recent growth, there are passages in Hebrew poetry and Greek drama which seem to show that the writers were not insensible to natural beauty. I am rather inclined, however, to think that about the time of the Reformation, the great mountains and the deep valleys between them, in which we rejoice, were regarded with repugnance by cultivated people. The highways, even in the level parts of Europe, were indifferent, and the Alpine tracks were wellnigh impassable. So that the mountains themselves came to be regarded simply as obstacles to traffic,—places which honest wayfarers, lay and clerical, found unnecessary and inconvenient. That, at least, was the view taken by the Bishop of Ely and Lord Montagu, who were sent as an embassy, by " bloody Mary," to the Pope, and who visited Mary Stuart at Fontainebleau, in the year 1555. They crossed the Alps by the Mont Cenis. " Passing over the great Mountain Cenis I was fain to hire one to lead my horse up before me, and I to come after him, holding by the tail, for fear of falling backwards, it was so steep to the top. There was such a noise of water beating upon the rocks, and such monstrous mountains to behold, of a huge height, being always in danger of some stone falling upon us, that *it seemed rather a hell than a highway to pass in.*" But the taste for the wilder aspects of nature had begun to revive a century at least before Mr Ruskin was born ; and even the poet Gray, to whom the trim lawns of England were dear, would spend his holidays among the lakes and mountains of the North—just as we do. Some of the descriptive passages in his letters indeed might not have been quite out of place in *Modern Painters*. He paid a visit to Lord Strathmore, at Glamis Castle, during the summer and autumn of 1765, where he saw something of the Perthshire Highlands. Here are a few scraps from a letter to Dr Wharton : " The ground now grew unequal ; the hills more rocky seemed to close in upon us, till the road came to the brow of a steep descent, and (the sun then setting) between two woods of oak, we saw far below us the river Tay come sweeping along at the bottom of a precipice, at least 150 feet deep, clear as glass, full to the brim, and very rapid in its course. It seemed to issue out of woods thick and tall, that rose on either hand, and were overhung by broken rocky crags of vast height ; above them to the west the tops of higher mountains appeared, on which the evening clouds reposed. . . . Next day we set forward to Taymouth, twenty - seven miles further west ; the road winding through beautiful woods, with the Tay almost always in full view to the right, being here from three to four hundred feet over. The Strath-Tay, from a mile to three miles or more wide, covered with corn and spotted with groups of people then in the midst of their harvest ; on either hand a vast chain of rocky mountains, that changed their face and opened something new every hundred yards, as the way turned, or the clouds passed. In

short, altogether it was one of the most pleasing days
I have passed these many years, and at every step I
wished for you. . . . The road is excellent, but
dangerous enough in conscience, the river often running directly under us at the bottom of a precipice
200 feet deep, sometimes masqued indeed by wood,
that finds means to grow where I could not stand;
but very often quite naked and without any defence;
in such places we walked for miles together, partly
for fear, and partly to admire the beauty of the country,
which the beauty of the weather set off to the greatest
advantage. . . . But my paper is deficient, and I
must say nothing of the Pass itself, the black river
Garry, the Blair of Athol, Mount Beni-gloe, my return
by another road to Dunkeld, the Hermitage, the Stra-
Brann, and the rumbling Brigg.   In short since I saw
the Alps, I have seen nothing sublime till now."

Gray had been among the Alps themselves with
Horace Walpole in 1739, and from his description of
the ascent to the Grande Chartreuse we may learn
how he regarded them : " It is six miles to the top;
the road runs winding up it, commonly not six feet
broad ; on one hand is the rock, with woods of pine-
trees hanging overhead, on the other a monstrous precipice, almost perpendicular, at the bottom of which rolls
a torrent, that sometimes tumbling among the fragments of stone that have fallen from on high, and
sometimes precipitating itself down vast descents with
a noise like thunder, which is still made greater by
the echo from the mountains on each side, concurs to

form one of the most solemn, the most romantic and
the most astonishing scenes I ever beheld; add to
this the strange views made by the crags and cliffs
on the other hand; the cascades that in many places
throw themselves from the very summit down into the
vale and the river below; you will conclude we had
no occasion to repent our pains."

All this is quite modern in a way; and yet, in
another way, it is a world away from us. Is it the
insistent note of sadness that is wanting? Compare
it with Matthew Arnold's *Stanzas from the Grande
Chartreuse* :—

> " Knock ; pass the wicket ! thou art come
> To the Carthusian's world-famed home ; "

or even with this extract from an old letter by Mr
Ruskin, now lying before me: " I climbed the Old
Man yesterday in curiously sunny and sweet air—
staying half an hour at the top.   It is two miles as the
bird flies from the lake shore, and 2400 feet up—which
means a very fair walk, and I find myself a good deal
better for it this morning.   Only I'm always good for
nothing in the evenings, and I find them rather sad,
all alone."   One cannot help feeling that the easy-
going comfort - loving eighteenth century had sometimes rather the better of *us* to whom "the something
that infects the world" is an ever-present burden—of
which, unlike Christian, we cannot divest ourselves.

*   *
*

We appear to have lost the taste for Prologues. Yet the prologue was once considered the most interesting part of the play. A prologue by Dryden drew the whole town; it was talked of at every coffee-house where the wits gathered; some of his best-known lines are to be found in his prologues; those, for instance, in which he indicates his preference for the loyal Oxford :—

> " Oxford to him a dearer name shall be
> Than his own mother-university.
> Thebes did his green unknowing youth engage ;
> He chooses Athens in his riper age : "

or those in which he pays a courtly compliment to the Duchess of York on her return from Scotland :—

> " When factious rage to cruel exile drove
> The Queen of Beauty and the Court of Love,
> The Muses drooped, with their forsaken arts,
> And the sad Cupids broke their useless darts.
> But now the illustrious nymph returned again,
> Brings every grace triumphant in her train."

A collection of the prologues of the last century would furnish a sparkling commentary on the social life of the time, and one wonders that it has not been made. But fashions change, and we have now only Prefaces and Prospectuses. The change is hardly to be commended; the *press* is more exacting and harder to please than the *pit;* it must have been a treat besides to listen to the most trivial or stilted verse declaimed with charming animation by a Woffington or a Bracegirdle. We must learn, however, to be content

with what is left us, and the unspoken prelude is not to
be despised. The overture to a musical piece is sometimes more suggestive than the completed work. It is
an intimation of what is coming, though the promise is
not always fulfilled. A finer note is occasionally struck
at the outset than is ever afterwards "recaptured."
And as youth is glorified by the pleasure of anticipa-
tion, so the prologue to poem or romance—nay, even
the prospectus of a limited company—has something of
the same attractive uncertainty. Will the promised
harvest be reaped, or will it end in insolvency and
liquidation? I have a note of the prologues which
have most impressed me since I began collecting thirty
years ago; Thackeray figures in the list, as does Mr
Ruskin, Lord Dufferin, the author of *Mark Rutherford*,
Rudyard Kipling, and many others who have only this
bond in common. There are epilogues too; but the
epilogue is too often the confession of failure and defeat, as indeed the preludes themselves sometimes are.
Here, for instance, is the first edition of Mr Ruskin's
Notes on his Turner drawings. The epilogue breaks off
abruptly—"left by Mr Ruskin in an incomplete state
at the time when he was taken ill," we are told; but he
had been able to finish the prelude before the cloud
came down, and these are its closing words. Sadder
words I think were never written. The date and place
are given—" Brantwood, 12th February 1878 ":—

"Morning breaks as I write, along those Coniston
Fells, and the level mist, motionless and grey beneath
the rose of the moorlands, veils the lower woods, and

the sleeping village, and the long lawns by the lake-
shore.

"Oh, that some one had but told me, in my youth,
when all my heart seemed to be set on these colours
and clouds, that appear for a little while and then van-
ish away, how little my love of them would serve me,
when the silence of lawn and wood in the dews of
morning should be completed; and all my thoughts
should be of those whom, by neither, I was to meet
more."

* *
*

The contribution of another great master of "our
English" to my collection is now almost as rare as the
books printed in Scotland three centuries ago, and
which for the most part have been *read* out of existence.   It is the leaflet in which Mr Thackeray
announced that he was about to commence the publication of a Magazine, to be called *The Cornhill.* The
date is "Nov. 1, 1859." Only Thackeray could have
written this delightful "foreword,"—in fact, it is
Thackeray all over. I suppose the copyright (if it
ever existed) has long ago expired, and that it may be
reprinted without fear of interdict or inhibition. How
characteristic is such a passage as this:—

"Our Store-House being in Cornhill, we date and
name our Magazine from its place of publication. We
might have assumed a title much more startling: for
example, 'The Thames on Fire' was a name suggested; and placarded in red letters about the city

and country, it would no doubt have excited some curiosity. But, on going to London Bridge, the expectant rustic would have found the stream rolling on its accustomed course, and would have turned away angry at being hoaxed. Sensible people are not to be misled by fine prospectuses and sounding names : the present writer has been for five-and-twenty years before the world, which has taken his measure pretty accurately. We are too long acquainted to try and deceive one another ; and, were I to propose any such astounding feat as that above announced, I know quite well how the schemer would be received, and the scheme would end.

"You then, who ask what *The Cornhill Magazine* is to be, and what sort of articles you shall supply for it ?—if you were told that the Editor, known hitherto only by his published writings, was in reality a great reformer, philosopher, and wiseacre, about to expound prodigious doctrines and truths until now unrevealed, to guide and direct the peoples, to pull down the existing order of things, to edify new social or political structures, and, in a word, to set the Thames on Fire ; if you heard such designs ascribed to him — *risum teneatis?* You know I have no such pretensions : but, as an author who has written long, and had the good fortune to find a very great number of readers, I think I am not mistaken in supposing that they give me credit for experience and observation, for having lived with educated people in many countries, and seen the world in no small variety; and, having heard me soliloquise, with so much kindness and favour, and say my own say about life, and men and women, they will not be unwilling to try me as conductor of a concert, in which I trust many skilful performers will take part."

* * *

Lord Dufferin has done much since he wrote his *Letters from High Latitudes*, but he has done nothing better. While, among great books of travel, it cannot compare with *Eōthen* (which is indeed a finished work of art, entitled to rank with the classics of our literature), its fresh and brilliant gaiety is still undimmed. The lines addressed *To the Figurehead of the Foam*, with which it opens, are as nimble and graceful as the little craft herself, and quite in character. This "sculptured image of as sweet a face as ever lighted up an English home" smooths, as Aphrodite herself might have smoothed, their path before them :—

"What marvel then if—when our wearied hull
  In some lone haven found a brief repose,
Rude hands, by love made delicate, would cull
  A grateful garland for your goddess' brows?

What marvel if their leader, too, would lay
  His fragile wreath of evanescent rhyme
At her dear feet whose image cheered his way,
  And warmed with old home thoughts the weary time?

When as he watched that sculptured lifelike smile,
  Through many an anxious hour of arctic gloom,
Its magic influence would half beguile
  The bleak and barren ocean tracts to bloom—

> With well-remembered woods, and Highland hills
> That cluster round a castle's stately towers ;
> And gleaming lawns, and glens, and murmuring rills,
> Where Edith plays amid the summer flowers !"

It is a tuneful and graceful prelude (with its ripple of laughter and touch of tender trifling), and ranks with the best. Who "Edith" may be we dare not venture to guess, any more than we can guess to whom Mr Rudyard Kipling addresses the dedicatory lines :—

> "The long *bazar* will praise—but Thou—
> Heart of my heart, have I done well?"

*   *
*

"Youth on the prow, and Pleasure at the helm," would have made a fit motto for Lord Dufferin— the Lord Dufferin of 1857. But in the remarkable books of the author of *Mark Rutherford* the "bloom of young desire and purple light of love" have no place. In them there is no room for the play of animal spirits. Though this sombre and powerful writer is in his own bleak and unlovely domain without a peer, it is difficult to account quite satisfactorily for the impression that he produces. To what is the fascination of his relentless inquisition into the spiritual ailments of unlettered nonconformity to be attributed? The light that falls upon the squalid company is not exactly lurid ("lurid" is rather too suggestive of stage-fire, if not of the pit), but it has a gloomy

intensity. There can be no doubt of the reality of
the conflict — a conflict as strenuous as Christian's
with Apollyon; and the record is drawn with uncom-
promising directness and pitiless simplicity. Had
John Bunyan lived in our slums among free-thinkers
and socialists, his story might have taken some such
turn. The prelude to *Mark Rutherford* is as striking
as the book itself, and may be regarded, indeed, as
its epitome. It strikes the note which is preserved
throughout.

> " 'There is no deed which I have done,
> There is no love which I have won,
> To make them for a moment grieve
> That I this night their earth must leave.'
>
> Thus, moaning at the break of day,
> A man upon his death-bed lay ;
> A moment more and all was still ;
> The Morning Star came o'er the hill.
>
> But when the dawn lay on his face,
> It kindled an immortal grace ;
> As if in death that Life were shown
> Which lives not in the great alone.
>
> Orion sank down in the west
> Just as he sank into his rest ;
> I closed in solitude his eyes,
> And watched him till the sun's uprise."

* * *

Let me close these selections with one taken from
a bright little volume which came to me the other

day. It is the prelude to Miss Symonds's *A Doge's Farm*, which she was writing when her father, who had been her companion in year-long wanderings by Alp and Apennine, died suddenly at Rome.

To

MY FATHER,

JOHN ADDINGTON SYMONDS.

"O Love, we two shall go no longer
To lands of summer across the sea."
TENNYSON.

That is all; but it is admirably effective and touching, though, of course, the prelude to *The Ring and the Book* has not yet been matched, nor is like to be :—

" O lyric love, half angel and half bird,
And all a wonder and a wild desire."

*   *
*

To-day, when, for good or for evil, the account of the Nineteenth Century is about closed, the century of prologues and epilogues begins to look remote. I am not sure that, at the bar of history, the pre-eminence, the literary pre-eminence, of our own sixty or seventy or eighty years will be admitted without protest or challenge. I have been reading a very admirable book by Mrs Oliphant, which somehow neither public nor critic has adequately appreciated, in which the douce and shrewd Eighteenth Century gets, as I think, scant justice. But indeed Mrs

Oliphant's view is not singular; is on the contrary
shared by many to whose judgment I readily defer—
when I agree with it.

* *
*

It has been said that its poetical style and methods
were stilted and artificial : and it is condemned accordingly. No ridicule can be too keen for a generation
which went into raptures over Pope's balanced couplets.
But if we regard it as an age in which the rational as
opposed to the romantic temper was skilfully and
sedulously cultivated, it seems to me that a good deal
may be said for the defence. The English literature
of the Eighteenth Century reached its highest level
in its *prose*. Hardly before the reign of good Queen
Anne, had Englishmen obtained a perfect mastery of
their mother tongue. Of course there were great prose
writers before her time—the prose of Jeremy Taylor
and Sir Thomas Browne is luminous and splendid—
but in the mere elementary matter of constructing
sentences they are often (if not as a rule) cumbrous
and involved. They want ease, simplicity, and directness. Now the prose of Swift, of Addison, and of
Goldsmith, is eminently easy, simple, and direct; and
I do not think that we can be said to have made any
appreciable advance, in these respects at least, since
they wrote. The tracts which Mr Gladstone discharged
at Lord Beaconsfield are not to be compared for finished invective with those which Lord Bolingbroke

directed against Walpole. But what of its poetry?
The finest poetry of Pope, it may be admitted at once,
is just the finest talk of the day, done into epigrammatic invective and epigrammatic eulogium. It is the
didactic and rationalistic spirit of the time presented
to us in a new form—the metrical. I cannot think
however, that poems which, though utterly destitute
it may be of the true lyrical movement, yet represent
in a not ignoble fashion, but on the contrary with the
brilliant distinction of a brilliant and potent pen, the
great movements of a great age—its soldiers and its
statesmen, its philosophy, its politics, and its social
life—are unworthy of our admiration. On the other
hand, let it be frankly recognised that the substance
of this poetry is prose, and that it seldom or never
ascends into the pure heaven of the imagination.
That the poetical style of Wordsworth is more natural
and unaffected than the poetical style of Pope, may
be admitted even by those who doubt whether it is as
natural and unaffected as (let us say) the prose of
Swift and Goldsmith. So that the change which
Cowper and Burns and Wordsworth effected, by sub-
stituting a more direct simplicity of speech for the
French polish of their predecessors, does not go very
deep—if that were all. But the change of style was
only a *symptom*,—a symptom of a change of spirit.
The romantic idealism which Puritanism and the Whig
Revolution had crushed into country parsonages and
Border peels was once more to make itself felt—not
in Border ballads only. The nation which had been

feeding itself for fifty, or sixty, or seventy years upon
the arid husks of Whig constitutionalism, was suddenly
roused by the first Pitt into the conception of a warmer
and more ideal patriotism.   It has been said that Lord
Chatham was almost the only man of his time who
read *The Faery Queen;* and it would not perhaps be
over-fanciful to maintain, that to him and to what he
did the renewal of our poetical life can be not remotely
ascribed.   But the genius of modern poetry, sole sitting by the shores of old Romance, did not draw her
inspiration exclusively or even mainly from the past.
She was taken possession of by a fiercer spirit, which
gave fire to her dreams and intensity to her music.
She represents the modern democracy as well as the
medieval minstrelsy.   This child of the Revolution,
who might have preached a Crusade, belongs to neither
age, or rather to both.   She has the mystical aspira-
tions of the one and the passionate directness of the
other.   What would the contemporaries of Pope have
thought of such a verse as this?—

> " This song was made to be sung at night,
> And he who reads it in broad daylight
> Will never read its mystery right,
> And yet—it is childlike easy."

Of all that is here implied they knew nothing,—they
were absolutely ignorant of those dim and obscure
pathways of the spiritual life on which the light of
common day does not shine.   Yet without its mystery
and its gloom, without its ideality and its romance,

modern poetry would cease to be characteristic. But then a revolutionary gospel, such as democracy is, insists upon a solemn and almost monumental simplicity of feeling and directness of expression. A rotten dynasty of kings and poets might be permitted to invoke the Loves and the Graces and the Muses; but those who proclaimed that human nature was always and everywhere the same, and who saw in the meanest hind a man and a brother, had no patience for laborious trifling. The tragedy of life could play itself out in a hovel as in a palace; and the characters in which it was recorded should be such as all could read. From these contrasted but interwoven influences none of the new poets escaped. The romantic force might be stronger in one, the revolutionary in another; but Wordsworth, Coleridge, and Scott, as well as Byron, Shelley, and Keats obeyed, consciously or unconsciously, and each in his own fashion, the inevitable impulse.

*   *
*

They are all great names to us still, however the tide of fame may ebb or flow hereafter. Mrs Oliphant has said many true and admirable things about each of them; but it strikes me that she is less than just to Scott and Keats. Scott became as rapidly popular as Byron; but whereas Byron's is complete and lasting, "Scott's can hardly be called a *genuine* poetical fame." *Don Juan* is, I admit, the most plastic, brilliant, and

vigorous "criticism of life" in our language, and Sir
Walter certainly could not have written *Don Juan*.
In that tremendous outbreak of the cruelly wounded
spirit we have, unfortunately, Byron at his best, and I
cannot at all agree with Mrs Oliphant when she says
that "according to all the laws of growth and development Juan should have come first and Childe Harold
later." Compared with the mature art and the bitterly
incisive insight of Don Juan, Childe Harold is absolutely boyish; and so also are the Giaours, and the
Laras, and the Corsairs, and the Parasinas who took
the world by storm. If Mrs Oliphant means to maintain
that this sickly and monotonous refrain upon a single
string is superior in any way to *Marmion*, and *The Lord
of the Isles*, and *The Lady of the Lake* (with their bright
and varied life and their high and martial music—as of
the sound of a trumpet), I can only say that I do not
agree with her. Byron like Shelley was one of the
distinctly revolutionary forces of the age—a mighty
elemental force; and after a period of neglect we are
again beginning to admit that he is also one of our
greatest singers; but in the placid strength and garrulous simplicity of Sir Walter there is something
of the Homeric calm to which Byron, restlessly and
recklessly egotistical, never attained.

*   *
   *

Nor do I think that Mrs Oliphant has formed any
quite adequate conception of the immense greatness of
Keats. That this apothecary's apprentice should have

given us, before he was well out of his teens, some of the most absolutely faultless poems in the language—faultless as a shell or a crystal—does not seem to strike her as very wonderful. It is hardly too much to say that not one immature line came from his pen; that his lyrical perfection of style and form has never been excelled; that the unfinished *Hyperion* moves on in nobly sustained majestic march, until the pen is dropped with an unavailing sigh, and the poet disappears into darkness like his own dejected King of Day;—

> " Then with a slow incline of his broad breast,
> Like to a diver in the pearly seas,
> Forward he stoop'd over the airy shore,
> And plunged all noiseless into the deep night."

Of those extraordinarily mature and finished poems Mrs Oliphant remarks that they are "more preludes and overtures in poetry than anything else;" and that their author is specifically "the favourite of *young* readers." Take any stanza of the *Ode to a Nightingale*, and the inadequacy of such an estimate will be apparent at once.

> " Thou wast not born for death, immortal Bird !
> No hungry generations tread thee down ;
> The voice I hear this passing night was heard
> In ancient days by emperor and clown :
> Perhaps the self-same song that found a path
> Through the sad heart of Ruth, when, sick for home,
> She stood in tears amid the alien corn ;
> The same that oft-times hath
> Charmed magic casements, opening on the foam
> Of perilous seas, in faery lands forlorn."

That is not the sort of poetry popular with "young people" only; that is not "more a prelude or over-ture than anything else;" that is performance of a kind which the most skilful and consummate art in the old world or the new has never very much surpassed.

Mrs Oliphant is of opinion that Shelley's work is more mature than Keats's, and many critics (especially at the present moment when Shelley is being raised to a higher pedestal, and a copy of the original edition of *Adonais* brings fifty guineas) will be ready to agree with her. In one sense the observation is just enough. Shelley, I fancy, had written his best before he died. His nature was passionate, not contemplative; and such poetry as he was capable of ripens early. But there were still vast possibilities for Keats. Had Keats been permitted to live on, it is almost certain that he would have gained steadier constructive force, and a mellower and more meditative insight. *Hyperion*, the last and greatest of the "astonishing remnants of his mind," is the best proof that his poetical powers were still growing. Though each is perfect in its way, there is an immense distance between his earlier and his later work,—the famous colour picture in *The Eve of St Agnes*, for instance, being to my mind mere surface work when compared with the pure intellectual majesty of *Hyperion*. Shelley, on the other hand, however long he had lived, would have changed little. He was too fervid, too eager, too oratorical, too passionate, too unstable, to learn how to utilise his gifts. Whether his poetry might have gained greater definiteness and a more distinctly human interest, — whether he could by-and-by have descended from the too rare air which he habitually breathed to the common earth and the common people—is also open to grave doubt; for the vagueness and obscurity of this "beautiful but ineffectual angel" were constitutional, and he would probably have gone on to the end "beating in the void his luminous wings in vain," as Matthew Arnold has said with equal truth and beauty.

***

The emotional wave which, so to speak, bore these men on its crest has not yet entirely spent itself. Most of the writers at least whose names occur in this book could not have been what they were but for its influence. Even Thackeray would not have been the Thackeray we know had he been a contemporary of Esmond. The Romantic School in a measure still maintains its ascendency; how long it may do so, who can tell? The younger men have really more in common with Pope than with Wordsworth. Belinda is resuming her airy empire, and honest Peter Bell is dismissed, if not with derision, yet with a pretty distinct intimation that he had better try his hand at steady work. The rising generation is falling away from the prophets; we are gently and daintily (for of course anything like violence is bad form) putting Carlyle and Ruskin aside. An age of Epigram and

Table-talk, of Little Comedies and Ballades in Blue China, is before us.   The modish Cupid of the day will shrill his tinsel shaft, and the rustle of Belinda's brocaded petticoat sound sweeter in courtly ears than song of thrush or skylark.

II.

MAINLY ABOUT THACKERAY.

I DO not know to what cause it is due; possibly to
the almost morbid reticence which his family have
thought fit to preserve;[1] but it seems to me that the
current ideas about Thackeray require to be revised.
The notion that he was an utterly heartless worldling,
curt, cynical, unsympathetic, finding his chief joy in
eating and drinking and the assiduous cultivation of
social " swells," must be dismissed. But a false impression once formed has a malignant vitality which
time does not impair. I should say that Thackeray
was constitutionally a shy man, and that his shyness
accounts for a good many traits (foibles, if you like)
which have been gravely rebuked by superior moralists.
For myself, I can only testify that on the rare occasions when I met him in the snuggery at Onslow
Square, or elsewhere, I found him one of the gentlest

---

[1] Silence since partly broken in *Chapters from some Memoirs*, by
Miss Thackeray (that was) herself; but we want more, much more, and
from the same hand.

of satirists. At the same time he was extremely outspoken; he had a childish inability to conceal, and,
like a child, he sometimes repeated what was not intended for repetition. In an old Diary I find it
written : " I found him sitting in his den at the top of
his house in Onslow Square. He has suffered much
and long, and the traces of suffering are visible in
his face. I fancy that even in his brightest moods it
is possible to detect these traces, sometimes in the
eyes, more frequently about the grave curves of the
mouth. Of course I was ushered into his den — of
course he told me how and from what he was suffering.
This perfect unreserve, this almost infantile openness
of nature, is characteristic of Thackeray. He is willing
that his whole life should be laid bare and looked
through. The clear, transparent simplicity of the boy
at the Charterhouse never deserts him. In fact, there
is much of the boy about him, in spite of the grey hairs
and the spectacles. On this very day he wore an old
shooting - coat much too short for him ; it fitted the
giant as a boy's jacket would fit an ordinary mortal.
Yet, with all his boyishness of manner, there is something leonine about Thackeray." " And there came
up a lion out of Judah ! " Charlotte Brontë said when
she first saw Lawrence's picture. So we know now;
and to the mass of silvery hair—the lion's mane—the
impression was possibly due.

* *
*

After Lord Macaulay died, leaving his prescribed task unfinished, I had vaguely thought of writing a history of the reign of Anne, for which, in connection more especially with the political career of Henry St John, I had accumulated a mass of material—rare Jacobite pamphlets and the like. Then an intimation, more or less authoritative in form, appeared in a literary journal, that Thackeray proposed to under-take the work. Of course, if the work was to be done at all, the author of *Esmond* was the right and the only man to do it; and I wrote to him inquiring if the report was true. I was barely known to him at the time (it was the year the *Cornhill* was started, when his spare minutes were few and precious), and yet a courteous reply, in which he apologised for his tardiness, was penned within a day or two:—

"36 ONSLOW SQUARE, S.W., *Dec.* 14, 1860.

"DEAR SIR,—I ask pardon for delaying to answer your note. Frequent illness, constant business, and want of system send my letters often deplorably into arrear, and I lose even more time in finding them than in answering them.

"Queen Anne has long been my ambition; but she will take many a long year's labour, and I can't ask any other writer to delay on my account. At the beginning of this year I had prepared an announce-ment stating that I was engaged on that history; but kept it back, as it was necessary that I should pursue my old trade of novelist for some time yet to come.

Meanwhile her image stands before St Paul's for all
the world to look at, and who knows but some one
else may be beforehand with both of us and sketch her
off while we are only laying the palette?

"Is all your spare time given to *Fraser*, and have
you any subject which you think would suit us at
Cornhill? I should be glad to have any suggestions
from you.—Truly yours,   W. M. THACKERAY."

                        * *
                          *

It was through the author of *Rab and his Friends*
that I came to know Thackeray. "Doctor John,"
for whom Thackeray had a warm regard, gave me
an introduction and pressed me to call on him—which
I did. I lunched with him, I remember, at the Gar-
rick, and he had other hospitalities in prospect. But
I was obliged unexpectedly to leave London; and the
notion that a friend of "Dr John" had not been more
abundantly entertained gave him really acute disquietude—expressed thereafter on more than one occasion with almost humorous insistence. Dallas, among
others, was commissioned to apologise. "My dear
Shirley," Dallas wrote, "just read your *Fraser* article.
. . . It is not to say this, however, that I write, but
to convey a message, or a *quasi*-message from Thackeray. I was dining with him at Greenwich and talking
about Edinburgh. He asked me if I knew you. I
owned the soft impeachment, and he wanted your
address, fancying you were still in town. When I

told him you were gone he could scarcely believe it, and seemed cut up. Several times he recurred to the subject, and lamented his not having had you at his house in such a way that, although he sent no direct message, I fancy he wished his feeling on the matter to be reported to you and to John Brown. I am in hopes that, in these days of Carlton Club bribery, you have been committing some awful political crime, and we shall soon again have you in London to answer for your sins before a committee of the House of Commons.—Ever yours truly, E. S. DALLAS."

* *
*

There was no one of his standing so quick to appreciate what he held to be a really sincere and kindly greeting as Thackeray. He was essentially a humble-minded man who was rather astonished at the fuss the world was beginning to make about him. I had made the most casual allusion to him in a *Fraser* article; here, indeed, are the very words: "Men, therefore, whose writings owe their fascination to the 'wise sad valour' which lies at the root of all true humour, and to the mellow autumnal hue which falls like the golden lights of harvest aslant the page; the moralists who take *Vanitas!* for their theme—Montaigne, Charles Lamb, William Thackeray—appear to gain a new force and faculty as they grow old. That tender sagacity and gentleness of touch which charm us so is long in being learned; 'tis a second nature, scarcely quite formed until the head is grey and the brow furrowed," — and I had no thought that they would meet his eye. But within a week of their publication there came a letter to " Dr John "—the ever dear " J. B."—in which grateful allusion was made to the half-dozen lines. Even now one wonders how he came to light upon them, or how they should have made the most fleeting impression on his mind. One cannot help contrasting the modesty of the author of *Vanity Fair* with the "gude conceit o' themselves" which the New Generation cultivate so successfully. There is no tribute, however florid, which our Homeric Smith, or our Horatian Brown, or our Shakesperian Jones, or our Miltonic Robinson would consider unduly laudatory.

The Cornhill Magazine,
Smith, Elder, & Co.

"36 ONSLOW SQUARE.

" MY DEAR J. B., — I see Mr Skelton has been saying kind things about me in *Fraser.* Is he full of work ? Could he do something for If you know his address will you send him this line on from yours,   W. M. T."

I was unable to comply with the request at the time; by-and-by came another invitation still more urgent, to which response was duly made. [I took advantage of the opportunity thus offered to introduce to the readers of the *Cornhill* a volume of translations recently published —surely among the most perfect in our language—a volume of which the title-page ran somewhat as follows —*The Early Italian Poets in the Original Metres, together with Dante's Vita Nuova. Translated by D. G. Rossetti. London : Smith, Elder, and Co.*, 1861.]

" *Wednesday*, 36 ONSLOW SQUARE.

" MY DEAR MR SKELTON,—Many thanks to Shirley. I like his writing so much, that I long to know whether we can't have some of it in the *C. H. M.?* About that Winter article ? Will Winter stay if you don't hold it by the beard ? If you have it, do send it to Cornhill, and write a line to my house warning,—Yours very faithfully, W. M. THACKERAY."

* *
*

How the friendship between Thackeray and John Brown took its rise has been told by the latter; the whole incident, from the purchase of the silver " Punch" with eighty half-crowns collected from Edinburgh admirers until it was duly packed and sent off with the inscription,—

GULIELMO MAKEPEACE THACKERAY.

ARMA VIRUMQUE

GRATI NECNON GRATÆ EDINENSES

LXXX.

D. D. D.

has been charmingly narrated ; the narrative is printed
as Dr Brown's contribution to a volume of essays and
reviews by the late Henry Lancaster, where also will
be found Thackeray's fine and characteristic reply.
I am afraid that Mr Lancaster's clever essays were
not so widely read as they deserved to be ; and many
who know their Thackeray well are ignorant that such
a letter exists. So I venture to reprint it here, for their
benefit. " The arms and the man arrived in safety
yesterday, and I am glad to know the names of two
of the eighty Edinburgh friends who have taken such
a kind method of showing their good-will towards me.
If you are *grati* I am *gratior*. Such tokens of regard
and sympathy are very precious to a writer like myself,
who have some difficulty still in making people understand what you have been good enough to find out
in Edinburgh, that under the mask satirical there
walks about a sentimental gentleman who means not
unkindly to any mortal person. . . . I assure you these
tokens of what I can't help acknowledging as popularity make me humble as well as grateful, and make
me feel an almost awful sense of the responsibility
which falls upon a man in such a station. Is it deserved or undeserved ? Who is this that sets up to
preach to mankind, and to laugh at many things which
men reverence ? I hope I may be able to tell the truth
always, and to see it aright, according to the eyes which
God Almighty gives me."

*   *
*

The volume from which this letter is taken fails
to convey (let me say in passing) any adequate impression of the inextinguishable vitality, the force and
vivacity, of Henry Lancaster. He ought to have
survived us all; and yet he died early. Death lays
his hand on the most unlikely subjects; why were
such athletes as Tulloch and Lancaster taken when
so many withered old fogies are left? Jowett con-
tributed the Preface; but it hardly did justice to the
" Rabelaisian Lancaster," as Dr John used to call
him. Yet this story is told very prettily. " The
last time I saw him was two years ago at Loch
Kennard. His two little girls, children of seven and
nine, went with us to the station, where we arrived
half an hour before the train started. This gave
occasion to a childish remark made by one of them
which greatly pleased him. The elder child had said,
' It was better to be too early than too late.' But
the younger one thought that ' It was better to be
too late than too early, because if you loved your
friend very much you went back and saw him again.' "
A really delightful remark; yet one is afraid that the
little lady may have learnt in the interval that to go
back after you are once fairly off (the boxes all packed,
and the farewells all said) is a doubtful experiment.

* *
*

When over the tea-table one turns to old letters one
is apt to grow garrulous, if not egotistic. To be grace-

C

fully, or even innocently egotistic, is a gift which belongs to few; I could count on my fingers those who during the last three centuries have succeeded. So I shall only add that on the 23d of December 1863, I called at the fine new house in Kensington Gardens. The man who opened the door told me that his master was in his bedroom, "lying down," or something to that effect; nothing seriously amiss, only he could not see visitors that afternoon. "I would come another day," I said, and left. But that other visit was not to be paid; for next morning I heard that he was dead. He had been a sufferer for years; but he treated his sufferings with a touch of humorous exaggeration that was apt to mislead; and his friends had looked forward with confidence to an Indian summer. Possibly with due vigilance he need not have died at fifty-one. He knew "Syme's method and high reputation," he wrote me; but he shrank from the cruel knife, however deftly handled. "We shall see," he added, writing on the last day of 1861. Perhaps the old year was dying while he wrote; for there is a brief postscript which seems to belong to 1862. "What a sad New Year with war to open it!" In these last months I fancy he was taking a silent farewell of much. "And oh, the delightful passages, the dear, the brief, the for ever remembered!" he exclaimed in almost his latest writing. The January *Cornhill* was on the bookstalls the day he died; Dallas was deputed to ask Charles Dickens to write a few pages for the February number; and the tribute from the great rival, " the old comrade and brother in arms," was happily expressed. But when I think of Thackeray, the lines I associate with him are taken from his own poetry; these from *The White Squall*—

> "And when its force expended,
> The harmless storm was ended,
> And as the sunrise splendid
>   Came blushing o'er the sea,
> I thought as day was breaking,
> My little girls were waking,
> And smiling, and making
>   A prayer at home for me ; "

and these from *The End of the Play*—

> " Come wealth or want, come good or ill,
>   Let young and old accept their part,
> And bow before the Awful Will,
>   And bear it with an honest heart.
> Who misses or who wins the prize,
>   Go, lose or conquer as you can ;
> But if you fail, or if you rise,
>   Be each, pray God, a gentleman."

These were the texts on which in his works and in his life this "cynic" discoursed; and he, however famous or however humble, who leaves a legacy of love and gentleness behind him, cannot be said to have lived in vain.

* *
*

Glancing through the *Roundabout Papers*, in the early numbers of *The Cornhill* (since this Table-Talk was in type), I came upon a few lines—perfectly finished as flower or shell, but tender, gracious, solemn as twilight —which are perhaps even more characteristic of the writer's habitual mood towards the end than either of the passages I have quoted. I cannot resist the temptation to copy this unconsidered masterpiece of a great literary artist :—

" It is night now: and here is home. Gathered under the quiet roof, elders and children lie alike at rest. In the midst of a great peace and calm, the stars look out from the heavens. The silence is peopled with the past; sorrowful remorses for sins and shortcomings—memories of passionate joys and griefs, rise out of their graves, both now alike calm and sad. Eyes, as I shut mine, look at me, that have long ceased to shine. The town and the fair landscape sleep under the starlight, wreathed in the autumn mists. Twinkling among the houses a light keeps watch here and there, in what may be a sick chamber or two. The clock tolls sweetly in the silent air. Here is night and rest. An awful sense of thanks makes the heart swell, and the head bow, as I pass to my room through the silent house, and feel as though a hushed blessing were upon it."

The ease, the simplicity, the sincerity of these lines are, to my mind, wonderful. The art is perfect (if it be art, it is the art which nature makes); the cadence dwells upon the ear. I know not where, in contemporary writing, they can be matched, except perhaps by the closing lines of *Tristram of Lyonesse* :—

> " But peace they have that none may gain who live,
> And rest about them that no love can give ;
> And over them, while death and life shall be,
> The light and sound and darkness of the sea."

III.

MAINLY ABOUT
THOMAS SPENCER BAYNES.

O F all men I have known, Thomas Spencer Baynes
was (I am tempted to use a word frequently
misused) the most *saintly*. I knew him intimately for
nearly forty years; so I had probably better oppor-
tunities for forming a judgment than any man now
living; and I can say with confidence that his friendship was one of the "mercies" for which I am most
grateful; and for which I never cease to return thanks.
To have known him was not a liberal education only—
it was *that*, and much more. After being with him a
little, one came to comprehend what self-sacrifice and
renunciation meant. Not that he was an ascetic; far
from it; he had a keen enjoyment of life, and a hearty
welcome for whatever tended to sweeten and beautify
it; but his greatest happiness, at whatever apparent
temporary cost to himself, was to serve a friend. In
his pure idealism, in his eager quest after the true and

the good, in the absence of all self-seeking, he was the Galahad of our society.

* *
*

Baynes and Dallas were in the early fifties (and long afterwards) bosom friends: but no friends could be more unlike. One cannot look back now on Dallas's meteoric career without recognising that his was one of the cases in which fine natural gifts have been reck-lessly and foolishly squandered. Baynes, on the other hand, was one of the most scrupulous and chivalrous of men. He was never weary in welldoing—in true sympathy, in unaffected kindness. He was very keen, satirical, intellectually incisive; quite a man of affairs, and accustomed to mix with all sorts and conditions of men—newspaper editors, literary ladies, stolid farmers, college dons; but he was one of those rare characters which, in the best sense, are without guile. He was not rich (not rich even as Dallas was—and Dallas was often in deep waters), but he was vigilantly honest and exact, and never owed any man a penny. He was all his life an invalid; he had a weak heart and only half a lung; he knew that he might die at any moment; but his spirit was so intrepid, so indomitable, that he never lost his habitual cheerfulness, but looked at the dread shadow that haunted him with an eye that kept a pleasant—I might say, a humorous—twinkle to the last. He was really a considerable, if not a great, metaphysician; he had a rarely catholic taste in letters; and his critical apprehension was singularly subtle. But he was unduly modest; while he admired his friends, and praised them far more than they deserved (and yet his enthusiasm was perfectly genuine), he made little of his own accomplishments, and kept himself habitually in the background. A nobler character in all ways it has not been my lot to meet in this world—the simplest, the gentlest, the manliest—the one in which self had least place. Those who knew him as I knew him know what "moral beauty" means, and are the better for the knowledge.

* *
*

A selection from his writings, to which a too brief memoir of his life, by Mr Lewis Campbell, is prefixed, has been quite lately published by the Longmans. It does not appear to me that the selection has been entirely fortunate. What has become of the bright and animated sketch of Sir William Hamilton which appeared in the volume of *Edinburgh Essays*? What of the subtle and ingenious essay on Shelley's poetry which was published in the *Edinburgh Review*, and is constantly referred to by Shelley experts as a contribution of permanent worth to the Shelley literature? What of the witty papers with which "Juniper Agate" enlivened the *Edinburgh Guardian*? The Shakespeare studies are good in their way; very good; but they fail to convey any adequate impression of the various gifts of an all-accomplished man. The Shelley text is notoriously corrupt; we have such astounding mis-prints as " The blue Ægean *girls*," for " The blue Ægean *girds* "; and Baynes's suggested readings were dictated by sound judgment and taste, and the finest critical discrimination.

* * *

When I first knew Baynes (about 1850, it must have been), he was assistant to Sir William Hamilton, and the *Port Royal Logic*, and *The New Analytic*, had already secured reputation for him in philosophical circles.   The fame of Edinburgh as a school of meta-physic and the belles lettres was then at its zenith; and to Sir William Hamilton, " Christopher North," and William Edmondstoune Aytoun, the University mainly owed its more than European distinction.   At all events, Wilson, Hamilton, and Aytoun were the three most potent personalities of our college life.   Wilson almost to the end was a grand athletic figure; in those days, when though age had crept upon him, the old man eloquent had lost none of his fire, one used to think of Mrs Browning's *Homer* :—

> " Homer with the broad suspense
> Of thund'rous brows, and lips intense
> With garrulous God-innocence ; "

but Sir William Hamilton, before I ever saw him, had been stricken by paralysis.   The massive brow and the calmly observant eye were clouded; the articula-

tion was defective and laborious; but he struggled
bravely on; and the moral effect on the students of
that shattered body sustained by an indomitable will
was immense. Aytoun was cast in a lighter mould;
but his plain face was bright with humour; and his
wit, his badinage, his fine taste, his common-sense,
his admirable lucidity, did us all a world of good.
Bombastic pretence or inflated rhetoric had no chance
with the author of *Glenmutchkin* and the *Fairshon*.
Yet—a poet himself—he liked to encourage any spark
of imagination there might be among us; and the
weekly exercises he set us tried our metal. The Edinburgh rhetoric class-room in the 'forties and 'fifties
might have been a school of the sophists. We were
generally invited to write on some classical theme—
Leonidas at Thermopylæ, the speech of Aristides to
the Athenian people, Dionysius and Damocles, Glad-
iators in the Roman arena, and suchlike. The worst
was that the best of these imaginative diversions were
generally read to the class; the honour was great no
doubt, but it was somewhat trying to the nerves, as
there was always a good deal of rather boisterous
comment, in the way of cheers and laughter, from a
crowd of students. Among all these men Baynes
held his own — modestly, manfully — as friend and
colleague.

*   *
*

Besides his work at college, Baynes had undertaken
to edit the *Edinburgh Guardian*, a literary, artistic,

and political paper which had been started about 1850, and in which much good work was done by men who afterwards attained considerable eminence. Among others, I remember E. S. Dallas, Sidney Dobell, Alexander Smith, Alexander Nicolson, Patrick Alexander;[1] and it was in the *Guardian* that a friend of my own, under the *nom-de-plume* of "Shirley," made his first literary venture. But the goodly company broke up about 1855. Baynes went to his native Somersetshire, Dallas to London, some of us (in poor David Gray's words) to "other kingdoms of a sweeter air," on the shores of the Mediterranean; and for ten years thereafter Baynes was my most constant correspondent. His letters were real letters; sometimes of many pages; capital letters; bright, animated, intensely sympathetic, picturesquely descriptive. I came upon a bundle of them the other day (they had somehow fallen out of sight, and were only accidentally recovered), and I read them over after all these years with an interest that never flagged; for they convey a wonderfully vivid impression of a time which is divided from the present day by a great gulf. No letters of any note are given in the *Memoir;* and yet, to his early friends, Baynes's most characteristic and personal convictions found expression in his letters, and in his letters only. They ought, for these

---

[1] All these college contemporaries (except Professor Calderwood) are gone,—Nicolson and Veitch the last. For many a day among the Border dales and the Dandie Dinmonts the memory of Veitch will be cherished ; and they have called one of the Coolins after Nicolson,—Sgurr Alasdair,— a monument more enduring than brass.

and other reasons, to be preserved in some permanent form (possibly in an enlarged edition of the *Memoir*); meantime a few selections may be made for the benefit of the audience I am privileged to address. The earliest that I quote is dated August 1854, when Baynes, living in Edinburgh, was still editing the *Guardian*. Most of the others are from the South; from Rumhill House, near Taunton, which the family to whom it belonged had occupied since the close of last century; thereafter from London, where, with Walker and Pigott,[1] he conducted the *Daily News* up to the time of his return to Scotland—a not altogether congenial occupation which he was glad to exchange for the lighter labours of a professor.

*   *
*

"23 DUNDAS STREET, EDINBURGH, *August* 14, 1854.

"There is no news. How can there be here after the 12th, when street-porters are the population, and shopkeepers represent society? Yes, by the way, there is some news — *Firmilian* was published last week. . . . You will find some capital passages and scenes in it. Perhaps the chief fault is that it is too good, too poetical. Some of the lines are remarkably fine—those about the moon, for instance; and what

---

[1] Edward Frederick Smyth-Pigott was appointed Examiner of Plays in 1874, and died 23d February 1895,—one of Baynes's warmest and most cherished friends.

could be more happy in expressing the action than
these :—

> 'Fling bullying Mars,
> With all his weight of armour on his back,
> *Down with a clatter on the heavenly floor.'*

The rattling fall is given in the very accent of the line.
However, here is the book, and you will enjoy it for
yourself.

"By the way, I must not forget when you come to
town on your way to the West—I have a mask of
Shakespeare's face that I want to show you. It is
taken in plaster from the bust in Stratford Church,
which Chantrey believed to have been executed from
a cast taken after death. However this may be, it
is to me self-identifying—the authentic Shakespeare.
In the busts and engravings we see about there are,
you know, two types of the Shakespeare head—one
with a broad, square, somewhat heavy brow, and an
expression almost coarse; the other with a high,
smooth oval brow, mild features, and a Grecian, god-
like calm upon the face—no strong individuality expressed, but infinite possibilities—the calm mirror of
all individuality—the universal poet. This is given in
the Stratford mask more perfectly than I have seen
it in any engraving. I have no place to hang it up
here, and, lying on the side-table, I can hardly tell
you the strange effect it has in different lights. Above
all, at midnight — more than once, when on raising
my head from a book, my eye has casually fallen upon
it lying pale and still in partial shadow, the calm face

has become as it were a presence, and I have been filled with a momentary awe in the consciousness that I was not alone. Positively the only ghost I have ever seen. You must see it too. . . . All are well, all heartily glad to hear of your arrival, and all earnestly hoping that, since you have come back, 'Shirley' has returned too. None more earnestly, I assure you, my dear S., than yours very faithfully,

"THOS. S. BAYNES."

*   *
*

"RUMHILL HOUSE [NEAR TAUNTON], *Feb.* 2, 1855.

"Now good-night; I will write again—I will not say when, but very soon, and tell you what I am thinking about and doing. I have not the sea here, as you have in the North, but I have all the glory of the midnight heaven—the unveiled moon, the clear blue depths of the frosty sky, and the winter stars glittering like gems amidst the leafless boughs. And I am continually struck afresh with the refined beauty and power of the winter landscape."

"RUMHILL HOUSE, *Feb.* 26, 1855.

"I confess I felt a certain malicious satisfaction in hearing that the influenza had got hold of you at last, for you were always in a severe state of riotous health that was offensive, not to say absolutely insulting, to a dyspeptic and bilious-minded man. Yet to do you

justice I must say you bore the visitation of severe
and long-continued health with as much modesty and
resignation as most men—

> 'Wearing all that weight
> Of *haleness* lightly like a flower.'

"With regard to myself—my occupation and way
of life—I hardly know what to say. I found a pleasant
kind of busy idleness for some days in unpacking and
arranging some boxes of old books which were sent
on here. Though I knew in general that they were
books collected while I was cracking stones on the
old scholastic road, yet it was so long since I had
seen them that I was quite aghast at the mass of
medieval lumber heaped up in dusty piles before me.
Vanitas vanitatum! Yet it was not all vanity either;
it was useful and instructive to get a good peep into
that strange medieval monastic life, into the world
of the school and the cloister. Every epoch of real
mental activity is worth looking into, and among many
epochs that of scholasticism is not the least interesting. It was, in fact, the feudal system established in
the domain of thought, the scholastic doctors being
the Great Barons, with Aristotle at their head as the
Suzerain, or supreme lord. . . . But I have cut out
for myself a wider course of investigation—the critical
study of Early English history, language, and literature, which, with health for the work, I hope to pursue
and make something of, having already made a beginning in the Anglo-Saxon period."

"RUMHILL HOUSE, TAUNTON, *March* 14, 1855.

" I send you a couple of newspapers containing the *Alfred and Guthorm* paper. . . . I have found it interesting to get an introduction to the old Chronicles, and through them an insight into the old Saxon way of life ; all the more so as definite traces of this life yet exist in the neighbourhood round—all through West Somerset, in fact.

" That display at the Opera was most indecent—quite the savage side of civilised life; and, perhaps, of all the barbarities connected with the war, the most barbarous.[1] It surely is not seemly to exult in the presence of death, even though the victim stricken be a foe, and an imperial one. For even while the crowned head that was a name of terror sinks, the King of Terrors stands before us vaster and more terrible from this conspicuous instance of his asserted power. And in the death of the Emperor there was a desperate calmness, a vast and terrible desolation of soul, which one can scarcely think of without an emotion of sadness and awe."

"LONDON, *May* 25, 1855.

" Dallas was not at home ; and, though I called again, and he was twice here yesterday, we missed each other till the evening, when I met him at the Standard Theatre, where Miss Glyn is now acting. I was late, but saw her in *Taming the Shrew*, as " Catherine,"

---

[1] The Czar died suddenly during the Crimean war.

which she acted with great spirit, throwing into the character so much of thoroughly human—nay, woman-like—petulance and contradiction as to make it essentially credible, which in the comedy it scarcely is.

"I went in for half an hour to the Royal Academy yesterday, but, as I was almost too tired to stand, and did not stay any time, I shall say nothing about it—save only this, that the face and form of that woman on the stairs of the burning house are—if not, as I am disposed to think, beyond all—quite equal to the best that Millais has ever done, not forgetting the look of unutterable love and life-deep yearning in the Huguenots. And those children—ah me!—I can hardly bear to think of it yet; the agony is too near, too intense, too awful, for present rejoicing, even at the deliverance; and that smile on the young mother's face has struggled up from such depths of speechless pain, and expresses such a sudden ecstasy of utter gratitude and over-mastering joy, that it quite unmans you to look at it. It is the most intense and pathetic utterance of pure human love I have ever met with."

"RUMHILL HOUSE, *June* 16, 1855.

"I got here a fortnight past on Monday, having spent four days in London, and a few hours at Oxford on my way down. Nothing has happened since I arrived here, except storm and sunshine, sheep-shearing, and local agricultural shows, with fat pigs awful to behold, and lean after-dinner speeches mournful to listen to.

" I have still unaltered my first and fresh impression
of the only picture at the Academy I went to see or
really looked at—' The Rescue.'   That impression I
shall not lose, and those faces are to me as much
realities—real, living, human facts—as any faces I ever
looked on almost.   There is a good deal about that
large picture of Leighton's[1] that I like, something of
the unconscious poetry of Italian, and especially of
Florentine, life—at least as I fancy it.   There is a lazy
splendour about the men, a dreamy light and moving
grace about the maidens, that has in it nothing akin to
sluggishness, but is rather the perfect bloom of a free
and finely tempered life.   Then, too, everything around
is in keeping;—the blue sky, the flowers, the tall trees
rising in the distance over the wall, and suggesting
shady walks and stately terraces, the fair street, the
rich dresses, and the music, harmonise perfectly with
the poetic ease of the people—people already instinct
with the grace and genius that soon made their city for
beauty the capital of the world—" Firenze la bella."
Of course, I am aware that I am utterly unintelligible,
but that is, you know, the great characteristic of all
art-criticism, the privilege and prerogative of all art-
critics.   You have seen Ruskin's *Notes*, by the by?
They at least are plain and tolerably pungent; but his
condemnation of Maclise's picture is most just."

[1] Cimabue's Madonna carried in procession through the streets of
Florence.

"RUMHILL HOUSE, *Oct.* 15, 1855.

"I suppose you know all about Dallas—his marriage and literary engagement. He is likely to succeed on *The Times,* I should fancy. Those articles of his have great spirit, breadth, and dash about them. Have you been able to move at all in the Working Man's College, of which we talked a little? I should be most glad to hear that something could be done in that direction. I feel more and more how important, how imperative some such movement is."

"RUMHILL HOUSE, *Nov.* 22, 1855.

"I saw, when in London, a good deal of Masson, something of Pigott (editor of *The Leader*), as also of Lewes, who is now living at Richmond, not in very strong health, but in good spirits at the completion of *Goethe's Life,* on which he has been occupied so long. He proposes to write a *Biographical History of Science,* after the fashion of his ditto of Philosophy. The tale might very well be told so, for the history of science is far more, even than that of philosophy, the history of individual men and their discoveries."

"RUMHILL, *May* 3, 1856.

"We have birds in these parts in whose doings I take some little interest, especially at this season; but their character and ways are not half so wild and varied, so rich and picturesque, so thoughtful, yet so courageous and so gay—in a word, not half so striking and individual as those sailor and sea - shore birds you talk about. Ours at best are mere barn-door fowls in comparison. I am glad you quote *Hiawatha*. It is perfect. Most marvellous, what music he brings out of that dull, straitened, unused, monotonous metre. Full of fire too, simple, fresh and vast as the woods, the rivers, and the mountains it reflects."

"RUMHILL, *July* 16, 1856.

"While in London I went down to Cambridge for three days on a visit to Brimley, who is in wretched health, but fighting bravely on, and doing his work in *The Spectator* every week as usual. I saw Frank Russell several times, and one night met at his rooms Dr Carlyle (the translator of Dante), who looks and talks wonderfully like his brother, only just a little milder."

[Towards the close of 1856 Baynes removed to London, where he remained, as assistant editor of the *Daily News*, till appointed, in 1864, to the Chair of Logic at St Andrews.]

"18 PRINCES STREET, HANOVER SQUARE, *New Year's Eve*, 1856.

"It is the last night of the old year, and I cannot let it pass without asking you to forgive my too long silence, and receive from me the good wishes of the season—a happy new year. I send it speeding across the Border in the silence and darkness of this cloudy night, hardly knowing where it may find you, whether watching the old year out in Edinburgh, or afar on the Northern Coast,

"Listening now to the tide in its broad-flung ship-wrecking roar, Now to the scream of a maddened beach dragged down by the wave."

But wherever to-night you may be smoking the pipe of peace, I say, in shaking hands over the grave of 1856, God bless you."

"18 PRINCES STREET, HANOVER SQUARE, *Feb.* 5, 1857.

"I am very glad you like the essay on Sir William [in the *Edinburgh Essays*].   Smith's essay is delightful, and shows poetic power sufficient to crush all the *Z*'s in the world.   His prose is quite peculiar for its condensed poetic strength.   That essay of Andrew Wilson's is very striking — too obviously Carlyleish, but containing capital stuff notwithstanding.   Only he ought to have included Satan among the *Infanti Perduti*, as he certainly made a powerful attempt (if we may believe Milton and others) to reconstruct the world on an imaginative basis.   St Thomas Aquinas' earnest prayer for his restoration would have come in well, too."

"98 MOUNT STREET, GROSVENOR SQUARE, *June* 12, 1857.

"Dallas is mad with Mrs Gaskell, and will hear no good of her.   So he thought you praised her too highly.   He has reviewed the life for *Blackwood*, and I suppose it will appear next month.   Mrs G. does seem

to have made rather a mess of it in that story about
——, but her friends say it is all true, notwithstanding
the public contradiction.

"I met Maurice the other day, and Mrs B. Stowe,
and heard a long talk between them on the drama,
which Mrs S. seems strongly disposed to revive—on
Christian principles. Only a day or two ago in looking over some papers I met with the note I received
when with you last year from poor Brimley, in which
he speaks so calmly, yet so despondingly, about his
health. He died last week, you know. This was to
be expected at any time, and I knew he was worse;
still it came like a shock. It was no surprise to him.
For a long time he had worked on at his post in the
immediate presence of death, waiting calmly amidst
pain and toil for the moment of release and rest. This
week Jerrold is gone, after only two or three days' illness—a most sincere and noble-hearted man, whose
loss will be sorely felt. So the days pass and the tale
is told."

"I will send you a copy of the *Somersetshire Dialect*
as soon as I get my number. Many thanks for your
inquiries after a Scotchman that knows his own tongue.
We can't resist the inevitable, but it does seem a pity
that the old expressive and picturesque Lowland tongue
should be dying out so fast. How is —— dear me,
what is his name?—the smallest of men and of advocates, the distracted and most rapid of speakers, the

subtle, discriminating, analytic — you know who I mean, the name has escaped me and won't come back in time."[1]

"16 WILTON PLACE, REGENT'S PARK, *Dec.* 24, 1860.

"Nine years ago my sister, with whom I had grown up, died. How earnestly we look into the darkness, and ache over the mystery of death, and how vainly. We can only trust in "the dear might of Him that walked the wave." Love is the only link that binds us to those who are gone, the only link that binds us to those who remain. Surely it *is* the spiritual world, the abiding kingdom of heaven not far from any one of us. There is the verse of an old hymn, often sung at home, which runs in my head, and seems rudely to embody this truth—

"The Church on earth and all the dead
But one communion make ;
All join in Christ their living Head,
And of His life partake."

"It is Christmas Eve, and I am here alone in my room. I am not much given to days and seasons, but there is something hallowed and gracious in the time, and it is good to be alone and fill an evening hour with thoughts of the absent. There is none I think of with truer, tenderer regard than yourself. Let me send you, dear S., across the frozen land lying white beneath the stars, the best wishes for the new year."

[1] Can this refer to my old friend Lord K—n—y?

"16 WILTON PLACE, *Nov.* 9, 1861.

"We have been taking holiday for rather more than a month, part of the time on the Continent, in Denmark, and a day and a half at Elsinore, where we visited the old castle and the traditional scenery connected with Hamlet. Amongst others we went to see the 'grave of Hamlet,' which the old man in attendance informed us had been recently made 'for the convenience of visitors.' The scenery in the island of Zealand is very like that of Scotland—large woods, bare uplands, and extensive inland lochs."

"16 WILTON PLACE, *June* 15, 1864.

"I had not heard the sad news of Ferrier's death, and though it might at any moment during the last six months have been looked for, it took me by surprise and was a painful shock. . . . He had talked of the South of England. He has taken a far quieter, a much shorter journey, and is better off than he could have been on any of our mortal shores. One of the noblest and most pure - hearted men I ever knew, a fine etherial intelligence, with a most gallant, tender, and courageous spirit. Hawthorne, too, has just gone; slept the peaceful sleep of the just and true; done with the veil of time and the mystery of incarnation."

It was in the autumn of this year that Baynes went to St Andrews, — where he was greatly beloved by

young and old, where he did much excellent work,
and where his memory is still cherished.

* *
*

Principal Tulloch died in the spring of 1886; and
the latest letters that I had from Baynes related to
the Memoir of the Principal, which he had asked
me to write for the *Encyclopædia Britannica*. (Baynes
was editor of the last edition of that exhaustive and
monumental work—a work which brought him into
pleasant editorial relations with all our best writers,
from Swinburne to Huxley.)

"St Andrews, *8th Sept.* 1886.

"I have been rather exercised in mind as to the
notice of our dear friend Tulloch for the *Encyclopædia*.
At first I had thought of attempting it myself, but
I have virtually relinquished this; and you naturally
occur to me as one of his most intimate lifelong
friends, who would be able to do justice to his
character, position, and especially to his historical
and literary labours. I daresay, if you needed any
help with regard to the Principal's ecclesiastical position and church work, Story would gladly give it.
Mrs Oliphant, as you know, is writing the Principal's
life, and she will be in possession of all the needful
materials, and would supply you with any facts you
might wish to use. . . . The Water-hens are old
friends of mine, and the moral (or rather morals)

you draw from their simple history is most salutary
and seasonable. As the years increase upon me, I
love more and more this quieter kind of literature,
sweetened and enlarged by direct contact with nature
and natural influences."

"UNIVERSITY, ST ANDREWS, 22d Sept. 1886.

"By all means take a week or two to consider the
matter. I am delighted to think there is a prospect
of your undertaking the work. What you say of the
difficulty of sketching the Principal's character is most
true. The charm of a personality so large and vital,
so strong and tender, so manly, and yet so exquisitely
sympathetic and humane, is not easily conveyed to
others who never saw his face, or heard his voice, or
felt his noble presence."

* * *

Baynes passed through Edinburgh in the spring
of 1887, when I saw him and persuaded him to write
the Memoir himself. But it was not to be. Three
weeks after we parted the news came that he had
died suddenly in the night. His life for long had
hung by a thread; he constantly realised that at any
moment he might be called away; and now it seemed
to those of us who had known him best that death
had only made his communion with the unseen world
somewhat closer. But, as I have indicated, he was
no speculative recluse; he liked to mix with his

fellows; he was keenly interested in politics; his appreciation of excellence of any kind, especially of a joke, was prompt and decisive; and he combined an almost feminine delicacy of sympathy with the most perfect manliness, and (where principle was involved) a courage as resolute as it was modest and undemonstrative.

IV.

MAINLY ABOUT OUR POOR RELATIONS.

WE have been blown away from our perch on the hillside. The yellow leaves are careering wildly before the November blast; mists hang about Benledi and Benvenue, and even the Lomonds are invisible; it is time for us to retreat into some more sheltered haven, and fortunately for us such a haven is at hand. Here, by the burnside, where the water-hens are waiting for their crusts, and with ivy-mantled rocks on either hand to shut the winter out, shall we abide until the spring returns.

*   *
*

Anything but unanimity prevails, I believe, among the people who make books as to the most propitious season of the year for composing. There are some men and women who work best in summer, whose ideas unfold with the leaves, and ripen with the straw-berries. Their imaginations are nipped by the frost;

whereas when the thermometer is at 70° in the shade, when the July breeze sighs softly through the half-closed venetian blind, and the shimmer of the sea through the open window is as a glimpse of Paradise, they shake off the intellectual torpor of the dark months, and grow busy as bees in the sunshine. But there are other writers to whom the long winter evenings are very precious. The keen nor'-easter, which heaps the snow round the doorways and hushes the tumult of the streets, braces their minds as it braces their bodies, stimulating their industry and sharpening their wits. Such people, indeed, are good for nothing in the way of intellectual work after the middle of March. With the first balmy breath of spring they throw aside their pens. The spirit of the gipsy takes possession of them, and thenceforth, till the days draw in and the leaves begin to yellow, they expend a vast amount of energy in going to and fro upon the earth. Something, to be sure, can be urged on behalf of the literary vagabond. Is it not shameful to waste the priceless summer days among musty books? "Better than all treasures that in books are found" is the fresh morning air upon the hillside or the pregnant silence of evening among the woods. The moods of Nature are incalculable; age cannot wither her nor custom stale her infinite variety; and we shall have to bid her a final adieu long before we have exhausted her surprises. This, I suppose, is substantially what the poet meant when he declared that Nature never did betray the heart that loved her. But though the love of Nature,

when assiduously cultivated, is the most enduring of
passions, yet, like other divinities, male and female,
she resents a divided allegiance, and unless summer
after summer we keep our hand in (as they say at
golf) she is apt to disown us as we grow old.   So
that, for my part, I agree with those who maintain
that for a steady spell of literary work the dead season
of the year, when the leaves, and the squirrels, and the
dormice are asleep, and the spirit of life has retreated
to its innermost sanctuary, is unquestionably the best.
Whatever is done in the dog-days is light, fugitive,
ephemeral—*pièces volantes*, as they say in France.

I once ventured to prefer a plea for Winter—winter
in the country—on which a trenchant critic observed
that winter in the country was all very well when you
lived within hail of the town, and could see your
friends daily to enlarge upon the charms of solitude.
Cowper, in a sly, humorous aside, had long ago made
a similar reply:—

> " How sweet, how passing sweet is solitude—
> But grant me still a friend in my retreat,
> Whom I may whisper solitude is sweet."

And it must be allowed that there is a certain aptness
in the retort.   The same delightful poet, however, has
elsewhere indicated the precise terms on which the
deep seclusion of the country in winter may be truly
and thoroughly enjoyed :—

> "'Tis pleasant through the loopholes of retreat
> To peep at such a world—*to see the stir*
> *Of the great Babel, and not feel the crowd."*

I am willing to admit, therefore, that the student should select a winter hermitage to which the noise of the city may come to him across the fields. The fierce pressure of the crowd is certainly unwholesome, but a man who lives all the year round among hedges and ditches is apt to grow mouldy. A little of both is best. If you spend your afternoon at your club in town, you will enjoy all the more the walk home beneath the leafless trees in the starlight, when the owls are hooting from the ivy; will listen with even keener zest to the narrative of winter adventure from eager lips—how a woodcock has been flushed in the copse, how a flock of wild-duck have pitched in the burn, how the water-hens have fraternised with the poultry, how the kingfisher and the water-ousels have been angling below the bridge, how the footprints of an otter have been seen upon the snow.

* * *

I must frankly own that there are seasons when I regard with possibly unchristian envy a sportsman and naturalist like Mr Harvie-Brown, who is watching wild creatures, the *feræ naturæ* of our moors and lochs, all day long and all the year round. Yet possibly my own brief peep into Arcadia, while the dew is still on the grass, is by reason of its brevity an even finer joy. There is only a single field between us and a great city; but our ivy-clad glen is still populous with the shy tenantry of the woods, and as I stroll up the avenue on my way to the day's work I hear the wild-fowl splashing in the burn, and bright eyes look at me through the leaves. I do not allude merely to winter days, when the frost is so hard that woodcock and mallard are driven from inland copses and marshes to the open springs beside the sea. Woodcock and mallard are our rare occasional visitors; but we have lots of poor relations who never leave us. When I came down this morning I found the water-hens wait-ing below the dining-room window for their crusts. Robins and tom-tits, and blackbirds and thrushes, gathered round them while they ate, and appropriated, not without controversy, the unconsidered fragments. On the bridge below the dam a pair of keenly alert water-ousels (their clean white bibs tucked under their chins) were bowing and bobbing as we passed. A little farther on a majestic heron rose stealthily from the margin of the stream; and close to the lodge a couple of squirrels at work among the acorns (what a year for acorns it has been!) seemed loath to be disturbed at their morning meal.

Happy the man who can find solace and refreshment in this innocent company! But with the fever of the nineteenth century in our blood, how can you or I pose as an Izaak Walton or a Gilbert White? "I too have been in Arcadia," you will say. Very good; but (between ourselves) did you not find it just a trifle dull?

* * *

The touch of cynical candour in the last sentence is, let us hope, partly or wholly affected; at any rate, I am bound to confess that I have hitherto found my own *Gallinula chloropus* a most agreeable and entertaining companion. This green hollow between the hills is, as Mr Courthope might say, "The Paradise of Birds." *Our* wood indeed is hardly so thick and tangled as that which enclosed the Sleeping Beauty; but, within the charmed circle, all these shy, sensitive, bright-eyed, flighty creatures feel that they are safe. Safe at least from the "auld enemy"; but whitrets, and water-rats, and hooded crows, and tabbies in whom the feline instinct is quite too keen for tranquil domesticity, cannot be excluded from a merely earthly Paradise. (One might as well try to exclude original sin from a theological treatise.) These however are the invariable incidents of bird-life,—mysteries which may be explained hereafter, but which, in the meantime, the mild-eyed Mavis and the philosophical Robin are prepared to accept as inevitable. We don't worry ourselves because we live in a world where there are hurricanes and thunderstorms and waterspouts and Radicals and railway accidents; and habit is as strong with birds as with men.

My own particular pair of water-hens are, as I have indicated, excellent company. The more we see of "our poor relations," the better we like them,—the intrinsic and inherent superiority of the unfeathered biped becoming, as time passes, more and more problematical. Wherein consists the coveted pre-eminence? We live together in families—so do the water-hens. We feed and educate our offspring—so do the water-hens. We vegetate in winter and migrate in summer for change of air—so do the water-hens. It is tolerably clear that the social and domestic economy of the coot is not inferior to our own. Then they have as sharp an ear, as quick an eye, as a Red Indian; and it may be said of them as of the swallow, that "where they most breed and haunt, I have observed the air is delicate." They are shy and sensitive, and reticent when it is judicious to be so; but, in defence of their little ones, they are as brave as the bravest warriors, and will attack a hawk or a rat without counting the cost. They have, it is true (so far as we know), no parliamentary debates, or ecclesiastical controversies, or late dinners—no telegraph, no telephone; but then, odd as it appears to us, they don't seem to miss them, or to feel that life without the evening paper, and a pretty matrimonial scandal in the Divorce Court, is vapid and colourless. In so far, therefore, as the chief ends of rational existence are involved, I really fear that our claim for precedence must be dismissed. To obey the laws of health; to rise at daybreak and go to bed with the sun; never to over-eat or over-drink or over-sleep themselves; but to lead in all respects a sober, vigilant, righteous, and cleanly life to the best of their ability—which of us can say as much? A water-hen two days old is incomparably cleverer than a year-old infant; before they are a month out of the shell they can wash and dress themselves; and at an age when the human baby is absolutely helpless, these water - babies are keenly alive to the stratagems of fraudulent magpies and felonious rats,—have begun in short to adapt themselves with marvellous readiness to the world in which they find themselves.

Our water-hens (the male, I suppose, strictly speaking, should be the water - cock) began their housekeeping in April. We had some lovely days during the month, and they took advantage of the fine weather. Their architectural education has been rather neglected; they have little of that delicate sense of colour and proportion which the wren and the linnet manifest; but they know exactly what they want, and they work with a will. If they are inclined to be somewhat more fussy and excited over their work than is absolutely necessary, it is the way of the world; and in the spring-time the flood of new life in the veins needs to be worked off somehow; and this is as good a way as any. The nest is built under the great Portugal laurel across the burn (where the ferns have been splendid this year), and you might see the cock any morning tugging frantically at the tough leaves of the iris, or racing up and down the bank with great bits of stick trailing behind him. Their round tower (it is round as an O) rises rapidly until it is a foot or two from the ground; then on the summit they spread a soft bed of moss and fern-leaves, where the spotted eggs are laid. The birds at that season come up to the window for their accustomed crumbs with a preoccupied air,—they say as plainly as possible,

—" We are so furiously busy that we have really no
time to eat." The cock condescends to aid the hen
in the process of incubation, and is (be it said in
passing) a model husband and father from the first.
One or other is never long absent; but when both are
away the eggs are deftly hidden. The nest, though
visible enough, is not calculated to excite the curiosity
of the passing tramp; its very roughness is in its
favour; any *spate* might have deposited that tangled
mass of rotten twig and withered sedge. During the
last day or two before the great event comes off the
birds are rarely visible, and for a day or two afterwards
the cock only appears for the matutinal crust, which
he carries along with him, soaking it in the water as
he crosses, so that it may be soft and pulpy for the
tender young bills of the little chicks who have
not yet quitted their cradle. These seven or eight
hairy little balls are eager, however, to try the water,
and one by one they scramble out of the nest, to
which they never return. There are few prettier sights
in this bad world than these tiny creatures gathered
round their mother, when, having plucked a mouthful
of the water-weed which they love, she holds it aloft
over the eager little heads. How daintily they peck
the dainty morsel from her bill! When quite young
the water-hen has a thoroughly aristocratic air, a Lady
Clara Vere de Vere tone of high breeding and delicate
upbringing: most young creatures have indeed; the
glories of the descent from aboriginal royalties not
being as yet obscured by plebeian surroundings and

vulgar cares. The old bird herself quivers with ex-
citement; she jerks her head, she flirts her tail; it
is a St Vitus' dance, in which the movement, though
characteristically abrupt and nervous, is not ungraceful.
During this time the cock is constantly on the watch;
for an ugly lot of vermin are about—hawks, hooded
crows, weasels, magpies,—and the little mites are juicy
mouthfuls. One day we saw him engage a great grey-
brown rat; he went at him in a fury of passion, and
routed him ignominiously. A bird, in a panic of parental
anxiety, becomes a formidable antagonist; the flapping
pinions, the strong beak and claws, do wonderful execution. But unhappily his unwearied vigilance is
rewarded with only moderate success. Night by night
the covey grows smaller; we hear through the open
window in the summer darkness an occasional chirp of
fright from the other side of the burn—a weak, ineffectual appeal; and then, as Hamlet says, "the rest
is silence." Next morning another member of the
little breakfast party is absent, and in the end not more
than two or three attain maturity.

But the old birds have little leisure for the indul-
gence of grief. Before the brown feathers of the first
brood are grown the hen is again hard at work, a new
nestful of eggs is ready to hatch, another lot of black
hairy mites are taking to the water. Then comes
an unexpected and altogether singular *dénouement*—the
prettiest scene of all. The survivors of the first brood
become the nurses and foster-mothers of the second!
They sit beside them; they follow them about; they

fetch them food; they build new nests for them in the
sedge (these birds, young and old, have a passion for
nest-building); they are altogether as jealous and care-
ful of their comfort as the parents themselves could be.
This premature development of the maternal instinct
leads to all kinds of unusual combinations and beautiful surprises.   It is like a picture by John Leech or
Thackeray,—Mary Anne, aged five, with the baby in
her arms, out for a walk.

One poor little brat of the second brood was obviously regarded with special tenderness by its nurse.
When it was about a fortnight old it had somehow
hurt its leg.   It had been bitten by a rat possibly;
anyhow, it could only limp painfully after the rest, and
clearly did not thrive.   A fine wealth of affection was
lavished upon the tiny invalid.   The parents, to do them
justice, did not neglect it; on the contrary, so far as
appeared, they were quite as fond of it as of the others;
but they were already making ready for a third family,
and divided duties naturally distracted their attention.
But the close friendship between the little fellow and
his big brother or sister was really touching.   They
were constantly together; they slept in the same nest
—a new one, which the elder bird had constructed
among the long grasses on the near bank; if the
wounded chick moved away ever so little, the other
took alarm, and was forthwith at its side.   But though
the leg seemed to mend a bit, so that the little thing
could swim quite deftly at last, it did not grow like the
rest.   Had it gone to the hospital, the doctors, I dare

say, would have made it out to be a case of blood-poisoning—the large category to which all diseases that do not admit of easy definition are at present referred. A rat's bite is an ugly wound, and even such a complete course of hydropathic treatment as a water-hen must be able to command may fail to effect a cure. By-and-by the nurse went away on her travels—as they all do sooner or later. Her little charge had disappeared (or died?) the day before she left us, and we had a fancy—I suppose it was only a fancy—that she had gone to seek the truant. *Sunt lacrymæ rerum*—to such a case of dumb devotion, of dimly recognised loss, Virgil might have applied the never-to-be-forgotten words.

I need not pursue this true history further. But, at the risk of repeating in substance what I have said before, I venture to add one other sentence. When I consider the really beautiful traits of character in these birds, I am absolutely filled with amazement when I find persons of no particular distinction talking with supercilious condescension of "the lower animals." The lower animals, indeed! Where will we find sweeter manners or purer laws than in these unlettered communities? They rebuke our pride of station, our Pharisaic assumption of superiority, as, with apostolic energy, it had been rebuked before. "I have not found such faith, no, not in Israel." I do not pretend, of course, that our feathered friends are faultless. Even the "lower animals," though controlled by natural piety and guided by inevitable instinct, are not perfect. The water-cocks, especially,

are by nature jealous and irritable, while, during the
courting season, it must be frankly admitted, they
fight like demons. They are, besides, extremely conservative, and have the dimmest and most confused
notions of liberty, equality, and fraternity. The theory
of "ransom" is not one that commends itself to their
intelligence. The cock who intrudes himself into the
territory which his rival has acquired by usage or
prescription fares badly. They are so exclusive, indeed, that even their own young, within a month or
two of birth, are turned into the wide world to shift
for themselves. Water-birds, as a rule, do not divide
their forces; but the coot is an exception. That the
old birds "throw themselves on their backs and strike
each other cruelly with their claws," is, let us hope,
a vulgar calumny; but, as I have said, I am not an
out-and-out or indiscriminate partisan; I am content
to maintain only that the moor-hen (as the Borderers
call him) has many intrinsically charming and winning
ways. Funnier young things than these black, hairy
little trots (about the size of a moderate-sized mouse),
with their big bills and their big feet, are not to be
met with anywhere; and to see a group of all ages
gathered on a mud-bank in mid-stream, sending the
water over their heads in jets of spray, or preening
their feathers after a swim, is to gain a glimpse of
simple domestic felicity which the matrimonial ex-
periences of mere men and women sometimes fail
to furnish.

*   *
*

But what of the "Moral"? I remember when, on a similar occasion, I ventured to moralise a little after the manner of Wordsworth, being taken to task by our most brilliant man of science. *Nature never did betray the heart that loved her.* "An egregious mistake," he replied. "Why, Nature is the most arrant jilt." Nor did Moral No. 2 fare any better. "I wish," he said, "that I could accept your Moral No. 2; but there is amazingly little evidence of 'reverential care for unoffending creatures,' in the arrangements of Nature that I can discover. If our ears were sharp enough to hear all the cries of pain that are uttered on the earth by men and beasts, we should be deafened by one continuous scream! And yet the wealth of superfluous loveliness in the world condemns pessimism. It's a hopeless riddle." So we won't, if you please, have any Moral to-day.

V.

MAINLY ABOUT ROSSETTI.

THE publication of Mr William Bell Scott's reminiscence of his contemporaries has been the
occasion of much painful, and more or less indignant,
comment. Into the more general controversy I do not
desire to enter; it is being fought out elsewhere; and
the living are well able to take care of themselves.
But another sufferer — Dante Gabriel Rossetti — is
dead; and as I knew him intimately during the years
to which Mr Bell Scott specially alludes, I may be
permitted to record, as briefly as may be but to the
best of my recollection, the *facts* on which a considerable superstructure of misunderstanding and mis-
representation, if not of absolute calumny, has been
raised. The passages to which attention has been
directed need not be quoted here. There are many
details of which, of course, I am ignorant, and in
regard to which, I presume, his nearest relative is
now the only competent authority. I believe that
Mr William Rossetti is scrupulously within the mark

when he observes in a studiously restrained and temperate letter that Mr Bell Scott's statements are "unkind, unhandsome, inaccurate, and practically incorrect and misleading." But in respect of my own intimacy with a poet and painter of rare if unequal powers, I am entitled and possibly bound to say that the general impressions conveyed by the reminiscences—viz., that Dante's temper was jealous and ungenerous, as well as moody and uncertain, and that he resorted to illegitimate methods to advertise himself and his works, are ludicrously and grotesquely unjust.

* *

It is now many years since I made Rossetti's acquaintance. In the spring of 1859 I went with the late Alexander Sellar to Oxford, and after a forenoon in the company of two illustrious professors (who continue to "pipe as though they would never grow old"), they took me to see the hall of the Union Debating Society, which had then been newly decorated by certain members of the Pre-Raphaelite brotherhood. The frescoes (if they were frescoes, but I have since been told that they were drawings in distemper) have long since mouldered away; then they were vivid and splendid — fresh from brush and pencil. Rossetti's contribution was by far the most striking; and for moral force and spiritual impressiveness I don't think he ever afterwards did anything much better. He had taken for his subject that vision of Guinevere

which arrests Lancelot in his quest for the San Grail;
and the face of the queen was simply wonderful.

* * *

Next morning I went to London to stay with Dallas
of *The Times*, and it turned out that he had already
met the artist, who, except to a select circle, was
then quite unknown. But it was clear that the man
who had drawn that unforgettable Guinevere must
be a man worth knowing; and in the course of four-
and-twenty hours—high up in an airy studio above
Blackfriars Bridge—I had been introduced to him,
and to the works on which he was engaged.

Rossetti's figure was not imposing;—short, squat,
bull-doggish, he belonged to the Cavour type; but
the sallow face was massive and powerful. The
impression of solidity is somehow toned down in
Watts' portrait, and the face is thinner and more
worn than it was when I knew him. Sleepless nights
and protracted pain may possibly have changed him
in later years, and made the ideal Rossetti more manifest. Except for the tranquil, meditative, ruminating
eye (one thought of the ox-eyed Juno) there was
nothing ideal about him then; he was intensely
Italian indeed; but it was the sleek and well-fed
citizen of Milan or Genoa that he recalled—not the
slim romantic hero of Verdi or Donizetti. For several
years thereafter, detained in London by Scotch Appeal
Cases and other business, I saw much of him. I

would call for him in the afternoon when the House
of Lords had risen, and we would ramble about the
river until it was time to dine at some homely restaur-
ant in the City; and then, if we did not go to the
theatre, we would knock up Dallas in Hanover Square
for a rubber—Rossetti liked a rubber, though he was
a poor player, and rather addicted to abstruse specu-
lations on the reasons which had induced him to play
the wrong card—and finish the evening with whisky-
and-soda and poetry over the fire.

Rossetti, as I have said, was in the early sixties
little known either as painter or poet outside the circle
of his friends. Yet some of his very finest work had
been finished years before. The Pre - Raphaelite
brethren were then regarded in many quarters with
unreasoning hostility; and Rossetti, who was very
sensitive to ridicule, had sedulously shunned publicity.
It was only by accident that I came to know that
he was a poet. He gave me some sheets of MS.
one day, and asked me to look at them. I found
among them more than one of his most perfect sonnets. He had a good memory, and at times he would
declaim in his slow deliberate manner scraps and fragments of verses which he would attribute to writers
of whom no record remains. When brought to book,
and obliged to confess that they were his own, he
would tell us that the pieces from which they were
taken had been unfortunately lost. (We came by-
and-by to understand what "lost" meant.) *The Early
Italian Poets* was published in 1861, and, of course,

from that time forward his wonderful facility for turning into English the most delicate and idiomatic felicities of a foreign tongue was pretty widely recognised. But of his own inspiration (though the true poetic faculty in some of its highest and most intense moods was unquestionably his) little was known till later.

It is difficult for us, in this year of grace 1894, to realise the vehemence of the hostility with which what was called "the Rossetti school" was regarded somewhere over thirty years ago. John Parker, though he could be righteously fierce at times no doubt, was one of the sweetest-tempered and mildest-mannered of men. Yet I came upon a letter of his the other day which curiously illustrates what I say. Parker was editor of *Fraser*, and he had good-naturedly complied with my request to be permitted to extend recognition, more or less cordial, to a young writer named William Morris, who had recently published a volume of poetry entitled *The Defence of Guinevere*. But he would only do it under protest; and this was his protest (which, after all these years, may be printed without offence to any one), of date May 14, 1860.

"I saw Morris's poems in MS. He wanted us to publish them. I confess I could make nothing of them. Nor could a very able man who looked at the MS. for me. Surely 19-20ths of them are of the most obscure, watery, mystical, affected stuff possible. The man who brought the MS. (himself well known as a poet) said 'that one of the poems which described a picture of Rossetti was a very fine poem; that the picture was not understandable, and the poem made it no clearer, but that it was a fine poem nevertheless.' For myself, I am sick of Rossetti and his whole school. I think them essentially unmanly, effeminate, mystical, affected, and obscure. You ought really to say more as to Morris's obscurity and affectation. Please to return the proof *at once*."

The world has decided that Parker was wrong; and yet it must be admitted that he had a vast mass of authority on his side, and a grain of truth at least.

* * *

To return to the present controversy.

If I am not much mistaken, all Rossetti's surviving friends will admit without qualification that his admiration of the genius of his contemporaries was spontaneous and unstinted; and that while singularly modest and reticent about his own poetic work, he was eager to secure recognition for the younger men. If he erred at all, it was in the persistency and imperativeness with which he urged their claims. I have preserved a number of his letters, and there is barely one, I think, which is not mainly devoted to warm commendation of obscure poets and painters,—obscure at the time of writing, but of whom more than one has

since become famous. As Rossetti was an admirable
letter-writer, no apology for printing one or two of the
most characteristic is needed. This from Paris is
among the earliest I can lay hand on. I may explain
that he had given me a copy of Mr Swinburne's first
volume — *The Queen Mother and Rosamond* — with a
view to a review [1] :—

"PARIS, 13*th Nov*. 1864.

" MY DEAR SKELTON,—You see your letter has been
sent on to me here, where I expect to be for a week or
so longer,—not more, as I find it impracticable after
two or three weeks' stay to set to work, though I
brought some work with me.

" I think I agree in every word you have said of
Swinburne's first volume ; but no doubt you, with me,
are astounded that, with all its faults, it should have
hitherto had no justice whatever done to its beauties.
It was published when he was not much more than
twenty, and mostly written even earlier. He has since
written abundance of things of many kinds, and of
quite another order from these early ones as regards
perfection. His principal fault now is perhaps abundance—exuberance it hardly is, for no one has more real
command of style than he has now acquired, and is
daily further acquiring. Among the mass of work he
has in MS. is a tragedy on the subject of Châtelard
and Mary Q. of Scots, which, I believe, you would
admit went far to answer your requirements, having

---

[1] Which afterwards appeared in *Fraser's Magazine*, June 1865.

been written and rewritten to avoid the faults of the two early plays. But he finds the greatest difficulty, or indeed hitherto impossibility, of getting his work accepted by a publisher. M—— took them into some consideration, but ended by funking it. Every one finds them too outspoken on the passionate side. I think nothing could serve him or please him better than such an article as you would be likely to write in *Fraser*, giving the first full recognition he has obtained in print — though, of course, not slurring the shortcomings of this early volume, of which he himself is well aware. In private he has made so large a circle of ardent admirers, that I cannot doubt his public reception would eventually be a most enthusiastic, though not a universal one. If you have a file of the *Spectator* anywhere attainable in Edinburgh, you would find (about summer and autumn of 1862, I think) the only short pieces he has printed yet; and also thereabouts, or rather later, various prose articles by him—such as several on Victor Hugo's *Misérables*—which are worth your reading. There is no present prospect of his fresh works appearing, but an article might help him on. My sister will bring out a new volume before long, I believe, but is of the unready order. She has it nearly got together, however.

"As for myself, I should really have published when I announced a volume at the end of my Italian poets, having it all fairly copied out—a big lump, and quite ready. However, I lost the fair copy by an accident, and do not know if I could ever recover the matter now from imperfect scrawls, even had I the patience. Here is a rigmarole from Yours very truly,

"D. G. ROSSETTI."

The next letter refers to some sketch which had disappeared—"if it ever existed it must long ago have reached the general gully-hole of things"—and to an illness from which Sir Noël Paton, whose noble aims in religious art he warmly appreciated, had not entirely recovered. Later on in 1865 (a copy of the Madox Brown Catalogue and a card for the private view on 11th March, filled in by Rossetti himself, having been previously forwarded), he writes:—

"16 CHEYNE WALK, CHELSEA, 13*th March* 1865.

"MY DEAR SKELTON,—I shall be very happy to see your friend whenever she is able to call. My best hour is towards dusk when the day's work is over, or else at about 11 A.M. But then or not then I shall welcome her visit.

"I fear I have given you reason to think me obtuse, and not sharp-sighted enough to see through a 'West Highland' fog. But I did though,—indeed it was 'Isabel' who tipped me a wink through the mist. Only I have been so busy lately that I have not had time to acknowledge your kind present of the little volume.

"The said Isabel is among my favourites. I am not sure, but she almost seems shorter to me than when I saw her last, and, strangely enough, not to her detriment! *Easter Bells* is one of the most striking pieces, and *Whither?* one of the most sustained in measure and manner. *My Dovecot* and *Rosamond* are, I think, equal to these; and I do not know that there is anything better in the gathering than (in their own way) *A Song for May* and *Soap-Bubbles for Baby.* I am glad you have collected all these, and am sure it is the way to do more.[1]

"Do write something concerning Swinburne. You will find his *Atalanta* a most noble thing, never surpassed to my thinking. I hope you will be in town during Madox Brown's admirable exhibition, and should like to visit it in your company. I am sure his *Catalogue Raisonnée* must interest you much.

"My sister Christina will soon have a new volume out.—With kind remembrances, I am, yours ever truly,

"D. G. ROSSETTI."

Then in 1866 he was much occupied with the George Cruikshank Memorial Fund. "Will you let

---

[1] This is the little poetry book to which allusion is also made in Charles Kingsley's *Life and Letters;* but both Rossetti and Kingsley were in error in attributing the collection to a single writer. To one of the reputed authors Kingsley wrote,—" You have given me a great pleasure. I knew most of your things through *Fraser*, and delighted in your drawing of West Highland shore scenery; but I did not know till now that you were the author of the little poetry book with the bull on it which was Mrs Kingsley's delight last year. Her especial favourites are *The Reply*, and *The E'en brings a' Hame;* and her praise is worth having. For I have never known a critic who combines so much common-sense and appreciation of good art with so much rich humanity and refinement and tenderness and purity."

your name appear on the Committee List," he wrote
on 17th April, "for the Cruikshank Testimonial? We
in London hope so, and I need not remind you how
invaluable the co-operation of a member able and willing to work the effort in Edinburgh to any possible
extent would prove." I have an impression that the
privately issued appeal was drawn by Rossetti, and it is
now an interesting document. The President was
"John Ruskin"; Thackeray had written, "Before the
century was actually in its teens, we believe that George
Cruikshank was amusing the public. Is there no way
in which the country could acknowledge the long services and brave career of such a friend and benefac-
tor?" and Rossetti (if it was Rossetti) continued:
"There can be few men who on reaching, as George
Cruikshank has now reached, the advanced age of
seventy-three, can look back with a clearer consciousness of great abilities used in more directions than one,
laboriously, fruitfully, honourably, and well."

The first series of Mr Swinburne's *Poems and Ballads* (1866) was withdrawn by Moxon shortly after
publication. Rossetti (who had wished, however,
on various grounds to exclude one or two of the
pieces, as he told me when I was engaged in writing
the protest against the irrational violence of the critics
which appeared in the November *Fraser*) was extremely
indignant:—

"My DEAR SKELTON,—Swinburne's book has been
withdrawn by Moxon, quite unjustifiably from a busi-

ness point of view. It will immediately be reissued (unaltered, I regret to say) by another publisher. The attack in the press has been stupid, for the most part, and though with some good grounds, shamefully one-sided.—Very truly yours,   D. G. ROSSETTI."

In *Fraser* for February 1869 I had a paper on Mr William Morris, which was promptly followed by the following letter, and a few weeks later by a parcel of admirable photographs of some of the artist's best known sketches :—

"16 CHEYNE WALK, CHELSEA, *7th Feb.* 1869.

"MY DEAR SKELTON,—The *Fraser* containing your article on Morris has been sent me,—doubtless through the same kind remembrance of me on your part which is apparent in the article itself.

"I think all you say of Morris is very completely and excellently said. It indicates, I should say, on the whole, the same estimate of him which I have long entertained, as being—all things considered—the greatest literary identity of our time. I say this chiefly on the ground of that highest quality in a poet—his width of relation to the mass of mankind ; for, in inexhaustible splendour of execution, who can stand beside Swin-burne ?—not to speak of older men.

"You know Morris is now only 35, and has done things in decorative art which take as high and exclus-ive a place in that field as his poetry does in its own. What may he not yet do ? The second volume of the

Earthly Paradise is getting forward, but will not be
ready, I should think, till the spring of next year.   In
some parts of it the poet goes deeper in the treatment
of intense personal passion than he has yet done.
After this work is finished, I trust his next step will be
in dramatic composition, in which I foresee some of
his highest triumphs.

" What you say of me comes curiously at a moment
when a spell of ill health has limited my painting, and
thrown me back a little on old poetic ideas. I fear I
shall find on examination that there is not much of the
MSS. I lost (a biggish vol. ready for the press) which
can be got together again.   There will be some sonnets
of mine in the *Fortnightly Review* next month. I shall
probably write some new things, and see whether they
seem worth anything among such poets as we have
now.—Ever yours,   D. G. ROSSETTI."

The extracts I have made are sufficient to show that
Rossetti was constantly and warmly interested in the
success and welfare of his friends, and that any in-
sinuation of indifference or jealousy ought not to be
listened to for a moment.

*   *
*

The specific charge that he employed illegitimate
methods to promote the circulation of his poems admits,
I think, of a complete answer. But to arrive at a just

conclusion, the whole circumstances attending their publication must be known.

I have already alluded to the fierce and persistently hostile criticism which had been directed against the Pre-Raphaelites and their works. The opposition had grown more feeble and less bitter before the end of the sixties; but there can be no doubt that it had told upon Rossetti. The aversion to publicity had increased; so much so that the mere rumour that one of his pictures was being exhibited would make him uneasy for days. He had grown morbidly sensitive to praise or blame. He was convinced that if he ventured to publish he would be pitilessly and wantonly assailed. The entreaties of his friends were for long disregarded. I ventured at length to appeal to him in public. I had said something to the same effect in an article on *The Winter Time* which had appeared in the *Cornhill*, Thackeray's *Cornhill* ("About that Winter article?" Thackeray wrote, "Will Winter stay if you don't hold it by the beard?"), but the passage to which Rossetti refers in his letter of 7th February 1869 appeared in *Fraser* for that month. Ten years, I wrote, had passed since *Dante in Verona* was promised, and the work was still unpublished. "It is said that an accident befell the manuscript; but surely from the rough drafts that Mr Rossetti must possess the poems might even yet be recovered and put together. Even in this prolific age the world can ill afford to lose a volume which would undoubtedly prove a substantial addition to its poetic literature." It was about the time the article appeared

that he said to me that if his friends would stand by
him he would run the risk.   He would consent to
publish because his friends had assured him that his
poems ought not to be hidden away; would we say to
the world what we had said to him in the confidence of
friendship?   To this of course there could be only one
reply; we were eager to get them on any terms; and I
cannot see that there was anything undignified, anything that reflects injuriously either on Rossetti or his
friends, in the assurance that we would be early in the
field.   It is easy of course to say that Rossetti was unduly disquieted, and that no man should be so morbidly
sensitive as he was; and I am quite willing to admit
the validity of the reply.   As it happens, however, we
are forced in this world to take men as we find them;
and although Rossetti was the most variously gifted
man it has ever been my privilege to know, he had his
weak points like the rest of us.

The letters which follow relate to the publication of
the poems, and must be read in connection with what
has been said.

"16 CHEYNE WALK, CHELSEA, 3d *February* 1870.

"MY DEAR SKELTON,—I am going to publish some
poems, as you have, I think, heard from M'Lennan,[1]
and have been meaning to write you thereanent.   After
your public *premura* about them, I daresay I may reckon,
without too much conceit, on an intention on your part
to review them fully in *Fraser*.   I am anxious that some

[1] J. F. M'Lennan, the author of *Primitive Marriage*.

influential article or articles by the well-affected should appear *at once* when the book comes out, for certain good reasons. If you thought you could secure the appearance of a notice all the sooner by my sending you proofs of the things as far as printed, and had time to think about it, I could do so very soon. If you then let me know how early you could secure the appearance in *Fraser* I would take this into consideration as to precise date of publishing. I suppose I cannot get out till April. I want to add a thing or two yet, if possible, but am much taken up with painting. Did you see some sonnets of mine in the *Fortnightly* nearly a year ago? I had tried to make them as perfect as in me lay, and have a good number in the volume.

"Swinburne wishes to 'do' my book in the *Fortnightly*, and Morris elsewhere; and if these and yours, with perhaps another or so, could appear *at once*, certain spite which I judge to be brewing in at least one quarter might find itself at fault. . . . A model just come in. Farewell in haste.—Yours very truly,

"D. G. ROSSETTI."

Then the proofs came,—there was a good deal of revision and alteration later on :—

"16 CHEYNE WALK [*5th March* 1870].

"MY DEAR SKELTON,—I'm sending you the proofs at last to-day—couldn't get them before. If too late, it will have to be put off to the June number, as I know the calls on your time must be many, and now

the thing *does* come out, should be specially sorry if
you were forced to hurry your notice. I'm going into
the country for three weeks, and may possibly add a
little more. I publish in April.—Ever yours,

"D. G. ROSSETTI."

"SCALANDS, ROBERTSBRIDGE, HAWKHURST,
"*Friday* [20*th March* 1870].

" MY DEAR SKELTON,—Your note has only just come
to me here. The picture you ask about must be a
'Venus' (now at Manchester). There is a sonnet
written for it in the book; but I did not get the roses
and honeysuckle into the sonnet.

"I am glad you like my book as well as any of its
size. This point of size is just the thing that I think
last finish concerned in rigorously limiting. Thus a
good deal has been excluded altogether from my
volume, and among other things included some had
originally been written to twice their present length.

"I judge that your article is to deal with my book
alone, which I shall much prefer if so, as studied work,
where unity is specially kept in view, suffers I think
by the associated plan of criticism, and the comparative treatment seems to me never quite a sound
one.—Very truly yours,   D. G. ROSSETTI."

" I have added a sheet more to the book, and shall
send you this soon—before fitting the things into their
places as a whole. I am now shifting the first poem
(*Troy Town*) further on, and opening with the *Blessed
Damozel*. I shall be out for certain by end of April."

The book itself (in its lovely binding of green and gold—what ails Sir Herbert Maxwell with the binding?) quickly followed. It was published towards the close of April, and in little more than a fortnight a thousand copies had been sold. The rapid success was very pleasant to Rossetti.

"Scalands, Robertsbridge, Sussex, 4*th May* 1870.

"My dear Skelton,—Let me thank you for being so early in the field with your friendly article on my poems. You will be glad to hear that the result of a few such timely notices has been that my publisher is already going to press with the second thousand.

"I have been out here for two months now, recruiting after a spell of queer health, and have benefited greatly. I shall return to town almost immediately, and get to my painting again; but it is possible that, after making a good start with a picture I am beginning, I may bring it to this neighbourhood, and go in for a summer's working and walking together, of which I still stand in much need.—Very truly yours,   D. G. Rossetti."

* * *

I saw little of Rossetti after the sixties. Between 1870 and 1880 my annual holiday was spent in Italy or among the Alps, and I was seldom in London except for a night in passing. I fancy that after the severe illness of 1872, Dante aged quickly. He was

surrounded till the end by many attached friends;
but, with one notable exception, they belonged to a
later generation. Though the occasional letters he
wrote were still frank and cordial, they had hardly
the earlier brightness (in the latest I had from him
he said, somewhat sadly, that he could now make
no new departure in art, "finding myself, as I grow
older, more than ever at the mercy of my first sources
of inspiration"), and one fancied, perhaps wrongly,
that the step was less elastic, the spirit more weary,
than of old.

My contribution to the debate is the merest frag-
ment. When Mr Theodore Watts' Memoir appears
we shall see Rossetti as he was, and any lingering
shred of cloud will be dispersed. But when are we
to have it?

*   *
*

One or two of the later letters may be added.

"ALDWICK LODGE, BOGNOR, 26th March 1876.

"MY DEAR SKELTON,—Yours of 22d has been sent
on to me here, but your book so kindly sent still lies
at Chelsea. When I have made acquaintance with it,
I hope to write again, but need not wait to thank you
for it. I have no foregone conclusions about Mary
Stuart, and could have no others, as I have never yet
gone into the involved subject. Your book will enable
me to do so.

Plenty of pictures do I paint (or at least I never do

anything else, though they are far from getting out of
hand in a mighty hurry), but never a photo gets taken.
I am so sick of them when they turn their backs at
last, and go to weary somebody else. Thus their departure is always a hurried one. If ever I have a record
of any tolerably worthy one, be sure I shall not forget
an old well-wisher like yourself. Another I should not
forget is Noël Paton. Indeed I will try to get something of the kind done, just for a few friends, from
some of my latest and only tolerable things. What
you tell me of Paton's having some picture of mine
by him makes me fidgety, as I know not whether it be
something (probably vile if so) offered him by some
dealer, or else some picture sent by an owner for the
R.S.A. exhibition. In either case I should like to
write him a line. I think his address is St George's
Square, but had better enclose the note with this, if
you will kindly post it.—Ever yours sincerely,

"D. G. ROSSETTI."

"19th Oct. [1880].

"MY DEAR SKELTON,—Thanks for still remembering
me when issuing *The Crookit Meg*. Even a first glance
shows me that it is full of the old spirit of your work.
I too jot a little now and then, though the brush is
oftenest to the fore.—Yours very truly,

"D. G. ROSSETTI."

* * *

I have spoken of the brief visit to Oxford in 1859, when I first saw Rossetti's handiwork. The impression then made was ineffaceable; but the first fine careless rapture found voice in *Thalatta*. Were it not that Oxford—"steeped in sentiment as she lies, spreading her gardens to the moonlight, and whispering from her towers the last enchantments of the Middle Age"—has since been touched by an incomparable pencil, I might have ventured to reprint a passage which is associated with some charming memories,—now memories only.

VI.

MAINLY ABOUT TYNDALL.

I SOMETIMES fancy (when one is inclined to be dismal) that the conventional associations with the seasons are curiously misplaced. There is something *inquisitorial* about the searching blaze of summer. It is like the fierce light which beats about the throne, striking pitilessly into the dark corners and obscure recesses of the conscience. Heine saw the young Spring God, — radiant, adorable, — standing on the summit of an Alp. A lovely picture! Yet many of us, who will not own that we are cursed by any over-morbid sensibilities, find ourselves willing, nay, eager, to delay his coming. One would put a drag on every month of the waning year if one could. Winter may be grim and inclement; but it does not take us to task, does not require us to examine ourselves, does not mark a new departure, as the spring does. The opening buds are the saddest moralists, the severest critics. To the very young, indeed, they may whisper of a good time coming, but to the old

they speak of the departed year. The 25th of March
used to be the first day of the year, and it had a real
and not a merely arbitrary claim to the distinction.
The old year had truly passed away, and a new one
was being ushered in. Under our present classification
there is an awkward interregnum. The old year dies
in December, but the new year makes no sign till long
after the 1st of January. *That* is why the Spring is
sad; it is a true Anniversary, reminding us with painful distinctness of duties unfulfilled, of work unfinished,
of ambitions more or less modest ungratified. The
25th of March is the great annual Day of Reckoning,
when we are called before the inner tribunal to render
an account up to date. *We speak to the wayside flowers
of our love, and to the fading leaves of our ambition.*
So Mr Ruskin says. For the russet leaves of autumn,
I would, for my part, be inclined to substitute the
firstlings of the Spring—the violet, the wood-sorrel,
the anemone. Here is another year visibly dead
and gone, and we are no further on than we were at
its birth. It is no wonder that a sort of hopelessness
should take possession of the man who feels at fifty
that he can do no better than he has done, and that
every new year now must diminish the vigour of mind
and body.

*   *
*

It is a matter of immense moment to retain as we
grow old a varied hold upon life. When we have
entered the fifties we get, as it were, a new horizon.

The comparative values are so completely altered that a fresh currency is needed. What used to seem solid ground becomes phantasmal — the stuff of which dreams are made. The uprooting of old associations and early limitations is often a perilous process. "Vanitas vanitatum, omnia vanitas." If we would not lapse into sheer cynicism it is very necessary that we should keep some of our illusions. When we find the walls of the universe, the *mœnia mundi*, as we esteemed them, falling around us at every turn, a sense of immense uncertainty and insecurity assails us. Our confidence is shaken—as in a city riddled by earthquake. Whether it is better for us or worse (as creatures accountable to a Supreme Judge whose verdict will be given hereafter — under quite other conditions) I do not stay to inquire; I am looking at the matter only from the homely standpoint of the merely mundane critic. But there can be no doubt that the man of fifty or sixty, whose attention is concentrated with eager curiosity upon any inquiry however microscopical or whimsical, is the man who, during what remains of life, will extract most good out of it. It has been said that whoever has no knowledge of whist is laying up for himself a miserable old age. This is only putting the fact with a somewhat truculent directness. The man who allows his interests to drop away from him when he begins to feel that he has taken the downward turn (which leads inevitably to ——what we know) will be very much in the same predicament as the man who allowed his friends to drop away from him when he fancied that he would not need them any more. We can hardly make new friends after middle life, nor can we strike out new lines of work or enjoyment. There are elderly people I meet every day who excite a gentle ripple of laughter among the younger members of our Society when they begin to discourse upon what is known as their favourite fad. For my own part (though some of them are ten years older than I am) I cannot look at them without envy. These hale old gentlemen are *so* fresh! —age does not wither them nor custom stale. Unfortunately the rest of the quotation is inapplicable— their "infinite variety" being confined to one foible apiece. Jones's craze (as the youngsters irreverently term it) is the Jones pedigree;—there is only one break in the chain which takes his family back in a direct line to an early Welsh ragamuffin; and this he is always on the very point of supplying. Poor old fellow, he will go down to the grave without finding the missing link, and probably without learning that it is well for him that he does not find it. His occupation gone, life would become utterly colourless. Brown has no personal ambition to gratify, but he nurses a highly abstract theory about the necessary connection between a *comes* and a *comitatus,* and he has gone through half the manuscripts in the Rolls House and the British Museum to prove that the single adverse decision (it is unfortunately dead against him) might be explained away, if we could only recover certain documents which were certainly destroyed (if they ever existed) not less than three centuries ago. Robin-son, who believes that Mary Stuart (in Mr Huxley's words) "blew up her husband only a little more thoroughly than other women do," and that Darnley committed suicide to compromise her,—who button-holes you in the middle of the street to inform you that that miscreant Smith (who classes her with Eve, Helen, Cleopatra, Delilah, and sundry other wicked sirens, who have lured men to their destruction) is hopelessly mad, and has been removed to a lunatic asylum,—what would become of him were he to solve the riddle? Ever to seek and never to find—the quest still retaining its attraction—*that*, I take it, is about as good a definition of human happiness as it is possible to hazard. Dear, dusty, dried-up mummies! I figure you to myself sometimes under the similitude of the lusty lover on Keats' imperishable urn :—

> " Bold lover, never, never canst thou kiss,
> Tho' winning near the goal—yet do not grieve ;
>   She cannot fade, tho' thou hast not thy bliss,
> For ever wilt thou love, and she be fair."

* * *

But the old (one is thankful to say) are not all dusty and dried-up mummies; and there is no pleasanter sight in this world than that of the profound philo-sopher or brilliant man of science who, spite of his threescore years and ten, is as bright, as alert, as keenly interested in the search after truth, as he was

in the vigour of his manhood. Of such men, I have
known more than one; and they serve to show us
that old age does not necessarily imply or involve
that failure of intellectual faculty, that exhaustion of
the soil of the mind, which we are apt to associate
with advancing years. I believe that Professor Tyndall, for instance, was really younger at seventy than
the severe moralist of five-and-twenty whose ripe experience assures him that life is vanity and happiness
a mirage.

                    *   *
                       *

I have said, in an earlier paragraph, that the passion
for mountaineering is of comparatively recent growth:
even while I write I learn that Professor Tyndall
has passed away; and Professor Tyndall was one of
the earliest, if not the earliest, of the great Alpine
climbers. What will the Aletsch glacier hereafter be
to those of us who have enjoyed the homely hospitality
of Alp Lusgen—what will it be without Professor Tyndall? He was the most conspicuous man of science
of his time; but it is as a mountaineer that he will
be most widely and affectionately remembered. A
week on the Bel Alp, with Tyndall as guide, philosopher, and friend, was an era in a life. He was
familiar with all the secrets of the wonder-world
that lies above the snow-line, and he had a rare
power, which he freely and graciously exercised, of
imparting them to others. Those summer nights,
when, from the terrace in front of his chalet, we heard

the thunder-cloud break over Italy, and saw the light-
ning play round Monte Rosa, are not to be forgotten.
It pleases one to think that he was able the autumn
of his death to revisit the altitudes which he loved so
well,—to pass, indeed, almost without a pause, from
the august company of the "silent summits" to "the
infinite azure" beyond.

> "Thither our path lies ; wind we up the heights ;
>   Wait ye the warning ?
> Our low life was the level's and the night's ;
>   He's for the morning.
> Step to a tune, square chests, erect each head,
>   'Ware the beholders !
> This is our master, famous, calm, and dead,
>   Borne on our shoulders."

* * *

I daresay you may remember some Swiss and Tyro-
lese sketches which appeared a good many years ago
now. One of the incidents in *Alpine Resting-Places*
(so they were named) I had from the Professor himself
—an incident in which he was the leading actor—
an incident, I may add, attended with the happiest
results. It occurred on the Aletsch glacier, not far,
fortunately, from the refuge, which was afterwards
known as the "Concordia Hut." May I, without im
propriety, transcribe the letters he then wrote me ?—

"*17th December* 1882.

"We still retain a very pleasant memory of your
visit to the Bel Alp. A slight amount of resentment

I confess survives when I remember the obvious distrust with which Mrs Skelton regarded my leadership
on the glacier. It was, I take it, this want of faith
on her part—the fear of being engulphed while in my
charge—which caused her to run away so rapidly from
the Bel Alp. We have chosen and succeeded in pur-
chasing a scrap of heather-land within less than two
hours of London—a spot surrounded by scenes of the
wildest beauty—for the building of a little nest in
England which will constitute a respectable set - off
to our eyrie in the Alps."

"*2d February* 1883.

" We were both charmed to see our little Alpine nest
depicted in *Good Words*, and surely could not be
otherwise than gratified with the friendly manner in
which you spoke of us. We ought to have been with
you on that occasion when you lunched at the foot
of the Aletschhorn. When breaking my crust there,
and drinking my glass of wine, I have often thought
of the words of Emerson,—' Give me health and a
day, and I will make the pomp of Emperors ridicu-
lous.' On one occasion especially, when the guns
were thundering in France in honour of Louis Napoleon, I thought of the unspeakable glory of my
surroundings as compared with his."

"*3d February* 1883.

"When I wrote to you I had not read your Alpine
letters through. I have now done so, and found them
bright and pleasant from beginning to end. But was

your escapade at the Concordia Hut a real event?
If so, I shall begin to entertain the possibility of
miraculous coincidences.

"Most of your scenes are familiar to me,—Stachel-
berg, the Pantenbrück, the Sand Alp, and the Clariden-
Grat. Over the Tödi I intended to go, but was turned
aside by an attempt at extortion.

"We are now again upon our moorland, having spent
the last two days in London. The storms were wild
here yesterday, and almost equally wild in the earlier
part of to-day; but they are now hushed, and instead
of flying scuds we have 'stars keen glancing from the
Immensities.'"

This letter supplies the keynote.

"To sit upon an Alp as on a throne"

was the master-passion; and even in England, even
in level England, he found such a home as he desired,
—where, high above the smoke of the great city, a
trifle nearer the stars, among furze, and bracken, and
heather, and Scotch firs on which the sunset lingered,
he could breathe freely,—almost as freely, indeed, as
on Dom or Weisshorn.

"1st April 1884.

"On this free moorland, with an outlook of incomparable beauty, we are building a house. By the end
of summer we hope to have it pretty complete. At
some future day I hope we shall enjoy the opportunity
of showing you and Mrs Skelton how nearly, within

forty miles of London, we have reached the wild-
ness of our Alpine home."

*   *

Nor can I forget that it was to one who writes the
most charming letters in the world (long may he write
them!) that we owed our introduction to the famous
mountaineer.   Huxley was Tyndall's lifelong friend,
and when he wrote—"So go boldly across the Aletsch,
and if they have a knocker (which I doubt) knock, and
it shall be opened unto you"—we felt that we had in
our possession a charm which would act as the "Open
sesame!" to Alp Lusgen.   As, indeed, it proved —
the little joke about the primitive simplicity of the
domestic arrangements being keenly appreciated.

*   *

But how, you ask, did this brilliant, busy, versatile,
eagerly - inquisitive man contrive to spend so many
months during each year on a remote Alp, in almost
absolute seclusion, without intolerable weariness?
Well; it was a really beautiful life that was led at Alp
Lusgen—simple, pastoral, actively beneficent.   Here
is a slight sketch of it—again in his own words:—

"31st *August* 1881.

"Huxley, for once in his life, was right when he
prophesied that you and Mrs Skelton would meet a

welcome here. Our only regret was that your visit was so short. Her first performance on the glacier caused me to hope that Mrs Skelton would return to Scotland a finished mountaineer. It is something, however, to have given her her first lesson among the crevasses.

"We went down to see you on the day of your departure, but were half an hour too late, which we regretted much.

"I have been mainly occupied since your departure in treating the wounds, bruises, and general sanitary shortcomings of the population here around me. They cut themselves and require plastering; they scald themselves and require swathing; and though clasped by this splendid air, they breathe the noisome emanations from their stables and cowhouses, and re-breathe, God knows how often, the exhalations of their own lungs. Hence premature age and debility. Gregory's powder, the virtues of which are known to Mrs Skelton, has in many cases done good, and in no case harm.

"One poor little boy, who had the skin of his leg removed from thigh to instep, and the muscles of the calf deeply attacked, by the overthrowing of a caldron of boiling water, I have managed to set completely on his legs. For a couple of days I had the invaluable assistance of a young surgeon from St Bartholomew's Hospital. His sudden departure made my position an anxious one, but, happily, all has turned out well, and the boy, who showed more fortitude than nine out of ten of our philosophers would have shown under the

circumstances, is now among the herds upon the hills.
He is a fine, intelligent little fellow, with a drunken
father and a good-for-nothing mother. I must keep
my eye upon him.

"My wife's mother has come, and we are very cosy
together. This morning we had bright sunshine. At
six P.M., which is the present hour, we are swathed in
fog. I wish you bright skies in Arran. Good-bye!"

VII.

MAINLY ABOUT A SUMMER NIGHT IN THE NORTH.

THERE was a good deal about the Jowett worship
that was incomprehensible to men who had not
been at Balliol. It was only the initiated, indeed, who
were permitted to penetrate the mysteries of the cult.
That it was a real and not a sham religion cannot be
denied by those of us who remember with what pious
horror the unwary scoffer was regarded. For him

> " The lifted axe, the agonising wheel,
> Luke's iron crown, or Damien's bed of steel,"

was too light a punishment. The author of *The New
Republic*, for instance, fared badly; he could not have
fared worse had he assailed a hornets' nest. His Doctor Jenkinson, to be sure, was cruelly clever. The weak
points of the Master's theology were emphasised with
really malignant enjoyment; but, in spite of the hostility
which it provoked, one is bound in fairness to admit
that it was a work of art of rare merit. The medium

may have been meretricious, and the author unscrupulous; but I do not know that there is any work in English satirical literature, since the *Dunciad*, which is worked out with the same industrious and felicitous animosity.

*   *
*

Jowett had a great talent for silence. I have seen him sit for hours (once, at Mürren, for days) without uttering a word. The discomfiture of the unhappy undergraduate, invited to join the Master in a country walk, has formed the theme of many legends. It is very difficult in this age to know what we are to believe —much more difficult indeed than it was before the invention of printing. The reporter of the penny or halfpenny paper lives habitually in the region of conjecture; and most of his stories of the living, as of the dead, are made only to be contradicted. Jowett could not have been consciously discourteous—even to an undergraduate; and the legend may safely be disregarded. Yet we can partly understand how the myth grew. A shy lad might have been driven entirely desperate (not to say fatuous) by that bland but invincible taciturnity. As no one could have been as wise as Lord Thurlow looked, so no one could have been as mild as Jowett looked. His face at the time I used to meet him (and, indeed, there were few lines to the last) was extremely like the faces we find on Titian's famous canvas of the ascending Madonna. It

was the face of a cherub—a chubby cherub, to whom
the inconveniences that attend and accompany a mortal
childhood are unknown. We were assured by those
who knew him best that there was a very bright and
virile intellect behind the infantile mask (as, indeed,
there was); but we had to take it mostly on trust.
The brilliant talkers—Sydney Smith in the last generation, Froude and Huxley in ours—carry their creden-
tials with them: Jowett did not. One characteristic
evening I have not forgotten. After dinner — it was
midsummer—we carried our glasses and the decanters
out to the lawn. The " Book-Hunter " was one of the
party, Sir Alexander Grant another. We got upon old
Scottish ecclesiastical scandals, and of these Burton
had an inexhaustible store, some of them barely fitted
for ears polite. The decanters were occasionally re-
plenished, but the summer night came down upon us
before he had exhausted his budget. Jowett was obviously entertained (hugely entertained, as we learned
afterwards); it was a new experience to him,—these
queer reminiscences of the Cameronian pulpit, these
samples of Presbyterian eloquence displayed; but during the whole evening he never opened his lips.

*　*
*

Those summer nights upon the slopes of the Pentlands were often magical. There was always a light
in the North, so that till midnight one might read the
smallest print. One such evening I walked with " the

Principal,"[1] across the fields to dine at the cottage which our friends from Heriot Row then occupied during the dog-days. It was from this cottage that possibly the most charming of our younger Scottish writers went out into the world to try his luck. He was only a lad at the time (he was not at home that night), and hardly any one except his mother guessed as yet what was in store. But she was prescient, as mothers are; and she lent us, I remember, a volume in which juvenile contributions to local journals had been carefully put together and preserved. We read them next morning — the Principal in his bedroom before breakfast, as was his way—and we then agreed that, whatever came of it, here was a fresh voice with a note delicate and unborrowed as the lark's. And, indeed, I am not sure that "Robert Louis" (as he was in these days) has ever done anything much better than, or possibly quite so good as, one or two of the trifles in that cherished volume of scraps.[2]

* * *

It is a thousand pities that the *Noctes Ambrosianæ* are now so little appreciated. Fashion is incalculable;

[1] For a quarter of a century, over broad Scotland, "the Principal" was Principal Tulloch.

[2] To the end (for the end has come since the text was written) "Robert Louis" never forgot the country, which he knew so well as a lad, between Edinburgh and the Pentlands;—

"The boyish rapture still survived the boy,
And Lochnagar with Ida looked o'er Troy."

The outlook from "topmost Allermuir" or "steep Caerketton" is pic-

but I cannot think that they will be permanently forgotten.   I tried once to disengage what was fugitive
and local from the perennial comedy, but I am afraid
the experiment failed — financially, at least.   (John
Blackwood, I see, wrote me six months afterwards,
when, on finding that it had not proved remunerative,
I returned the cheque he sent me,—" I can now say of
you as Don Dugald said of his friends of the Mist, ' I
have even known them to refuse coined money, a tale
seldom to be told in a Christian land.'")   And yet it
was well spoken of at the time; and I am pleased to
remember that one of Louis Stevenson's earliest Essays
in Criticism was directly due to the publication of the
Comedy.   His appreciation was singularly sound and
discriminating; and I cannot but feel that the "inter-
locutor" of so competent a judge ought to be affirmed.
If it is just (and, coming from a great master of style,
he would be a bold man who would dissent), what are
we to think of the critical insight of a generation to
which this perfect fooling is mere foolishness?

This is the substance of Mr Stevenson's judgment:
" Of the more perennial part of the *Noctes* we have
here what is perhaps the most durable monument to

tured with Homeric force and breadth in the lines " To S. C."; and the
road to the cottage at Swanston by Braid and the Boro'muir (where the
Scottish nobles and their men gathered for Flodden) inspired his latest
lyric :—

> " I gang nae mair where ance I gaed,
> By Brunston, Fairmilehead, or Braid ;
>   But far frae Kirk and Tron ;
> O still ayont the muckle sea
> Still are ye dear, and dear to me,
>   Auld Reekie, still and on ! "

Wilson's fame.   In it we find the immortal trio at
their best throughout.   From beginning to end their
meetings are inspired and sanctified by Bacchus and
Apollo.   North can always lay aside his crutch; Tick-
ler is always six feet high; and the Shepherd is always
the Shepherd.   For how is it possible to praise that
adorable creation but in terms of himself?   He is the
last expression of sophisticated rusticity; at once a
poet, a journalist, a Scotchman, and a shepherd; oscil-
lating between Burns and the *Daily Telegraph* in things
literary; and in things moral occupying all sorts of
intermediate stations between a prize-fighter and Peden
the Prophet.   If it were lawful to marry words of so
incongruous a strain, we might classify him as a Presbyterian Faun. . . . And this book is not only welcome
because it takes us on a visit to Wilson when he is in
his best vein, but because Wilson in all his veins is the
antidote, or at least the antithesis, of much contemporary cant.   Here is a book full of the salt of youth;
a red-hot shell of animal spirits, calculated, if anybody
reads it, to set up a fine conflagration among the dry
heather of present-day Phariseeism.   Touch it as you
will, it gives out shrewd galvanic shocks, which may,
perhaps, brighten and shake up this smoke-dried and
punctilious generation."

*   *
*

There were others, however, besides Stevenson who
held that the venture should have succeeded — the

author of *Rab and his Friends* being among them.
"Dr John," indeed, welcomed it in a characteristic
letter.   "Let me thank you for the *Noctes Comedy;* if
the execution is half as good as the idea (as doubtless
I'll find it to be all that), you have done a thing for
ever, and have saved Wilson from being 'strangled in
his waste fertility.'   The portraits are excellent ; Wilson's by far the best thing of him ; and the coarse and
fine (strange mixture) Shepherd genius is very good—
from its pawky e'en to its plaid."

But a "smoke-dried and punctilious generation"
would not listen to the Shepherd's piping.   John
Blackwood, a fine critic and a staunch friend who
had been bred in the traditions of the house, fancied,
rightly or wrongly, that the old sores were not healed.
The ghosts of the Cockneys who had fallen in the fight
were not yet appeased—*Hinc illæ lacrymæ!*   "There is
a strange hatred and want of appreciation of Professor
Wilson in the London press.   Cockney venom is very
long-lived.   I took the *Comedy of the Noctes* with me in
the Flying Scotsman, and it kept me laughing all the
way to London, except when old recollections almost
moved me to tears."

*   *
*

From the familiar letters of Sir Walter Scott (which
have been so admirably selected by Mr David Douglas,
that Prince of Editors), I gather that the wild animal
spirits of the Free Lances of *Maga, in consule Planco,*

H

rather startled the douce clerk of Session. He appreciated the excessive brilliancy of the assault ; but was
it safe ? The erudite if rather ponderous respectability
of the *Quarterly* was more to his mind. And yet the
Quarterly could be coldly and icily bitter; whereas
North's "bark was aye waur than his bite." Christopher, at the worst, was a generous savage, who did
not scalp his foes—except when the provocation was
excessive! I do not know that these letters throw
much light upon what must still be regarded as the
unsolved problem of Scott's life. Here is one who was
at once a wizard and a simple country gentleman ! He
built, he planted, he drained, he married his son to an
heiress, he wrote fairly interesting letters to persons of
quality, as country gentlemen have done before and
since. But, withal, his imagination was peopled as
Shakespeare's was peopled, and over the creations of
his brain he exercised a hardly less high and absolute
supremacy. How is the riddle to be read ? For my own
part it seems to me that every new contribution to the
solution of the problem only renders it more obscure.
The evidence that goes to show that the laird of
Abbotsford could not have written the Waverley Novels
is absolutely overwhelming; and we are driven to say
with Tertullian and Sir Thomas Browne, *Certum est
quia impossibile est.*

*　*
*

The perfect sanity of Scott is hardly consistent with
that land hunger from which, in common with the

Irish Celt, he suffered.   It is a passion that, like dram-
drinking, cannot be indulged with impunity.   It grows
with what it feeds on; and Scott, who started modestly
with a summer cottage and a couple of fields on Tweedside, was ready ere many months had passed to pay a
fancy price for every acre of land in the neighbourhood
that came into the market.   Had it not been that they
ministered to the master-passion, Scott would have
looked more narrowly into his accounts with printer
and publisher, and the financial crash might have been
averted.   Miss Jobson appears to have been a singularly silent and reticent young person; but she was
an heiress; and Scott lost no time in securing her for
his eldest son.   Lochore was clearly the attraction.
Yet no one would venture to say that Scott was
mercenary in the baser sense of the word.   He wanted
to be a laird himself; he wanted his son to be a laird.
To be Scott of Abbotsford was a much finer ambition
for a Borderer by birth and breeding than to be Scott
the poet or Scott the novelist.   I believe that the true
reason why he did not wish to be known as the
"Author of *Waverley*" was that he did not regard
the novelist's craft as entirely respectable.   Among
Lords of Session and territorial magnates the writer
of mere stories in verse or prose was little better than
a tramp or a gipsy.   Had it not been that the amazing
profits of the novels enabled him to add acre after acre
to Abbotsford, one doubts whether he would have continued to write.   The motives that put that magnificent
imagination in motion were not consciously sordid;

but they were of the earth, earthy; and it is foolish to maintain that they were not. It is because Sir Walter was so weak that he was so human; and his follies only make him more lovable to those who are not afraid to recognise that their idol had feet of clay.

*   *
*

The day is nearly over, and the birds in our narrow glen are singing their Evensong. The Woodland Vespers are as pure as any that ascend to heaven, and I should feel it a greater compliment to be on good terms with these feathered minstrels than with a good many of my fellow-creatures. The exquisite croon of the wood-pigeon is better than the best of old ballads. It is a note that must have been learnt before envy, hatred, malice, and uncharitableness first visited our planet. The pitiful plaint of the curlew is the wail of a lost spirit;[1] but the coo of the cushat, in its pure and confident tenderness, is even yet not unmeet for Paradise. Then there are two or three

---

[1] My poor little comparison (ten years old) has been since ridden to death; *e.g.*, in a volume published this year I find ;—"Far on the moors a curlew cried out that its soul was lost." "It sounded mysterious and unknown, the cry of a lost soul." "But only the wild bird wailed like a lost soul, too bad for heaven, too good for hell." (The first of these is the worst—fancy a curlew *crying out* that its soul was lost !) I sometimes wonder why Mr Samuel Butler's writings are not better known and liked. He at least is a true artist. Whilst others are painfully striving, he says the right thing with more than papal infallibility. " *Plaintive creatures who pity themselves on moorlands*," is clearly unapproachable.

timid water-hens among the sedges by the burn-side,
who are now nearly tame, and with whom I hope to
cultivate a still closer intimacy when they have got
their little ones fairly started in life.   They have had
a hard fight to bring them up so far.   There were
eight to begin with—downy little brats, black as coal,
with great patches of red on their prodigious bills.
They insisted on leaving the nest before they were
well out of the shell, and got stuck in holes and washed
away by *spates,* so that their numbers were quickly
reduced.   To see the old ones rushing into the water,
fishing up weeds and insects, and feeding the little
mites on the bank, was one of the prettiest sights
imaginable.   And to add to his worries, the male
bird had forthwith to begin the construction in mid-
stream of a new nest for the reception of the youngsters — a work which ought to have been completed
at an earlier date, I suspect, and before the little
ones had been allowed to get scattered about a bad
world where rats and magpies abound.   Now the
owl begins to declaim from the ivy (the poet must
have had a singularly unmusical ear who first formulated that weird expostulation into the conventional
" Tuwhit, tuwhoo ")—why or wherefore who can tell ?
Does he hoot the impostor and the charlatan, or, like
our popular assemblies, is his unmusical protest directed
against those only who are honest enough to speak the
truth ?   " What song the Sirens sang, or what name
Achilles assumed when he hid himself among women,

though puzzling questions, are not beyond all conjecture." But the Bohemia of the woods and fields
is still almost a *terra incognita* to us, and we have as
little real communion with these " poor relations " who
have been placed on our own special planet as if they
occupied Arcturus or Orion. There must be a mistake
somewhere.

VIII.

MAINLY ABOUT
JAMES ANTHONY FROUDE.

I FANCY that I shall always hereafter associate the plaintive strains of Gluck's *Orpheo* with the fatal illness of one of my dearest friends. I was on my way to hear Julia Ravoglio at a morning performance of the *Orpheo*, when I learnt that Froude was dying. Julia Ravoglio, as Orpheus, has always been and is still (as I think) without a rival; but that day it seemed as if the news I had just received added a keen, a poignant, pathos to music which I never hear unmoved. While one was being recalled from Hades, another high and pure spirit was passing away! Somehow the tender appeal, the exquisite pain and passion, the lofty consecration of a love stronger than death, elicited a responsive echo. Were it possible to revoke the sentence that had gone forth! Might not Death be appeased once more? Even at the eleventh hour might he not be persuaded to relent?

But in our prosaic modern world (where even the piping of an Orpheus would be unregarded) there is no relenting. Science has felt her way too surely: when she tells us with impartial composure, with cruel serenity, that there is no hope, we ask in vain for a reprieve. Froude, if we count by years, was an old man; yet it was wellnigh impossible to believe that he could be dying. Until a year or two ago he had retained much of his youthful vigour. His eye was not dim, nor his natural force abated. He could still land his salmon; and he had been a famous angler. He could still handle a gun; and he had been a crack shot in his time. When aboard the tidy little craft that he kept at Salcombe, especially if the waves ran high, he was almost boyishly elate. Sometimes, no doubt, he was sad; but it was the sadness of one who, looking before and after, has found that the riddle is hard to read. He had indeed an ever-present sense of the mysteries of existence, and of the awful responsibility of the creature to the unknown and invisible lawgiver. I have heard him described as "taciturn" and "saturnine." No two words could be less descriptive. He was a singularly bright and vivacious companion; his smile was winning as a woman's; possibly he did not always unbend, but when he unbent he unbent wholly. In congenial society he was ready to discourse on every topic in the heaven above or on the earth beneath; and when at his best he was not only a brilliant and picturesque but a really suggestive talker. I would not have it thought that he was not sometimes severe. He had a very high standard of right and wrong. He hated all shams, religious, literary, political. The casuistry of the rhetorician, the sophistical make-believe of the worldly ecclesiastic, he could not abide. In public as in private they were abhorrent to him. But while he had a passionate scorn of meanness and truckling, he had an equally passionate reverence for truth, as he understood it, whatever guise it assumed. The mask might be sometimes as impassive as Disraeli's; but behind it was an almost tremulous sensitiveness—a tenderness easily wounded. His presence was striking and impressive,—coal-black eyes,[1] wonderfully lustrous and luminous ("eyes full of genius—the glow from within," —as Dr John Brown wrote[2]); coal-black hair, only latterly streaked with grey; massive features strongly lined,—massive yet mobile, and capable of the subtlest play of expression. For myself I can say without any reserve that he was, upon the whole, the most interesting man I have ever known. To me, moreover,

---

[1] Coal-black they seemed, yet I am assured that they were the rare brown of the "ox-eyed Juno."

[2] "I greatly fear I shall not get to you to-night. I am never sure of Monday, owing to my Insurance work, which cannot be gainsaid. So if I do not appear at seven, you will know how sorry I am for myself. Give my best regards and admiration to your friend. What a noble utterance that was and is—as full of genius as are his eyes—the glow from within. He and Carlyle are our only Rectors of Genius. I shall be very vex'd if I don't see him."—Letter from Dr John Brown, 1867. On another occasion "Dr John" writes that he is afraid he will not be able to come, as possibly old Mrs Brewster is to dine with him. "But I hope to learn to-day the will of that beautifullest and oldest of women."

not only the most interesting, but the most steadfastly
friendly.   I have fished with him in the English
Channel, have yachted with him on the Kenmare
river, have acted as his assessor in University courts,
have been his guest and his host for five-and-thirty
years; and I found him ever the same,—the most
loyal and lovable of friends, the frankest but most
genial of critics.

That what may be roughly called the popular impression is very different I am well aware.   That this
silent, reserved, cynical, sardonic Timon held aloof
from his fellows, and regarded them with tacit or even
Swiftian disapprobation, we have been assured again
and again.   Against such a confirmed misunderstanding, the assurance of friends is comparatively valueless.
But even yet the true man is disclosed in his letters;
and of his letters I have preserved many.   He wrote
with surprising ease; and the sunshine or storm of the
moment was reflected in them as in a glass.   His "ver-
bal magic" was not an accomplishment but a natural
grace; Carlyle might hammer away painfully at his
Frederick in the Valley of the Shadow; but Froude,
however lofty or however lowly the theme, was never
embarrassed; and the rhythmical rise and fall, the
musical flow, of his written words was as noticeable in
familiar epistle as in finished "study."   I venture to
think that even a limited selection, a provisional instal-
ment, of his charming and characteristic letters will
serve to dissipate many prejudices.   Some of them are

too intimate and confidential for publication.[1]   There
are passages of flattering personal appreciation which
must, wherever practicable, be omitted, while on the
other hand there are humorously savage denunciations
of clerical impostors and political charlatans which
might be taken too seriously by the unwary.   Froude,
though constitutionally good-humoured, could hit very
hard when roused.   And there were occasions when he
did not hesitate to speak his mind to friend and foe,—
though I honestly believe that he never penned a line
which, so far as he was concerned, the world was not
welcome to read.   His opinions might change—as they
no doubt did; but he wrote always with the most
absolute sincerity.   He did not pride himself on " con-
sistency,"—which indeed is not seldom only a euphu-
ism for obstinacy or unteachableness.   Of a certain
eminent politician he wrote to me long ago, that he
was "a man of the believing temperament, without a
single conviction that can stand a strain "; but (though
sensitive as an aneroid to all the moods of the weather)
his own vital convictions were never lightly shaken.
There was an apparent fickleness, no doubt, about his
judgments of men; but it was apparent only.   He
judged them as—week by week, session after session—
they approached or fell short of his ideal.   He had, for

[1] As there is to be no "life" of Mr Froude, and no further publication
of his letters, I have retained a few sentences here and there, not of any
public interest it may be, yet without which this slight sketch of a singularly
sweet and friendly nature would be incomplete.

example, no confidence in the divine wisdom of democracies; the *vox populi* was not the *vox Dei*—quite the
reverse indeed as a rule; and just as the statesman
when he resisted ignorant popular clamour was blessed,
so when he yielded was he banned.

The letters cover a wide range—literature, history,
poetry, philosophy, and politics. Browning, Carlyle,
Matthew Arnold, Swinburne, Freeman, Disraeli, Gladstone, are among the men who figure most prominently
in this vivid record of five-and-thirty years. The
Russian troubles, the Irish troubles, the Carlyle
troubles,—there is hardly a single incident of our
time on which they do not touch. One page will be
devoted to the struggle between Moslem and Slav;
the next to the contest between rat and water-hen,
or "the fate of the magpie's nest." A singularly
sensitive and receptive eye watches with unwearied
curiosity the game that is being played! The watcher
sometimes becomes the worker; and then — once at
least, and possibly more than once — the interest
deepens into tragedy.

I did not know Froude except through his books (the
first two volumes of the *History of England* had been
published in 1856) until, on John Parker's death in
1860, he undertook the management of *Fraser's Magazine*. He had nursed Parker on his death-bed; he was
with him to the end; and it was to Froude that
Parker's aged father naturally looked for help when the
blow fell. For twenty years thereafter Froude, though
much occupied (till 1870 at least) on the successive vol-

umes of his history, continued to edit the Magazine,—
Charles Kingsley and Sir Theodore Martin occasionally
taking the duty when he had to be at Simancas or
elsewhere abroad.   It was in 1860, consequently, that
our correspondence began ; and it did not close till the
summer of the present year.   His last letter to me is
dated 22d June 1894.   I need only add that I had been
a frequent contributor to *Fraser* for several years before
Parker's death ; and that the manuscript of a political
sketch (now dead and buried), entitled *Thalatta*, was in
his hands at the time.

"6 CLIFTON PLACE, HYDE PARK, *December* 17 [1860].

"DEAR SIR,—You must excuse the silence of the
Editor of *Fraser;* when there was no editor, you could
receive no letter from such a person. . . . Am I addressing 'Shirley'?   At present even the names of
most of the contributors are unknown to me.   I hope,
however, that I may become better acquainted with
them in a little while.   I have often heard John Parker
mention your name.—Faithfully yours,

"J. A. FROUDE."

"The papers are sent to me in handfuls from the
Strand.   I get not what I wish to see, but what the
porter's hands happen to close upon when they dive
into poor young Parker's chest.   Chest and all, I
believe, come to me to-morrow.   I hope when you
come to London you will give me the pleasure of your
acquaintance, and will call on me."

"6 CLIFTON PLACE, HYDE PARK, *Jan.* 12 [1861].

"I have read *Thalatta;* and now what shall I say? for it is so charming, and it might be so much more charming. There is no mistake about its value. The yacht scene made me groan over the recollection of days and occupation exactly the same. To wander round the world in a hundred-ton schooner would be my highest realisation of human felicity."

"6 CLIFTON PLACE, HYDE PARK, W., *March* 27 [1861].

"*The Sphinx* is a very interesting paper. I will put it in gladly, or rather I will leave directions for it to be put in. I go myself to Spain for two months and leave on Saturday. Theodore Martin manages for me while I am away. I return the first week in June, when I hope to commence *Thalatta.*"

"BEMBRIDGE, ISLE OF WIGHT, *August* 12 [1862].

"We were driven at last to a shorter flight for our summer than we had intended. . . . You will see me, however, at Edinburgh *alone* before I begin to write out my first copy. Even on so old and vexed a subject as Mary Stuart, I have much to tell that is new. Alas! that Knox's Kirk should have sunk down into the thing which is represented in those verses. I dare not print them. The horrible creed is not new. Thomas Aquinas says much the same. And after all, if it is once allowed that God Almighty will torture poor Devils for ever and ever for making mistakes on the nature of the Trinity, I don't see why any quantity of capricious horrors may not be equally true. Given the truth of what all English orthodox parsons profess to believe, and Hephzibah Jones may believe as much more in the same line as she pleases. Only I think our opinion ought to have been asked as to whether we would accept existence on such terms before we were sent into the world."

"6 CLIFTON PLACE, *May* 18 [1862].

"If it will not give you too much trouble, will you tell me, quite briefly, the relation in which 'the Lords of the Articles' stood to a Scotch Parliament, and how in theory they were chosen?"

"6 CLIFTON PLACE, HYDE PARK, *May* 22 [1862].

"MY DEAR SKELTON,—Thank you much. You tell me exactly what I wanted to know. I fear my book will bring all your people about my ears. Mary Stuart, from my point of view, was something between Rachel and a pantheress.—Ever sincerely yours,

"J. A. FROUDE."

"RAMSGATE, *Easter Monday*, 1862.

"I know very little of Browning's poetry; but Browning himself I admire extremely, and I have often wished for leisure to read him. I tried *Paracelsus* twenty years ago unsuccessfully, and this, I suppose, has prevented me from exciting myself about him as

I ought. By all means let me have your article. Kingsley was very sorry not to see you."

"BEMBRIDGE, ISLE OF WIGHT, *Sep.* 13 [1862].

"MY DEAR SKELTON,—I suppose you are right about the Maclachlan story [1]—in some degree. But in that the offence was treason and not creed (though I incline to think the tradition true as to the public execution), yet creed and treason ran inevitably one into the other. The two metals, quite separate in the cold days, fused together in the melting heat of passion. I wish you or some competent person would take a look at your Scotch history as a whole from the Reformation downwards, showing how Queen Mary's Catholics became the Montrose and the Claverhouse of the next century. Men divide themselves into orthodox and unorthodox quite irrespective of the special creed they profess. The types of character and the contrasts of character remain constant, while the subject-matter is infinitely varied. Your orthodox latitudinarian Sadducee joined in condemning our Lord, just as your orthodox latitudinarian Doctor Lushington condemns the Essayists. No mind could be further from a Covenanter's, judged by its separate detailed opinions, than Macaulay's; yet the essential resemblance of sympathy was stronger than the opposed views of which he was conscious. The remarkable thing in Scotland was the intense

---

[1] The article referred to was on the Wigtown Martyrs' controversy.

hatred of the two parties for each other. It was not altogether Highlander and Lowlander. It was not patrician and plebeian, though in some degree these divisions followed the religious division.

"All mankind, Coleridge says, are either Nominalist or Realist. This was a metaphysical way of expressing two opposed classes which in one form or other divide the world; and which in your Scotland took such picturesque and romantic forms.—Ever faithfully yours,   J. A. FROUDE.

"On controverted points I approve myself of the practice of the Reformation. When St Paul's Cross pulpit was occupied one Sunday by a Lutheran, the next by a Catholic, the next by a Calvinist, all sides had a hearing, and the preachers knew that they would be pulled up before the same audience for what they might say."

"*December* 13 [1862].

"You will let me keep Browning till Feb.—will you not?"

[Froude in his conduct of the Magazine followed the "Reformation practice"; though Browning, I am afraid, was a hard nut to crack. But the prolonged unpopularity of our great poet is now a commonplace.]

"6 CLIFTON PLACE, *Jan.* 3 [1863].

"MY DEAR SKELTON,—I am very sorry about Browning. The length has been the difficulty. Were

I

it made up of your own work it should have gone
in long ago, without a day's delay. But Browning's
verse!—with intellect, thought, power, grace, all the
charms in detail which poetry should have, it rings
after all like a bell of lead. However, it shall go in
next time—for your sake. No doubt he deserves all
you say; yet it will be vain. To this generation
Browning is as uninteresting as Shakespeare's Sonnets
were to the last century. In making the comparison
you see I admit that you may be right. I have no idea
of giving up *Fraser* unless it changes hands, and goes
to some publisher whose views about it may be different
from mine. Parker, as you know, wishes to sell it.
Thalatta came duly, very much improved, I think,
by the additions. Thank you most warmly for your
words about me in the Preface. I wish I could deserve them. I hope to be in Edinburgh the end of
the month. I suppose I had better go through at
once, and see Dunbar and Berwick on my way back.
Surely I shall be delighted with *The Seaside Sketch*.—
Faithfully yours,   J. A. FROUDE."

"*March* 8 [1863].

"The Magazine prospers. The circulation now ex-
ceeds 3000, and more copies must be printed."

"*April* 16 [1863].

"I was highly complimented by Carlyle last night
on the management of *Fraser*."

" I read the notice in the paper which you sent me with deep regret for you—for I know what they were to you. My memory does not distinguish sufficiently between them to enable me to tell which you have lost.   I remember with greatest clearness one bright sunny face, running over with intelligence and kindliness. The other a genuine, true, but rather sadder person. . . . The old familiar faces which we recollect from childhood have a hold over us peculiar of its kind ; and as they drop off one by one the roots of our own hold on life seem shaken. . . . But somehow when successes of this kind do come to us, they come at a time when we have ceased to care for them, and are beginning to think as much of the other world as the present."

" *December* 12 [1863].

" I want you some day to go with me to Lochleven, and then to Stirling, Perth, and Glasgow.   Before I go further I must have a personal knowledge of Lochleven Castle and the grounds at Langside.   Also I must look at the street at Linlithgow where Murray was shot."

" *December* 22 [1863].

" I go to Ireland on the 27th for a few days' shooting, but I shall be here again by the 5th or 6th of January. As to Darnley. Yes, it was too certain that she would kill him. He was a poor wretched worm ; but they had better have let him crawl away to England, and the

manner of it was so piteous.   Still, considering the
times, there was nothing about a mere murder of an
inconvenient scoundrel so very wonderful.   It was
made important by the political consequences.   On the
ground that 'a blunder is worse than a crime,' it was
unpardonable."

"*February* 28 [1864].

" We have got into a sort of scrape by our Theological misdoings.   The world takes the message, but still
at the expense of the bringer of it. . . . Lord Stanhope
tells me that he [Joseph Robertson] has just brought
out for the *Bannatyne Club* a curious book about Queen
Mary.   If you see Mr Robertson, will you kindly tell
him that if he will lend me the book I will take the
greatest care of it. . . . I send you a lecture which I
gave at the Royal Institution, and for which I was
called an Atheist."

"6 CLIFTON PLACE, *June* 29 [1864].

" I almost regret that I did not choose Scotland this
year, as local knowledge of many places is growing
more and more necessary to me.   If we are alive next
year, you must take me to Lochleven.   I want to make
out Carberry Hill, and to seat myself on Queen Mary's
stone. . . . The story grows wilder and grander the
more I know of it ; but like most wild countries it
has bad roads through it, and the travelling is dangerous."

"Salcombe, *August* 14 [1864].

"I am only sorry to hear that the Campaigner[1] is so near his retirement. Let it be only on furlough, and let us by all means hope for more of him by-and-by. If your own travels bring you this way it will be most delightful, only if you come let it be before this splendid weather ends. We have no grouse, but we have a sea like the Mediterranean, and estuaries beautiful as Loch Fyne, the green water washing our garden wall, and boats and mackerel. I, alas! instead of enjoying it, have been floundering all the summer among the extinct mine-shafts of Scotch politics,—the most damnable set of pitfalls mortal man was ever put to blunder through in the dark. Nothing but blind paths ending each of them in a chasm with no bottom, and in the place of guides with good horn lanthorns to show the way, nothing but Protestant and Catholic Will-o'-the-wisps. I believe still that the Regent Murray was the honestest man in the whole island; but there was much pitch which he could not help handling. I shall want you next May to show me Carberry Hill, Lochleven, and Langside. Afterwards I must go to Carlisle, and see Naworth and the Border-line to Berwick.—Ever most truly yours,   J. A. Froude."

"6 Clifton Place, *June* 6 [1864].

"My dear Skelton,— Thanks about the *Campaigner*, which is quite faultless. If you care for praise,

---

[1] *A Campaigner at Home* (Longmans, 1865) originally appeared in *Fraser's Magazine*.

you will be satisfied with what is said by all whose good word is valuable. You shall have your proof as soon as possible. I did my work in Spain ; and except that I found I should have to go there many times again, I should be well satisfied. Just now my chief interest is in a number of ballads in the Record Office on the death of Darnley, and again on that of the Regent Murray. The whole tragedy told in that wild musical Scotch, which is like a voice out of another world. There are ten or twelve of them, some written or nominally written by Robert Semple, but there is more than one hand. Will you ask any of your antiquarian friends if they know anything about them ? They are printed on loose sheets at the time—1567 and 1570. There is no doubt of their being the genuine expression of the emotions of the time, and although strongly Puritan, they are equally beautiful. I am having them copied, and shall print them in a volume[1] if you or Laing or some one will help me with the Scotch.—Most truly yours,   J. A. FROUDE."

" December 4 [1864].

"Theodore Martin will, I hope, undertake the life of Maitland of Lethington, which I have been so long wishing to have written. Will the trout rise in Loch-leven in May? Then, or about then, I hope for my fortnight with you in the North."

---

[1] Since this letter was written these poems have been issued by the Scottish Text Society in a volume edited by Dr Cranstoun, entitled *Satirical Poems of the Time of the Reformation.*

"WESTCLIFF HOUSE, RAMSGATE, *August* 8 [1865].

" Pam. cares for nothing but popularity ; he will do what the people most interested wish ; and he would appoint the Devil over the head of Gabriel if he could gain a vote by it."

" WESTCLIFF, *August* 25 [1865].

" If you have time, I wish you would write half-a-dozen pages for October in review of two little books of poetry—one Allingham's *Fifty Modern Poems ;* the other another volume of our Devonshire Postman Capern, whom I reviewed in *Fraser* seven years ago, when he first appeared. Art has done nothing for him, but he is a fine musician by nature, and found out his faculties merely by being employed to write songs for the farmers' festivities at Christmas, and sonnets or elegies for despairing lover and friend. It is wildflower growth, but *real* as far as it goes. Shall I send you the book or books ? For Allingham I know not what can be said. All he seems to me to have succeeded in is in proving that with many fine faculties, which he certainly has, he will fail to the end of the chapter."

" 5 ONSLOW GARDENS, *October* 16 [1865].

" I hope to be with you on the second. Pray do not ask people to meet me. I am sorry about A.—on public grounds as well as private. But he will make a fair professor ; a leaden bottom and a wooden head seem the established qualifications."

[This is the first letter from the pleasant house in

Onslow Gardens, where Froude remained until he went
to Oxford in 1892.]

[In June 1865 I had reviewed Mr Swinburne's
earliest volume, *The Queen-Mother and Rosamond;* and
on the appearance of the first series of *Poems and
Ballads* in 1866, Froude permitted me, after some
hesitation, and in spite of, or rather in consequence
of, the extravagant and irrational violence of the
critics, to insert a qualified "apology." He had at
first, having seen only garbled extracts, been rather
carried away.]

"BABBICOMBE, TORQUAY, *August* 15 [1866].

"You are coming round to my opinion of Swinburne. . . . I have looked at his late poems, but I
have not got a copy of them. Your difficulty will
be in choosing passages to justify your interpretation.
. . . What about Dallas? Is the book ever coming
out, or is the article to be broken up?—Most truly
yours,   J. A. FROUDE."

"BABBICOMBE, TORQUAY, *August* 19 [1866].

"Since I wrote you I have seen Swinburne's volume,
and also the *Saturday* and the *Athenæum* reviews of
it. There is much, of course, which is highly ob-
jectionable in it, but much also of real beauty. He
convinces me in fact for the first time that he has
real stuff in him, and I think, considering the fatuous
stupidity with which the critics have hitherto flattered

him, considering that he is still very young, and that
the London intellectual life is perhaps the very worst
soil which has ever existed in the world for a young
. poet to be planted in,—considering all this, I am very
unwilling to follow the crew of Philistines, and bite
his heels like the rest of them. The *Saturday Review*
temperament is ten thousand thousand times more
damnable than the worst of Swinburne's skits. Modern respectability is so utterly without God, faith,
heart ; it shows so singular ingenuity in assailing and
injuring everything that is noble and good, and so
systematic a preference for what is mean and paltry,
that I am not surprised at a young fellow dashing
his heels into the face of it. If he is to be cut up
for what he has done, I would lay the blame far
more heavily on others than on him, and I would
and especially praise the many things which
deserve praise. When there is any kind of
genius, we have no right to drive it mad. We
deal with it wisely, justly, fairly.—Ever yours,
"J. A. FROUDE."

"5 ONSLOW GARDENS, *December* 15 [1866].
. . . tirely except to your view that there is no
the country beyond what is occupying itself
nging words together in prose or verse. I
say, on the contrary, that genius intuitively
practical, and only by accident gets squeezed
bad into book-writing. The ablest men in
the country at this time, I believe, are lawyers, en-

gineers, men of science, doctors, statesmen, anything
but authors. If we have only four supreme men at
present alive among us, and if Browning and Ruskin
are two of those, the sooner you and I emigrate the
better."

"5 ONSLOW GARDENS, *Feb.* 6 [1867].

"Your paper is with the printers. I don't agree
with it; but why should I? Could you not prefix
to the proof two or three words intimating that you
don't agree with the line which we are taking, and
that you wish to say a little on the other side? and
then I can put a note saying that I have the greatest
possible pleasure in acceding to the wishes of an old
and deeply valued contributor. I am grieved to hear
about your side. If I were you, and *could* manage
it, I would go right away to Algiers or some such
place.—Most truly yours,   J. A. FROUDE."

"5 ONSLOW GARDENS, *July* 7 [1867].

"I had a pleasant time in Spain, finishing my work
there, I fear, for good and all. A great deal which
is curious and unlooked for comes out about the relations between James VI. and Spain. They were
more intimate than anybody in Scotland knew, and
fresh vivid light is thrown by them on the Raid of
Ruthven. I have a weary time before me, however,
before I can begin to write. The book will be finished
in the next two volumes."

"5 ONSLOW GARDENS, *December* 26 [1867].

" I was on the point of writing to you to stir your memory. You shall gather material in Kerry next year for splendid ' Riverside' papers. The likenesses and the unlikenesses to Scotland will not fail to strike you; also the remains of the Anglo-Franco-Scoto-Hispano - Hibernico private establishments which swarmed on those coasts in the 16th century. What a subject for a novel!"

[Froude was much gratified when the St Andrews students in 1868 elected him their Rector, and his Inaugural Address was delivered on 23d March 1869.]

"5 ONSLOW GARDENS, *Feb.* 23 [1869].

" If I can spend a day and night with you going or coming I will; but it will be infinitely more agreeable, if Mrs Skelton will let it be so, to see you and have a chat with you without company. Consider what I shall just have escaped from, or shall be about to undergo. I am writing my lecture, which I alternately believe to be profoundly wise and absolute nonsense. I suppose it is neither one nor the other, but considerably nearer the last."

"5 ONSLOW GARDENS, *Feb.* 26 [1869].

" Matt. wishes your article on him to be postponed till the appearance of the new edition of his poems. He knows that he is strongest in criticism, and there-

fore cares most to be praised for his verses. Enough
can be said justly in praise of this side of him without
flattery, and therefore it will be perhaps wise to confine
yourself to it; but we can talk him over when I see
you. About my address. The subject will be modern
education; the burden, that all education, high and
low, ought to be of a kind to help men to earn their
livelihood. The useful first, the beautiful, and the good
even, afterwards. Or if men choose to devote themselves to the beautiful and good, &c., it should be
with the conditions attached to that sort of thing by
the old scholars of prospective poverty. Indirectly
it will be a compliment to your system at the expense
of ours. After four years of Oxford or Cambridge,
and an expenditure of two or three thousand pounds,
we turn young fellows out unable to earn a sixpence,
and with habits of luxury which will be a misery and
temptation to them all their lives. Of course there
will be more in the lecture than this. I give you
merely a sketch of the main drift. . . . Faithfully
yours,   J. A. FROUDE."

"5 ONSLOW GARDENS, *Jan.* 11 [1870].

"Thanks for your good wishes and a hearty return
of them. We were grieved to hear of your loss. It
was a cloud over your beautiful home which must have
thrown a heavy shadow there. I am glad you liked
what I said about the Colonies. It will be well if you
will work to the same purpose in *Blackwood*. Every
nerve ought to be strained, or it will be too late."

[From this time onwards, the policy of Imperial
Federation—or at least of a closer connection between
the mother country and the Colonies—was urgently
advocated by Mr Froude.   There can be no doubt that
to his urgent advocacy the sounder views that now
prevail are in some measure due.]

"5 ONSLOW GARDENS, *Feb.* 10 [1870].

"You might put Morris's last poem with Rossetti's
volume.   Also, could you not throw a general retrospective glance over the last ten years' produce in this
line,—gathering some kind of unity of tendency from
it.   *The Ring and the Book* requires mention.   Clough's
Dipsychus I consider the most really remarkable contribution we have had; but the poetry, like all else, is
going post-haste to the Devil just now, and Alfred's
last volume is the most signal instance of it.   He too
has been swept into the general stream.   You might
say as much as this—much as I like and honour him.

"I have been among some of the Tory magnates
lately.   They distrust Disraeli still, and will never
again be led by him.   So they are as sheep that have
no shepherd.   Lord Salisbury's time may come; but
not yet.   I am going in with *Fraser* for the reconsti-
tuting 'authority' somehow."

"5 ONSLOW GARDENS, *March* 9 [1870].

"I am to lecture at Edinburgh next winter on
Calvin. . . .   Hearty thanks for your invitation, of

which I shall not fail to avail myself. Remember, on the other hand, that you and Mrs Skelton promised yourselves to us this summer at Derreen. It is our last season; we are to be evicted without compensation at the end of our lease. . . . I want a crusade against party government. That lies at the bottom of every mischief under which we groan."

"5 ONSLOW GARDENS, *April* 12 [1870].

"Rossetti has gone to press. I was going to write to you to ask if you would review *Lothair* for the June number. It will be a labour of love to you, and you may praise Dizzy as much as you please. G—— and Co. deliberately intend to shake off the Colonies. They are privately using their command of the situation to make the separation inevitable."

"DERREEN, *June* 21 [1870].

"Don't bother yourself. My only vexation was lest S. and M. should construe the passage into retaliation for their own good-for-nothing attack on me in the Q——. I never resented anything more than that article. I felt as if I was tied to a post, and a mere ass was brought up to kick me. Some day I think I shall take my reviewers all round, and give them a piece of my mind. I acknowledge to five real mistakes in the whole book—*twelve volumes*—about twenty trifling slips, equivalent to i's not dotted and t's not crossed; and that is all that the utmost malignity has discovered.

Every one of the rascals has made a dozen blunders of
his own, too, while detecting one of mine.   Pray come
on here—we shall so much like to see you, and come
while the weather is fine and the sea moderate.   After
October sailing becomes dangerous work."

[This is almost the only letter in which Froude
alluded to the charges of inaccuracy that were freely
brought against him by Mr Freeman and others.   It
seems to me that the charge, even when stated in far
more temperate language than was used at the time,
rests on no sufficient basis.   We must remember that
he was to some extent a pioneer, and that he was the
first (for instance) to utilise the treasures of Simancas.
He transcribed, from the Spanish, masses of papers
which even a Spaniard would have read with difficulty,
and I am assured that his translations (with rare ex-
ceptions) render the original with singular exactness.
As regards Scottish history, I could not accept his
conclusions, and I had more than once to examine his
statements sentence by sentence; but I have seen no
reason to change the opinion I expressed in the Preface
to *Maitland of Lethington* : " Only the man or woman
who has had to work upon the mass of Scottish
material in the Record Office can properly appreciate
Mr Froude's inexhaustible industry and substantial
accuracy.   His point of view is very different from
mine; but I am bound to say that his acquaintance
with the intricacies of Scottish politics during the
reign of Mary appears to me to be almost, if not quite,

unrivalled." And with this view, I may add, John Hill Burton concurred.[1]]

"DERREEN, August 24 [1870].

"We expect you anxiously, and shall be most disappointed if you and Mrs Skelton do not come. At present the weather is most beautiful. Bring your gun or not as you please. I can furnish you if you don't. Our grouse have been a failure so far as we have yet seen. . . . You misunderstand me about the [Calvin] lecture. I don't mean to meddle with the metaphysical puzzle, but to insist on the fact historically that this particular idea has several times appeared in the world under different forms, and always with the most powerful moral effect. The last reappearance of it in Spinoza, and virtually in Goethe, is the most singular of all. . . . They have believed in Election, Predestination, and, generally, the absolute arbitrary sovereignty of God; and these, and not the moderate Liberals and the reasonable prudent people who seem to us most commendable, have had the shaping of the world's destinies. In fact I suppose if there is such a thing as a Personal God at all, this sort of theory is the true one, and most consistent with facts."

"DERREEN, KENMARE, Sep. 4 [1870].

"You will come from Killarney, and will therefore be at Kenmare about one. If the wind is East or

---

[1] An admirable letter by Sir Theodore Martin on the subject of the alleged "inaccuracies" appeared in the Times of November 7, 1894.

North, the yacht shall go up and meet you, and the men will be at the Lansdowne Arms. If you do not find them there, you will understand that it would not do, and come on in a car."

[Of that memorable visit to the wild glens of Kerry some record remains in an old Note-book, and the pages devoted to the pleasant days spent on the bay of Kill-mackillog still retain a touch of colour—though out of all the rest it has faded. As the happiest of Froude's later summers were passed at Derreen, those who knew him only in London drawing-rooms may like to see him in his shooting-jacket among the Paddies, for whom, in spite of all political heartburnings, he retained a warm liking to the last. Here, then, is one of these pages :—

We were on our way to visit a friend whose name has long been, and long will be, illustrious in English literature; and the week which we spent with him on the bay of Killmackillog will not be quickly forgotten. The "harbour" on which the house stands is surrounded on all sides by lofty mountains, which shut off the profane world. Their sides are bare of timber; but around the lawn forest-trees and rare shrubs, hollies, laurels, hedges of fuchsias, the pampas grass, the hydrangea, the myrtle, and the arbutus flourish luxuriantly. The woods are carpeted with ferns in autumn, and the loveliest wild-flowers imaginable are found in spring. Great dragon-flies sweep across the heather, and the curious humming-bird moth flutters among the roses and geraniums. Nor are more material attractions wanting—the land flows, so to speak, with milk and honey. There are real Scotch grouse on the mountain-tops (2000 feet above us), where they find it cooler than in the valleys. There are hares and rabbits and wild-duck; salmon lying by the score in the long still reaches of the river; an oyster-bed on the beach; plaice, soles, turbot, lobster in the bay. There are water-birds, moreover, of various kinds; but no one cares to meddle with them: so that, at twilight, you hear close at hand the wild plaint of the curlew, and next morning, when you go down to bathe, the cormorants gaze at you with the utmost composure.

On this side of the bay, for twenty miles, our host has no neighbours except the Kerry cottars and fishermen; but on the other side there are a few country houses: Dromore, the residence of the last representative of a great old Irish house; Parknacilla, where the most genial, tolerant, and learned member of the Irish hierarchy enjoys his summer holiday; and Garinish, which the taste and munificence of a Catholic peer have transformed from a desolate rocky island into a veritable piece of fairyland. The Kerry cottars and fishermen are an interesting study, and they are best studied on Sunday. The Catholic chapel and its vicinity on that day present a curious scene. The people assemble on the highroad and in the neighbouring fields. The donkeys and ponies are taken out of the carts and tethered to the bushes. Through the birch-trees that bend over the stream one sees young women, who have walked without shoes eight or ten or twelve miles, washing their feet in the running water. (They don't wear shoes in rainy Ireland, on the principle that it is *dryer* to wet their feet only, than their feet *plus* shoes and stockings.) Men and women and children are sitting about everywhere, a profusion of bright reds blazing through the green. Within the unfinished and unfurnished chapel the service is conducted in the most primitive fashion. The hum of voices comes in with the autumn sunshine until the host is raised, when for a few seconds there is deep stillness both within and without. Then the congregation leave the chapel—gathering into groups as at a fair—eating, drinking, buying, selling, winding up with a dance on the green. If you are looking on, some pretty, swift-footed Kerry girl will insist on your dancing with her—it is the custom of the country—and you must submit with the best grace you can. Then, late in the afternoon, the inhabitants of each district leave together in a body, and the loneliest glens are startled at dusk by the sounds of what always seemed to me in Southern Ireland a harsh and discordant merriment.

Respecting the other incidents of that pleasant visit, much might be written. How, in our host's yacht, we beat up and down the wide estuary from one point of vantage to another; how we visited the old churchyard where "The last remains of MacFinnan Dhu, Pater Patriæ!" are deposited; how we were lost in the mist among the mountains; how, aided by the most charm-

ing of antiquaries (since Monkbarns), we opened a *rath*
(or underground dwelling of the old natives), and how,
on hands and feet, the great historian disappeared from
our gaze into the bowels of the earth, and reappeared
——heavens! if all the mud that the *Saturday Review*
has cast at him had *stuck*, he could not have presented
a more appalling spectacle; how we ascended Knockatee, and inspected the Holy Loch and its rude shrine
and ruder offerings; how we walked and rowed and
sketched, and were happy in that glorious Kerry sunshine, will be known hereafter, perhaps, when A.'s
private diary is published by Mr Blackwood.

Mr Froude and his household remained at Derreen
till the beginning of November. " We leave Ireland
in a fortnight or three weeks. The weather has been
tremendous. No other word will do for it."
I return again to the letters.]

"5 ONSLOW GARDENS, Jan. 12 [1871].

" Carlyle has been angry too,—a strong Calvinism
lies at the bottom of his nature. He knows perfectly
that the life has gone out of modern Calvinistic
theology, but he likes to see the shell of the flown
bird still treated with reverence. . . . B—— is vexed
with me because I will not let him use *Fraser* to preach
up toleration of Ritualism. I grow more and more
intolerant of certain things; and conscious humbug
in religious matters is one of them."

[Froude delivered his closing address to the St Andrews students on 17th March 1871.   The subject was " Calvinism."]

" 5 ONSLOW GARDENS, March 24 [1871].

" I enjoyed my trip exceedingly; you were all very kind to me.   I shall ever retain a grateful recollection of the St Andrews students, from whom alone I have yet received any public recognition.   I suppose I shall as usual be made a spread-eagle of by the <i>Saturday</i>, but I have survived so many operations of that kind that I have ceased to be curious about them, and do not even look to see what has been done to me.   The Yankees have written to me about going out to lecture to them. I am strongly tempted; but I could not tell the truth about Ireland without reflecting in a good many ways on my own country.   I don't fancy doing that, however justly, to amuse Jonathan.   I liked the notice in the <i>Scotsman</i> very much.   It is a paradox to say that old Calvinism was not doctrinal in the face of the Institute ; but it is astonishing to find how little in ordinary life they talked or wrote about doctrine.   The doctrine was never more than the dress.   The living creature was wholly moral and political,—so at least I think myself."

" 5 ONSLOW GARDENS, June 8 [1871].

" I remain in office till December, so by all means let me have the <i>Mary Stuart</i>.   I shall be extremely interested in reading it. . . .   I am working away at the Irish book.   I found vast stores of material of a curious

kind in Dublin; and at any rate I hope to produce
something readable. I fear, however, that it will not
conduce to the agreeableness of my future visits to
Celtic Ireland. If G—— could have his way, there
would be no Ireland but a Celtic one in a few years;
but there are happy signs of approximation between
the Church and the Presbyterians, which may be the
beginning of a wholesome reaction. Protestants pull-
ing together may still hold out, and even recover the
reins."

"5 ONSLOW GARDENS, Nov. 17 [1871].

" I am to continue editor after all. Dasent declines
at the last moment, and the house of Longman petition
me to go on with it. I trust you will go on with me
also. Driven out of Derreen, I am thinking of trying
to get Garinish. Lord Dunraven is dead, and his
successor does not care to keep it."

"5 ONSLOW GARDENS, April 11 [1871].

" Don't you think the introduction into newspapers
of remarks upon our private affairs ought to be action-
able? You are very kind to have so far noticed that
unnecessary paragraph as to write and ask about it.
All I hope is well at the Hermitage. St Andrews is
at last provided of a Rector, and well provided. I was
heartily glad of the choice. I have changed my political mind about Dizzy, and shall be heartily glad of a
laudatory article upon him if you care to write it."

"WESTCLIFF HOUSE, RAMSGATE, *Sep.* 7 [1872].

" I sail in a fortnight [for the States], and I know
not what I have before me.   I go like an Arab of the
desert: my hand will be against every man, and therefore every man's hand will be against me.   Protestant
and Catholic, English, English-Irish, and Celtic—my
one hope will be, like St Paul's, to fling in some word
or words among them which will set them by the ears
among themselves. . . .   I have been cruising with
Lord Ducie in a big schooner.   We were for several
days in the Kenmare river, and I again walked over
Knockatee, with Campbell of Isla for my companion
—an extremely interesting man.   Derreen was beautiful
as ever." [1]

"5 ONSLOW GARDENS, *Feb.* 15 [1873].

" *Fraser* no longer brings us into correspondence,
for you have found better encouragement, I fear, in
the rival firm.   But that is no reason why I should
never hear from you.   My American experience has
been more than interesting.   They are good people—
very unlike what I looked for."

[This year I find he was looking out for a country-
house in Scotland,—" where we can have our three or
four months of gypsy life like the Irish one.   A stream

---

[1] Mr Froude did not return to Derreen again,—though I fancy that it had
a unique fascination for him.   So late as the autumn of 1888, he wrote
me,—"Derreen is offered me again.   I wish—and I dread—for Derreen
has associations for me which I hardly dare to revive."

with trout and an odd salmon would add to the pleasure, or still better the sea or a salt-water loch." But nothing came of it.]

"ATHENÆUM CLUB, *April* 2 [1873].

"Some time ago you offered to do a panegyric on Dizzy. I declined, but I have come round to your way of thinking. I am one of the weak-minded beings who are carried away by the Conservative reaction. Rather, I see plainly that G—— is driving the ship into the breakers. . . . I mentioned at a party of M.P.'s the other night that throughout human history the *great orators* had been invariably proved wrong. There were shrieks of indignation; but at last it was allowed that facts looked as if it were true. Will you write on Dizzy now?—Ever yours, J. A. FROUDE."

"5 ONSLOW GARDENS, *December* 16 [1873].

"I am working hard to finish my Irish book, which I have grown to hate. It will make the poor Paddies hate me too, which I do not wish, as I cannot return the feeling. . . . Anyway, I am satisfied to feel that the great Revolutionary wave has spent its force, and that the next fifty years will probably be more and more Conservative."

[In the spring of 1874 a great calamity overtook Mr Froude. Mrs Froude died suddenly early in March. Sir James Stephen, writing to me on April 1, informed me that he had been constantly with him since her death. " It is a terrible blow for him, poor fellow, and I think I am the only person (except Mr Carlyle) whom he has seen since it happened."]

" You will not expect me to say anything of what has befallen me. Rigid silence is my only present resource. . . . I am unable just now to attend to the Magazine work. We go in a fortnight to Wales, to remain there till the end of the year."

[Early next year Lord Carnarvon requested Mr Froude to visit South Africa, and ascertain the state of political feeling throughout the colony. He returned in December.]

" A word of thanks for your note, though I am overwhelmed with business. Yes, I am at home again, after strange adventures. We know what we are, but we know not what we shall be. If anybody had told me two years ago that I should be leading an agitation within Cape Colony, I should have thought my informant delirious. And though the world cannot yet understand what has happened, I have picked the one Diamond out of the rubbish-heap, and brought it home with me. The Ministers have the appearance of victory, but we have the substance.

" Pray send your Essays. I shall delight in them.
I have seen your hand from time to time in *Blackwood*
—specially in praise of Green's book at my expense.[1]
I will back my view to outlive Green's; though I
haven't had it, and don't know what he says. My
best regards to Mrs Skelton.—Yours most warmly,
                              " J. A. FROUDE."

[In 1876 Mr Froude and Professor Huxley were appointed members of the Scottish Universities Commission. For several years thereafter they paid frequent
visits to Edinburgh,—Mr Froude being my guest at
the Hermitage. Both of the English Commissioners
were brilliant talkers; and while the shadows gathered
outside in the glen, there was the sparkle of keen wit
and ready repartee within. For these unconventional
festivities, the injunction was "not to dress"; and I
find the Professor, *more suo*, proposing to come in
a kilt,—"to be as little dressed as possible."]

                "5 ONSLOW GARDENS, *May* 20 [1876].

" I would not be an inconvenience to either of you
for the world. And least of all think of inviting
any one to meet me. An evening or two with you
in your beautiful glen will be better than any quantity
of idle dinner-party talk. Abana and Pharpar are
not better than the waters of Israel or the murmur
of Lothianburn."

                    [1] Certainly not.

"5 ONSLOW GARDENS, *May* 27 [1876].

"Some time ago, before I knew that I was to be a Commissioner, I promised Henry Bowie that I would open the annual course at the Philosophical Institution by a lecture upon landlords and landed property. I had been much interested by what Mr Smith had done at Scilly, and I wanted to show Radical Scotland how beneficent a fairy a landlord still might and may be, in spite of battues and Deer-Forests. It occurs to me that my being a University Commissioner may be inconsistent with my performing on platforms. Will you think this over?"

"5 ONSLOW GARDENS, *November* 16 [1876].

"After I left, you seem to have had pleasant weather! Here we had only frost and fog; you had snow and a gale of wind. To-day it is like summer."

"5 ONSLOW GARDENS, *March* 24 [1877].

"This accursed Turkish business is still in the air. I met Lord and Lady Derby last night. They lay the blame on Ignatieff. I suppose, in fact, that the Russians mean to go to war unless Europe will efficiently back them in controlling the Turkish Government; and that the object of all their diplomacy is to put them in the right before Europe, and England in the wrong. A few weeks must end the uncertainty. When the roads in Bulgaria become practicable, the Russian army will either advance or show clearly that it does not mean to advance."

"5 ONSLOW GARDENS, *March* 29 [1877].

"I cannot make up my mind to go to B——. It would be like being shut up in a cage with a benevolent white bear. . . . The Essays come out to-morrow."

"CLARENDON HOTEL [*April* 2, 1877], *Tuesday*.

"The sacrifice has been thrown away. I ought to stay for the Friday meeting of the Commission, but I am so forlorn that if I continue in the Hotel the , temptation of the train will be too strong, and I shall find myself in the Flying Scotsman before I know it."

"5 ONSLOW GARDENS, *Sept.* 17 [1877].

"The Edinburgh duty is inconvenient, and if I was certain that you would be absent, I might after all resolve to shirk—but it would lie on my conscience.

"This Eastern business is very frightful, and will bring an ugly train of mischiefs behind it, worse than any which were anticipated. No European Government can allow Moslem fanaticism to come off completely victorious. The Turk, I fear, is like the Bull in a Spanish circus. However splendidly he fights, and however many men and horses he kills, he is none the less finished off in the end by *somebody*. Providence, that 'loves to disappoint the Devil,' will probably bring one good out of it all—a reform of the Russian administration. That democracies should promote the wrong man to high place is natural enough; but there is no excuse for an autocrat."

"5 ONSLOW GARDENS, *November* 23 [1877].

" I have never been in Scotland in mid-winter, and am curious to see what it is like.   Curling is one of the Scotch mysteries in which I am still uninitiated, and I may have a chance of witnessing it.   Also, there may be a woodcock or woodcocks in your glen. But whether or no, there will be warm Scotch firesides and warm friends whom I shall be glad to see again, and who will perhaps be moderately glad to see me.   This Commission work, thanks chiefly to you and Mrs Skelton, has been a real enjoyment to me."

"5 ONSLOW GARDENS, *December* 4 [1877].

" Anyway, pray order a frost.   I have never seen Scotland in her snow drapery and icy jewels."

"5 ONSLOW GARDENS, *May* 3 [1878].

" We will talk about Salcombe when we meet.   Seabathing, sailing, and fishing will do more to set you up than the French doctors.   What a nice temper we are all getting into, and how delightfully the cards are shuffled!—Bradlaugh and Liddon shaking hands on one side, and Lord Beaconsfield and General Cluseret on the other.   I have letters from the latter (who is now in Turkey) on the text of 'il faut humilier le Russie,' which explains the tenderness with which the 'General' is treated in *Lothair*. . . . I am reading up Cæsar and his times, with a view to writing a book about him.   Imagine a few years hence faction growing hot here ;—England governed by troops from

India, with Mr Hardy for Sylla; and then, by-and-by,
Chamberlain and Bright for Cinna and Marius!—
one's mouth waters at the prospect, and nothing less
is foretold by hot correspondents of the Radical
papers. Seriously, I believe things will end quietly.
The prospect on the Continent is so ugly on all sides
that all the Powers are frightened at the look of it."

"5 ONSLOW GARDENS, Feb. 7 [1878].

" I was at the club this evening, took up <i>Blackwood</i>,
as you recommended, and found your kind handiwork.
Of course it is yours—no one else would say such
pretty things of me, or give Freeman a kick on my
behalf.   But I was more pleased with your evident
liking for my poor little volume of <i>Studies</i>.   It contains
things which have been on my mind these thirty
years, and could never get themselves uttered before.
A 'Tory'!   I don't know what I am.   Nobody rejoiced
more than I did when the Tories came in, or wished
them longer life.   But they seem to me to be no wiser
than their predecessors, and to be working steadily on
the lines which will bring on the catastrophe, which
I fear as much as you.   But what am I?   and what
do I know?   I have lived long enough to distrust my
own judgment beyond that of most reasonable men.
I have been often wrong before, and I hope I am
wrong now.   And yet I hated the Crimean War, and
I saw every one (a few years ago) come round to my
old opinion.   Now, the country seems to me to have
been bitten by the same mad dog."

" I congratulate you on your deserved honour.   The
laurel is welcome when it comes; and though, as with
Cæsar, it serves sometimes to conceal the thin locks,
which tell us that we are older than we were, it is
evergreen, and defies age.   I should like to hear a little
more of you and of the Glen, where I have spent so
many happy hours.   How are you, and how is Mrs
Skelton, and May, and Jim, and the little fellow with
the round face? . . . You may have seen Freeman's
papers in the *Contemporary*.   The only answer which
I shall make will be to republish my own articles with
a few notes. . . . You will be glad to hear that he is
changing his mind on the Eastern question.   That
I should be on the same side has satisfied him that
he must be wrong.   Meantime I am undertaking a
Life of Cæsar.   What do you think? "

"5 ONSLOW GARDENS, *May* 9 [1878].

"The political atmosphere has grown cooler.   I
wrote to my Russian friends to warn them that the
Liberal party here was divided and powerless, and
that they must not count on the slightest help from
that quarter.   I suppose I may have helped in con-
verting the Russian *Press* with which my correspondents are connected.   But I have got into Cæsar, and
think no more of this storm in a slop-basin."

"THE MOLT, *Sep.* 19 [1878].

"We have been very quiet; a few visitors have
looked in upon us, among them Bret Harte, who

charmed us all; occasional yachts have come in with
glimpses of the outside world; and as long as the
weather allowed I had a *trawler*, which gave us an
occasional sail and found us in fish; but I cannot
respond to your encomiums on the season. August
was wet and stormy; the harvest was ruined; and an
incessant heavy sea, rolling in from the south-west,
interfered with our water amusements more than we
could wish. But I have been very happy and very
busy, . . . steadily at work on Cæsar. . . . I can
form no conjecture of what the world will say. I find
the kite rises equally well whichever way the wind
blows, if only there is enough of it. But, indeed, I
shall have trod on nobody's toes this time, unless it be
a few Republican fanatics—modern Catos like Frank
Newman."

"5 ONSLOW GARDENS, *December* 27 [1878].

"My hearty thanks for your kind card of good
wishes. We make many acquaintances as we grow
old, but few or no new friends. Those that are left of
the old ones we cling to closer than ever, and you and
yours I look upon as among the nearest now belonging
to me. . . . I have taken to my skates again, and I
should have enjoyed the change from the open winters
which we have had so long if it was not that so many
poor wretched creatures are starving, and that I have
to drive twice a-week with Carlyle in a fly with wide
open windows. The ten generations of his Annandale
ancestors have given him a constitution as hard as
granite. Disraeli's cards are still made of trumps.

Even when his hand is bad he plays it so well that I admire his skill, though I disbelieve in his foreign politics. He is more popular than ever. You see how well the people like him, in the absence of all complaints against the Government in the midst of so much suffering; and after all I would sooner see him Minister than G——."

"5 ONSLOW GARDENS, *Feb.* 6 [1879].

" I have been so busy up to this moment that I have not had time to read the *Essays in Romance* as I wished to read them. Yesterday I spent a delightful evening with you over the Prelude and Martin Holdfast. The Prelude is quite excellent,—your own Hermitage, with the rocks and the trees, and the ivy and the owls, and the cocks and hens. Can I ever forget poor blind Bellerophon — eating his soul — can I ever cease to feel for him? The picture made me long to be with you again. Martin Holdfast I of course remembered; but in the new good type it was fresh and young again.

" Those old times in Johnny Parker's room are wae to think on—so many dead and gone ;—Whyte-Melville went the last, and how characteristically! The rest of us will soon be over-ripened fruit ; but what is the use of complaining? We must go on and defy the Devil as long as we can stand and speak. Whether we shall have any more of that work *beyond* remains to be seen.

" Tulloch takes *Fraser*—what will C—— say to this ? I had an odd dream about Tulloch last night. I heard him say, with one of his jolly laughs, that his breeks were bigger than my ——. May it prove pro- phetic! Anyway I am glad that Longman has settled at last. I would not have given it up had you and Melville, and Lawrence even, been willing and able to help.

"*Cæsar* is in the press. I believe it is the best book which I have ever written. But how can I know? You say so truly that as we grow old we hold our con- victions conditionally, and lose the confidence with which we stept out when we knew less and felt more.

"I will write to you again when I have finished the Essays. My warmest regards to Mrs Skelton and the Boys and the little bright May. — Yours most truly,   J. A. FROUDE."

"5 ONSLOW GARDENS, *June* 2 [1879].

"I have been building a large boat, and we could have some sails, and forget that we are literary mor- tals, subject to wrath and the *Saturday Review*. I begin to think it is my fate to fly my kite against the wind. If by any chance the wind came favourable I should fall collapsed. Has Tulloch tempted you back to *Fraser?*"

"5 ONSLOW GARDENS, *July* 28 [1879].

"I am tired out with work and want of sleep. The salt water will set me up again. The *Short Studies* have done better than I had expected; a large edition is sold, and another is coming. But my poor Divus Cæsar falls flat: nobody cares about it."

[We were at The Molt this August,—a place almost as lovely and romantic as Derreen. Then we went to North Devon.]

"The Molt, Salcombe, *September* 2 [1879].

"I am glad you have seen Clovelly and the Hobby. I, as South Devon born, am fondest of our own coast; but I like the north of the county next best to my own side, as I like Yankees next best to Englishmen. . . . I have promised Morley an article on South Africa. It seemed easy at a distance. Now that the time has come to write it, I am like a pump which can draw no water. It is painfully brought home to me that as we grow old, the soil will not bear as it did."

"5 Onslow Gardens, *December* 5 [1879].

"The world has nibbled at my Railway Siding like minnows round a worm, as if they were afraid there was a hook inside of some kind. Francis Newman seems morally shocked at my pretending to believe in a day of judgment. It was just a fancy that came into my head; part of it was a real dream. . . . There should be cock and wild-duck in your glen, though you don't mention them. I have a fine preserve of sparrows under my window. A London sparrow, if he is aware of his advantages, should know that he is on the whole the best off of all mortal beings."

[Of one subject even Mr Freeman would have been forced to admit that the historian of the Reformation was a master. Froude was a born sailor, and could manage a yacht or yawl in the ugliest sea as if he had been bred to the business. So he was quick to detect any slip that his friends, who were less expert, might make. The workmanship of *Crookit Meg*, he was pleased to say, was as good as could be—with one exception. "If you mean to take us to sea in this questionable little vessel, you must have your sea-dialect looked over. The main sheet is a rope, not a sail. The jib is 'loosed' when you get under weigh, and is the first sail taken in when you are coming to your moorings" (January 30, 1880). The next letter refers to a proposal to republish *The Nemesis of Faith*, which (happily it may be) came to nothing. The *Nemesis* as a psychological study is extremely interesting; but it does not reach the high-water mark of his more mature work.]

"5 ONSLOW GARDENS, March 19 [1880].

"MY DEAR SKELTON,—Your letter encourages a half-formed purpose to ripen into Act. It seems that there is a *demand* for the poor *Nemesis*. The Longmans apply for leave to bring out a new edition of it. As yet I have said No,—but why may I not change it to *Yes*, and show the world for what slight cause they expelled from Oxford and half ruined the now visibly innocent author of the thing?

"I am hard at work on Carlyle's Life. As soon as

the leaves are on the trees, I must make a little tour
about Dumfriesshire—chiefly in Annandale—looking at
places where C. lived and Irving lived.   Don't you
think that you might meet me at Carlisle or Moffat,
and that we might do the investigation together?   If
the Annandale dialect is what it was sixty years ago,
I may want a *construe* now and then.   Three days
would exhaust it all; and if the Howards are at
Naworth Castle, as they perhaps will be, we could
give another day or two to that.

"I take M—— to Paris next Saturday; we shall
stay a week.   As to the elections, I had meant to vote
for Brown, a Conservative, but a stanch Colonist, who
shares my views on that subject.   But as he must
support the Colonial Office about the South African
policy, and as I cannot induce Beach to do as I think
he ought, I shall not vote at all.

"I do not love Beaconsfield; but I love Gladstone
less.—Ever warmly yours,   J. A. FROUDE.

"I have a charming little cutter—13 tons—building
at Salcombe.   We count on you and Mrs Skelton
coming."

Here in the meantime I must pause.   The fifteen
years that followed were not the least eventful in Mr
Froude's career; and the letters belonging to them are
(to say the least) as direct and graphic as any of the
earlier.   Sir George Trevelyan remarked at Dundee
the other day that Mr Froude had "a personal charm

and a personal force which were above anything that
he put on paper." The personal charm and the
personal force were unquestionably very great; but I
would have been inclined to say that they were
reflected with quite exceptional felicity and faithful-
ness in his familiar *Studies*, and, still more so, in his
familiar letters.

IX.

MAINLY ABOUT
JAMES ANTHONY FROUDE.

I AM hopeful that the extracts from Mr Froude's
letters, which I made the other day, have sufficed
to convince the reader who is not incurably prejudiced
that this much-maligned " Timon " of dyspeptic Critics
and Dryasdust Professors was not so much of a Timon
after all,—except, it may be, in his love for the sea.
We have seen him in his " happier hour "; clouds
gather in every life that temporarily obscure the sunshine, and Froude was not more fortunate than his
fellow-men. But these clouds passed away, as all
clouds do when we wait long enough; and the closing
years of his life were among the peacefullest and the
most prolific. He died in harness (only taking to
his bed when he had corrected the last sheets of his
Erasmus), as he had always desired to die, being
indeed (if we are driven for comparison to poet and
playwright) rather a Ulysses than a Timon :—

"Come, my friends,
'Tis not too late to seek a newer world ;
Push off, and sitting well in order smite
The sounding furrows ; for my purpose holds
To sail beyond the sunset, and the baths
Of all the Western Stars, until I die.
It may be that the gulfs will wash us down ;
It may be we shall touch the Happy Isles,
And see the great Achilles, whom we knew."

"*I have more than half a mind,*" he wrote to me in his
last letter, "*to accept an invitation from Sir George Grey,
and go back with him in the autumn to the Antipodes.*"
But there were to be no more voyages—on seas familiar or unfamiliar.

One or two dates may be here given before I continue
these reminiscences. James Anthony Froude was born
on April 23, 1818; he died on October 20, 1894; so
that he was in his seventy-seventh year. He belonged
to a clever and brilliant family. His father, the Arch-
deacon of Totness, was an admirable though self-taught
artist—some of his pencil-drawings which I have seen
are highly esteemed by Mr Ruskin. To his elder
brother—Richard Hurrell Froude—Anthony was profoundly attached; and he resented Mr Freeman's
insulting comments on their opposite views of the
Reformation with more than ordinary warmth: " I
look back upon my brother as on the whole the most
remarkable man I have ever met in my life. I have
never seen any person—not one—in whom, as I now
think of him, the excellences of intellect and character

were combined in fuller measure. Of my personal
feeling towards him I cannot speak. I am ashamed
to have been compelled by what I can describe only
as an inexcusable insult, to say what I have said."

The letters which immediately follow those from
which I have already quoted refer mainly to the Mary
Stuart controversy and the publication of Mr Carlyle's
remains. Of the Carlyle trouble I do not desire to say
a single word. Nor do I mean to enter again on our
protracted debate over the unhappy Queen of Scots. I
may string together a few sentences which will serve to
indicate what in Froude's view was the key of the position ; but these will come in better later on. Meanwhile I take up the narrative where I left off: 1880
was the year—the year of Lord Beaconsfield's defeat
at the polling-booths.

"5 ONSLOW GARDENS, *April* 28 [1880].

"Let us say nothing of the election and its consequences. Do not think I triumph in it. I was interested in the Eastern question for itself, but [not in the
men who have come in]. . . . My disliking extends to
the whole blessed system of government by party. You
are in the rapids in a two-oared boat, and your idea of
managing it is to pull one oar desperately and then the
other, or to back water with one while you pull with
the other. . . . The chief object of this is to tell you
that I am meditating a *final* flight from London into
the country. I stay only for Carlyle's sake, and when

he is gone I shall turn my back on it. It suits none of us in the matter of health. A—— must be going soon to the University, and must have some better place to spend his vacation in. I want to bring him up, as I was brought up, to open-air life—boats, hills, rides, guns, and fishing-rods in the old wild scratch way, when the keeper was the rabbit-catcher, and sporting was enjoyed more for the adventure than for the bag. Could I not find some old place of this kind by a Scotch lake?—a house as big as The Molt or Derreen, and shootings, all of the plain *winter* type which are over-looked in the August letting. G—— has immense par-liamentary dexterity, and is inevitable, at least for a year or two. But I bother myself no more with politics, and believe that in fifty years or sooner a vulgar Cæsar will be the outcome of it. Longman was here this morning; he gives an indifferent account of the health of poor *Fraser*. The change of clothes, taking him at a weak moment, brought on a chill from which he may not recover. *Sic transit Regina.*"

" The *Crookit Meg* shall have an honourable place in my own whatnot close to my arm-chair. She has not arrived—owing to the long calm weather, I suppose: but she will probably report herself before evening. Trench is tempting me back to the Kenmare river, and I have half decided to go there. If a Paddy shoots me—well, it will be dying in harness, and I, for my part, shouldn't so much care. The world will not move

to my mind for the next quarter of a century; and by
that time I shall have done with it anyway.   Ruskin's
letter has taken people's breath away.   I have read
nothing with so much pleasure these many years.
We returned from Salcombe last night, and most of
us are settled in for the winter.   M—— and I go for a
few days to Lord Carnarvon's on Monday, and towards
the end of the month I am going North to stay with
George Howard at Naworth, and examine the farm-
house at Ecclefechan where Carlyle was brought up.   I
may be tempted to run on for the mere pleasure of
spending a night at the Hermitage.   What should you
say if I turned up?   We had plenty of sailing in the
summer, though not under such fine conditions as
yours.   I was not particularly well, however.   Ireland
had got into my stomach and disagreed with me."

"5 ONSLOW GARDENS, *November* 16 [1880].

"We had a very interesting day in Annandale, saw
all that we wanted, and made the necessary sketches.
We were favoured by the weather, nine fine hours in a
week of snow and storm.   It was all very strange to
me and very pathetic. . . . I cannot talk of what I
shall do two years hence with the free confidence of
thirty.   Like enough I shall have made a change of
lodging still more considerable, and have begun existence again the other side. . . . I have read *Endymion*;
quite unexpectedly the author expressed a wish that I
should review it.   *Lothair* had so much delighted me
that I was rather pleased with the prospect; but when

I came to the reality I found it could not be. You will understand why when the book reaches you. We had two days' shooting at Naworth. A good many pheasants and a fine sprinkling of woodcocks. Considering how rarely I now take a gun in hand, I was rather pleased with my performance. I am astonished at the apathy of England and Scotland about this Irish business. I try to hope that the wood is only damp, and that it will kindle before long. Among educated people the wrath is loud and deep against 'the very worst Government that ever existed in this country.'"

[On December 23, 1880, Froude informed me that he had begun to print Carlyle's *Reminiscences*. He had allowed me to read the earlier sketches some years previously, and I had been delighted by their idiomatic force and freshness. The pictures of that old homely Scottish life were, it seemed to me, racy of the soil. Now he asked me to revise them as they went through the press, with reference more particularly to various Scotch names and idioms in the early sheets. " I therefore venture to hope that you will look through the pages, and mark anything that seems doubtful to you." This I did, aided by Dr John Brown. Only the proofs of the Scotch section of the book were corrected by me: had I seen the others I might possibly have suggested the omission of one or two passages; but surely the "ootbrak" of outraged decorum which followed the publication was out of all proportion to the offence,—if offence there was.]

" I am dreadfully busy," he continues, " bringing out
a new edition of *The English in Ireland,* with a supple-
mentary chapter on the present crisis.   No one knows
what is to be done,—the Government, I believe, as
little as any one.   The Whigs everywhere are kicking,
and so are those dear beings the Political Economists.
The worst symptom is the total absence of *courage* on
all sides. . . . I am at home alone, tied fast by
work while my children are away for Christmas.   I go
occasionally to the Athenæum, but only meet doleful
creatures there who are worse than nothing.   My
Christmas is not a bright one; I wish — I wish — I
could pass it with you at the ever delightful Hermitage."

"5 ONSLOW GARDENS, *December* 26 [1880].

"I send a few more sheets.   I have marked one or two
words specially, which seem to me doubtful.   Carlyle
himself is not in a condition to be asked questions.   I
fear the end cannot now be very distant.   Indeed one
can hardly wish it.   I have said out my own mind on
this Irish business in a concluding chapter to my new
edition of *The English in Ireland.*   This new business
in South Africa is almost as dangerous.   I think we
shall lose that country.   We are teaching every section
of the people to hate us there—English, Dutch, natives
alike—and unless we determine to hold the whole place
by force, there will soon be nothing for us but to take
ourselves off with shame."

"5 ONSLOW GARDENS, *Feb.* 3 [1881].

" What can I feel but pleasure at your proposal?
Small as the opinion which I have of my aspect (I
study it daily in the process of shaving), I should
like to have it remembered (if anywhere) in the house
of so old and warm a friend. I will do my part of the
business when the time comes, and I hope that I shall
not turn out quite so hideous as Sam Laurence made
me fifteen years ago.

" I was about to write you when your letter came.
I have waited, however, two days to answer it, that
I might tell you something authentic about Carlyle.
He is alive, I believe, at this moment, but will hardly
see another morning. His morning, if there is one,
will break elsewhere. He is to be buried beside his
mother and father in Ecclefechan kirkyard. The
funeral will be as private as possible. The family
particularly wish this, I believe, and the day will
purposely be kept unknown. But I am going down ;
and it strikes me that *you*, perhaps, might wish to be
present. If I am right, telegraph to me. During
his illness he has talked (when he has talked at all)
of his father and mother as if they were near him. His
niece he has called ' Jeanie '—his wife! Good-bye."

"5 ONSLOW GARDENS, *Feb.* 8 [1881].

" I did not gather from your telegram that you
would be able to attend. The day has been left
undetermined purposely to prevent a crowd. It is
now settled for Thursday (the day after to-morrow) ;

but do not mention it to others.   They will, I am
sure, be very glad that you should come as a friend
of mine; but the time is short to enable you to make
arrangements.   The funeral will be at 12.   I, Tyndall,
and Lecky will sleep at Carlisle the night before, and
go over in the morning.   If the weather is fine we
can walk up in the afternoon to *Mainhill,* where
Wilhelm Meister was translated (the last part of it),
and where it was read and wondered over by his
mother. . . .   We had a storm here last night, and
I fear it will be all bleak and dreary."

[After seeing the *Reminiscences* through the press,
Froude, who had been ailing, took a sea voyage,
which as usual set him up.   But he came back to
find "the heather on fire."]

"5 ONSLOW GARDENS, *April* 7 [1881].

"I had a pleasant idle month at sea and at Madeira,
but I came back to find such a complication of worries
that I have not yet felt equal to Mr Reid's studio.
When I am fit to be seen again I will go.   I am more
surprised than I should have been at the reception of
the *Reminiscences.*   It is Carlyle himself,—the same
Carlyle precisely that I have known for thirty years;
and it seemed to me that my duty was to represent
him (or let him represent himself) as near the truth
as possible.   To me in no one of his writings does
he appear under a more beautiful aspect; and so, I
am still convinced, will all mankind eventually think.

I cut out everything which could *injure* anybody. To have cut out his general estimates of men and things would have turned the book into a *caput mortuum*."

[Sir George Reid, P.R.S.A., was good enough to paint a portrait of Froude for me during April and May of this year. It is an admirable likeness, and a fine piece of work.]

"5 ONSLOW GARDENS, *June* 17 [1881].

" If you like the picture as much as I like the painter you will be very well satisfied. . . . The storm, which broke over me, has pretty well passed. You were wise and kind in taking no notice of it. In a year or two every one whose opinion is worth having will be grateful for having a true Carlyle before them, and not a mutilated and incredible one. A—— has entered at Oxford, and I expect will do well there. I have been at Chenies with him for a few days' fishing. We did little, though I succeeded in catching one big fellow—3½ lb. In Norway I shall get enough to last the rest of my life."

"SALCOMBE, *Sept.* 11 [1881].

" Here I am at last, after ten weeks on the Fiords. . . . I have come back *set up* in mind and body, and ready for such work as may offer. . . . We saw the old *Viking ship* at Christiania. The identical old timbers with marks of the caulking still in them ; and the vessel itself, 80 feet long, an open boat with

as fine lines and laid as surely down for speed as
Thorneycroft himself could not beat.   There was the
great copper caldron where they stewed their dinners
too—all very genuine and instructive.   One sees why
the Normans took to the sea.   In that country the
Fiords are the only roads.   The mountains are impassable.   But all this will keep.   I was shocked to
hear of the death of poor Miss B——, that bright
young creature with so fair a life opening out before
her.   How the fruit drops off (the best first), ripe or
unripe; while we old fellows are left scrambling on.
Burton gone—Stanley gone—Carlyle gone—all in this
last year.   I care not how soon I follow, if I may only
live to finish Carlyle's Life.   I have had a most hearty
letter from the one surviving brother in Annandale.
I will write again before long.   Just now, as you
may suppose, I have endless little matters calling for
attention.   This is only to report that I am at home
again. . . . The sketch of Burton is excellent."[1]

"THE MOLT, *October* 7 [1881].

"Ireland! Yes! More power to G——'s elbow. He
has ripened the fruit. It will hang no longer on the
old terms; and he will have to choose whether he
will fight the League at last or give up the country.
Sir Stafford Northcote was here the other day. He

---

[1] Froude refers to the sketch in *Maga*. Burton, who with all his quaint
oddities of dress and manner was finely simple and sincere, was much attached to Froude, and was always zealous in his defence,—no petty
jealousies disturbing their friendship.

was not supremely happy at the prospect of things. May the Devil fly away with Party Government. 'A plague o' both your houses!'"

"5 ONSLOW GARDENS, *Feby.* 17 [1882].

"Five years ago I said to Lady R—— that the English constitution was now flying like a shuttlecock between two adventurers. *She* was furious at me for calling the one an adventurer; *you* will not approve of my using such a name for the other. . . . Carlyle's Life—the Scotch part of it—will be out in three weeks or a month. I shall perhaps go abroad till the tongues have done wagging. . . . The end will be that C. will stand higher than ever, and will be loved more than ever. When a man's faults are not such as dishonour him, we are all the nearer to him because of them, and because we feel the common pulse of humanity in him."

"5 ONSLOW GARDENS, *June* 15, 1882.

"I saw the news of your father's death in the paper which you sent me. He was full of years. . . . *That,* if there be such a thing, is *euthanasia.* I did not write, partly because you would know that I felt for you, partly because I could not tell from your silence whether you did not share in the feeling of disappointment of Carlyle's Life, which Tulloch and Boyd led me to suppose is general in Scotland. Judge then if your letter has not given me pleasure.

"What motive could I have in writing as I have

done except to do what I believe Carlyle to have wished? It would have been idle folly to have kept anything back.

"I shall be heartily glad to see you; but we leave London for The Molt on 1st of July, and I fear we shall be gone before you pass through. May we not hope that you and Mrs Skelton will again find your way to us? My little yacht has now a lead keel, sails well, and fears no weather. We can meet you at *Dartmouth*, bring you round the Start, and spare you the long Kingsbridge drive. Do think of it and come while the days are long, before you go abroad.— Ever yours most truly,   J. A. FROUDE.

"The fetish-worship continues. . . . More than ever I regret Lord Beaconsfield's adventure into foreign policy. *He* might have settled Ireland, or at least might have made the present state of things impossible. I can hardly write—my fingers are numbed by this north wind—within a week of midsummer!"

"5 ONSLOW GARDENS, *December* 10 [1882].

"Your volume has come, a pleasant Christmas remembrance of an old and very dear friend. I will not argue about Mary Stuart. . . . In return I send you the concluding volume of my *Short Studies*. I have brought my confessions to the Day of Judgment; and with our present means of information we can, none of us, carry them farther. The rest of my working life, short or long, must be given to Carlyle. I

believe no biographer had ever a more difficult or
troublesome task bequeathed to him."

"5 ONSLOW GARDENS, *Feb.* 20 [1883].

" You will be more edified than surprised by the
Dublin revelations. There is nothing new in them
either to you or to me. Your friend Dizzy was the
only English statesman who knew anything about
Ireland. I had assured myself that when he came
into office in 1874 he would tackle the thing, and I
cannot yet forgive him for having rushed into an
'adventurous foreign policy' when he had such serious work cut out for him at home. It is sorrowfully
plain that as long as we are cursed with Parliamentary
Government, the Liberals only can hang Irish mur-
derers. If the Tories try it, the whole pack of idiots,
English and Irish, howl together. Still, Lord Beaconsfield would have stood higher as a statesman if he had
tried. A really wise man will put his hand to the
thing which ought to be done without minding much
what others say of him. *He* might have established
a just Land Court with the support of all the best
landowners in Ireland. Now who can say what will
happen ? "

[I paid a long visit to Froude during February and
March of this year, when I had the pleasure of reading
the proof-sheets of Mrs Carlyle's brilliant and remarkable letters. From notes made at the time, I take a

few extracts, descriptive of the impression which a
first reading produced on my mind :—

"Their true and main interest is of the personal
kind;—they are the letters of a strangely powerful
and brilliant woman, who expressed herself always
with absolute sincerity and the most relentless directness. She was singularly gifted, the humour and the
pathos being each unique in its way. She was the
companion of one of the most remarkable men of her
time : can we say that she was in any way his inferior ?
Nothing, indeed, can be more striking than the contrast between his involved and rugged commentary
and her sparkling lucidity. The play of her ready
and nimble wit is as incessant as sheet-lightning of
a summer night in the tropics, and it spares nothing
—not even her husband. Yet, on the other hand, her
heart was as tender as her humour was caustic and
incisive. She was not happy. Her marriage, it may
now be frankly admitted, was a mistake. I do not
know anything sadder or more touching than the
narrative of her return to Haddington after many
years of married life; a lost spirit revisiting the
glimpses of the moon might have indulged in just
such a strain of pathetic reminiscence. . . . This is
the story which, with wonderful spirit—with almost
cynical mockery and almost tremulous tenderness, the
tears and the laughter never being very far apart—
is related in these pages. It is a sad story, if you
will : but the 'bitter jests and bearing free' of this
curious cross between the Calvinist and the gipsy—

for she had the blood both of John Knox and Matthew Baillie in her veins—gives it a piquant and original charm that partly disguises its sadness."

So I wrote at the time; and our literature, I still believe, would have suffered an irreparable loss had "little Jeanie Welsh's" letters, like Byron's Memoirs, been reduced to ashes.]

"5 ONSLOW GARDENS, *April* 14 [1883].

"Mary Austin, one of Carlyle's sisters, has written me a most kind understanding letter. My German Translator is driven wild by Scotch phrases. 'Malt in shaft' means 'Meal in the box,' does it not? 'Jook and let the jaw gae by' is intelligible enough, but what is 'Jook' etymologically? The Duke of Bedford has written to ask on what days I would like him to *reserve!!* his fishing for me—the best in England. I wish you could be with me to enjoy it. You will see what it is like in the last volume of *Short Studies*."

"5 ONSLOW GARDENS, *November* 27 [1883].

"As to Lethington, I take him to have been in everything a Scotsman determined to secure to a Scottish Prince (Mary or James, as it might be) the English succession. This was the ruling principle, and explains all. As to religion, it was a 'devout imagination.' In Calderwood, as you know, he is always called Mitchell Wylie. It was a long time before I could guess what it meant (*Machiavelli*)."

"5 ONSLOW GARDENS, *Jan.* 3 [1884].

"A word of the usual wishes of the season to you
and yours.   I am your countryman in *this*, that I
dislike 'times and seasons,' and do not observe them.
You are *always* in a near corner of my memory, and
every day in one form or another I find myself thinking about you. . . . Carlyle in his Journal, speaking
of *his* foundation,[1] says very beautifully, 'It is his
Abbey of Cor Dulce for the burying of his loved one's
heart.'   The Cor Dulce seemed familiar to me: so far
as I remember, it refers to Devorgilla burying John de
Baliol, but I can find nothing about it in any one
of the hundred books into which I have looked, and
I fear my memory must have played me false.   Can
you help me?   I hope your pigeons and water-hens,
also the descendants of the poor blind Œdipus in
the farmyard, and all your other live stock, are pros-
pering in this charming winter.   I am as well as
a man can be who is dining out nowhere, and working from morning to night.   You will find you
have a fine portrait of Carlyle after all, which will
be a true one also."

"5 ONSLOW GARDENS, *March* 15 [1884].

"In two months, if I continue able to work, I shall
have written the last line of a business which has been
a perplexity and worry to me for the last fourteen
years.   All however is well now.   Arcturus is not

[1] The bequest to Edinburgh University in memory of his wife.

the less brilliant or beautiful because he flashes red and green instead of shining pale and calm as angelic stars ought to do."

[This was the year of the festivities in Edinburgh on the occasion of the University Tercentenary. For some reason Froude's name was omitted by the University authorities from the list of those on whom it was proposed to confer the honorary degree of LL.D. I pointed out the omission to my old and dear friend Professor Sellar, and one or two other members of the Senatus, and at their instance the blunder was rectified. But neither Froude nor Tyndall, who were to have been my guests, were able to attend.]

"5 ONSLOW GARDENS, *April* 1 [1884].

" Of course I cannot but accept so 'distinguished an honour,' &c. I owe it to you, and shall remember that I do; but I am very much obliged to the Senatus too. A great part of the personal attraction in the matter lies in your offer of hospitality. I shall be delighted to see the old Hermitage again, and you and Mrs Skelton and your little ones, now grown into big ones. Your house, I am afraid, like every other, will be crammed, and we shall have no pleasant saunters in the woods."[1]

---

[1] Many of Mr Froude's favourite walks are no longer recognisable,—the neighbourhood of the poor Hermitage having been badly disfigured of late by the speculative builder. Ought not outrages on the landscape to be punishable by Act of Parliament?

[On April 5 he writes as to cap and gown for the Tercentenary. "I am five feet eleven, and my head is 23 inches round, about half as big as yours!"]

"5 ONSLOW GARDENS, *May* 2 [1884].

" I cannot help you to a portrait of Carlyle, for none was ever made of him fit to be seen. I found in a letter an account of one in which the face, he says, is 'a cross between a Demon and a flayed Horse.' This, if it could be had, might be valuable, with C.'s description attached to it. . . . I am sleeping better; but go to bed each night in alarm how it may be. The brain, however, must be in a more quiet state, for my eyes, which were dark with soot-spots, are clearing again. Edinburgh would have done for me. Nor did I regret any part of the business, except the loss of a sight of you and Mrs Skelton. I creep more and more into my shell, love my friends better every day, and care less for the rest of mankind."

"5 ONSLOW GARDENS, *May* 16 [1884].

" You will be glad to hear that yesterday I *finished* the MS. of Carlyle. I really do think that when it comes out certain persons will be ashamed of them-selves. How ill A., B., and C. have behaved to me, no one will know, and no one could conjecture.

"THE MOLT, *Sept.* 14 [1884].

" This week the printing of Carlyle will be finished; and now the thing is done, Carlyle himself will be

more loved and honoured than ever. I do not believe,
and Sir James Stephen (who has read the proofs) does
not believe that there will be any more row. Stephen
in fact is *complimentary*. We came here at the beginning of August, and have been basking and sailing
ever since in this most delicious of all remembered
summers."

"5 ONSLOW GARDENS, *November* 1 [1884].

"Your letter does me good. It is not the sort of
letter which a man writes when he merely wishes to
pay a perfunctory compliment. You mean it all,
and it is a 'good joy,' as Mrs Carlyle used to say.
I have seen very few reviews. The *Times*, though
civil enough to me, is hard and unappreciative with
Carlyle. I do not think that the world, stupid as it
is, will accept such a view as that. . . . As to the
politics, I know well how unavailing it will be. We
are to drink the cup of the Lord's fury to the bottom.
But when the drunken fit is over, and we are sick
and sorry again, amidst the fragments of a ruined
empire, it will remain to show that Carlyle was a
true seer. No quilting of vanity is thick enough
to keep out entirely an arrow from such a hand.
I *hope* God knows what is going to become of us.
If He does, it is all right; but there is a wild time
before us."

[The winter of 1884-85 was spent by Froude in the
Australian Colonies. He came home by the States,—
crossing the Rockies he was caught in a blizzard.

"It was as if some one had hit me in the face, knocked me down, kicked me with mailed boots about my head, and gouged out my right eye."]

"ONSLOW GARDENS, *May* 28 [1885].

"Yes—I have been 'the other side.' It is very much like this side, except that it is warm and bright and full of flowers and plums and peaches, and you never see a discontented face or a hungry one. . . . Our Reformed Parliament plays fine antics. This has been the worst ever known in English history. The next will be worse still; and so on till the world is weary of them, and they get their necks wrung. Your account of Haddington is very interesting."

"THE MOLT, SALCOMBE, *August* 2 [1885].

"M—— told me generally what was coming.[1] The delightful Freeman too! You will have given him a stomach-ache. He will sit down and write another article about the Bishop of Lexovia. From you, my dear friend, who so widely differ from me on the subject and on the person that beyond all others exasperate controversy, these Good Words are doubly grateful. . . . Is it idle to hope that you and Mrs Skelton may once again pay us a visit here? It can be but once, and *this year*, if it is to be at all, for my

---

[1] M——, I think, hits the nail on the head when he says in a recent letter,—"Poor Froude! I loved him. A tender fine spirit finely touched and often misunderstood. Historical grubs feeding on parchment may say what they like as to inaccuracies; but he had what a whole brigade of them cannot furnish—the historical imagination. I believe his judgments are in the broad correct."

hard-hearted and tyrannical landlord wishes actually to occupy his own house in future summers! What a detestable institution Landlordism is ! ! I am writing my Colonial Notes — a book which I shall call *Oceana*. I am in the extraordinary position of having to speak nothing but well of everything and everybody. Having nobody to abuse, I am like trying to fly a kite without wind."

THE MOLT, SALCOMBE, *September* 3 [1885].

" You have spoken good sound truth. It is taking already, and will take more and more. The true figure of a true man will in the end interest all true men, —and who else ought to be considered ? My little *Romsdal Fiord* too! That too you are picking up out of oblivion. Do you observe that the special inspirer of it has been sunbeaming it in those same quarters? I wonder what he thought of the Old Ganger! . . . I am working hard at my *Oceana*. We shall get it out early in the winter. I will send you the sheets. I am very glad indeed that you are at work on Maitland. There is no figure in Scotch history more interesting in the best sense. *Mitchell Wylie,* as they called him. It was long before I could guess what the name meant. The 4th thousand (I think) of the *Life in London* is sold, and Longman writes that he must print again."

[The *Romsdal Fiord* to which Froude alludes appeared in *Maga*[1] and was, I think, the only poem he ever

---

[1] See *Maga* for April 1883.

wrote. It is very spirited, and it inculcates his favourite moral :—

> " Yet men will still be ruled by men,
>   And talk will have its day,
>   And other Rolfs will come again
>   To sweep the rogues away." .

Here, where we part finally with the Carlyle diffi-culties, I may be permitted to extract from the old Note-book, to which I have more than once referred, an entry which, interesting in itself, lies outside the region of controversy :—

" The reader of *Thomas Carlyle* will remember that during the time he resided in 3 Moray Street, off Leith Walk, he kept a Diary or Journal, occasional extracts from which are given. Under date 31st December 1823, this entry occurs: ‘December 31st. The year is closing. This time eight-and-twenty years ago I was a child of three weeks old sleeping on my mother's bosom.

> " ‘Oh ! little did my mother think,
>   That day she cradled me,
>   The lands that I should travel in,
>   The death I was to dee.’

" This entry, on the publication of Froude's volumes, attracted the attention of a respected citizen of Edin-burgh. When a lad at College (some few years after Carlyle had ‘flitted’) he had lodged at 3 Moray Street with his uncle, who still lives there. It at once recalled to him that on a pane of glass in the window of the sitting-room the four lines quoted in the Journal had been rudely scratched by some previous occupant. Could the writer have been Carlyle? He wrote to Froude, and at Froude's request I have visited the house. We were courteously received, and the writing minutely examined. There were other scratches upon the glass —mostly illegible, but made apparently by the same hand. The writing is somewhat cramped and an-gular; but any writing on glass, I presume, must be somewhat cramped and angular. But immediately below the lines three significant words are added. They are now barely legible, and had not been noticed until I drew attention to them; but they seem to me to be essentially Carlylian. The words are—'*Oh! foolish thee!*' The complete inscription then runs thus :—

> " ' Little did my mother think,
>   That day she cradled me,
>   What land I was to travel in,
>   Or what death I should dee.
>
>   Oh ! foolish thee !'

" Froude was satisfied that the inscription was genu-ine, and would have liked to have had the glass removed and preserved. ' I have not the smallest doubt,' he wrote, ' that the lines on the window *were* scratched by Carlyle; and some means ought to be used to preserve so precious a relic. Properly it should remain in the house. In years to come perhaps the room will be a place of pilgrimage. But if sufficient interest is not felt at present to allow any steps to be taken, I will myself gladly buy the pane (if the owner of the house will sell it), and will preserve it, with a note of what it is, that it may be restored if demanded hereafter.'"—(October 11, 1882.)

I have scrupulously refrained from making any extracts from the papers beside me which could serve as an excuse for reopening a bitter controversy; but I do not know any reason why the view I took at the time as to the ultimate effect of Froude's treatment of his subject should not be restated. For this purpose I turn again to the old Note-book which I have had occasion so frequently to consult. I find in it the record of a discussion on board the "Gael" (one of the steamers which then plied among the Western Islands) with a "Scotch Professor,"—who (if he was not altogether a man of straw—set up only to be bowled over) must by no means be identified with my lamented friend, the late Professor Nichol of Glasgow. John Nichol might have taken his motto from the *Faery Queen*,—"Fierce warres and faithful loves" (a motto, by the way, not altogether inappropriate for Froude himself); and he did not hesitate to denounce with characteristic ardour in the Preface to *his Carlyle* (in his own words, "with a feeling akin to indignation"), "the persistent and often virulent attacks" which had been directed against the friend and biographer of their common master. Time has been on our side. The conclusions we then formulated now pass as commonplaces. Though rather bluntly expressed, and deemed rankly heterodox at the moment, they have come to

be accepted without demur or serious protest by all
rational critics.

It would appear that the "Scotch Professor," as the
"Gael" steamed up the Sound of Jura, had entertained
his travelling companions by a comparison of Froude's
Carlyle with the biography or autobiography of a grave
ecclesiastical dignitary recently deceased—not to the
advantage of the former.   Who the Priest or Presbyter
was is now of no moment,—the book has been long
laid on the shelf, and is utterly forgotten; but, as a
model of "exemplary reticence" and discreet dulness,
it appears to have had its use at the time.   Any stick
will do to beat a dog.   The company are represented
to have listened in silence, until the patience (his stock
possibly was not large) of one of our party was exhausted.
It is to him that the speech which follows is attributed,
—a speech which might quite possibly have been spoken
by John Nichol, or some equally ardent and unconventional controversialist.

"Look here, sir," he said, "I have read both books,
and I'll tell you exactly what I think.   The one is
bright, vivid, incisive, vital; the other wooden and
ponderous beyond belief.   You say that Froude has
been indiscreet; but, after all, what harm has he done?
He has hurt Carlyle, you believe; pray do not believe
anything of the kind.   The Titanic force of the man
was never more manifest than at the end of the last
volume.   In the fierce light that has been brought to
bear upon him the mud and clay drop off, and only the
pure gold remains.   His head rises clear out of the

vapours, and touches the stars. I tell you frankly that I had no conception of the massive and elemental greatness of Carlyle—his immeasurable superiority to every contemporary—till I had read these familiar letters and journals,—letters and journals brimful of humour, of pathos, of intense insight, of immense tenderness. Out of harsh and jarring accompaniments, what subtlest, softest music is evolved! A sardonic humour, you say, that ought not to be tolerated by a polite society? Be it so; yet observe, my friend, there is nothing sardonic in the *heart*, and every word is illuminating—a revelation. *Verily this whole world grows magical and hypermagical to me; death written on all, yet everlasting life also written on all.— Death! the unknown sea of rest! who knows what harmonies lie there to wrap us in softness, in eternal peace? —The half-moon, clear as silver, looked out as from eternity, and the great dawn came streaming up.* Compare with these grains of diamond dust the hard, pompous, didactic platitudes of the Divine! From the one you have letters dull as ditch-water; from the other letters written in fire, and instinct in every line with *life*. To be sure, everything of the D.D.'s has been removed (as we are assured with the glow of superior rectitude) which could hurt the feelings of any one—his own included. Yet in spite of this ostentatious prudery, the 'unseemly disclosures,' as you call them, of Carlyle's domestic and other difficulties (mainly dyspeptic,—his own mother admitting that he was 'gey ill to live wi'') strike me as intrinsically more wholesome. In short—

N

begging your pardon, sir—to compare the one with the other is sheer fatuity. A contemplative cuddy giving utterance to the obscure feelings he has about the universe is entitled to some consideration, for his *bray* is genuine; but what are we to say of critics who are morally obtuse as well as mentally dense?"

It was no wonder, perhaps, that after such an address the Professor should have "landed at Lochmaddy"; and it is possible, I admit, that the deliverance, and others to the like effect, may have been pitched in a key somewhat too shrill, somewhat too aggressive. But I fancy that no competent critic now ventures to deny that the four volumes of *Thomas Carlyle* contain one of the half-dozen great biographies in the English language. Froude refused, and rightly refused, to listen to the threats and appeals of fanatical devotees, —though, in view of the storm they raised, he may have been sometimes tempted to wish that the prophet (whose love of silence was, as his wife said, purely Platonic) had done his penance in person, and not by proxy. But with unshrinking fidelity, which no clamour could shake, he resolved to set, and did set, Carlyle before us exactly as he appeared to him, assured that he could do so safely, and that the essential greatness of the man would only be brought into clearer relief when the truth, the whole truth, and nothing but the truth, was known. "She sleeps in a pure grave; and our peasant maiden to us who knew her is more than a king's daughter." So Carlyle said of his sister Margaret who died in girlhood; so, with the necessary variations, may we say of the brother who earned a world-wide fame, and died in extreme old age. " He sleeps in a pure grave." It is difficult to determine what of the Victorian era will live or die ; but I do not think that we shall greatly err if we assert that Froude's *Carlyle* is one of its imperishable bequests.]

"5 ONSLOW GARDENS, *Feb.* 11 [1886].

" I hope to be with you on the evening of the 22d. . . . *Oceana* is selling fast. It has answered to a particular condition of public feeling, and may, I really hope, prove of some service. . . . The scene in the streets last Monday astonishes people. Why should they be astonished ? The Irish have been shown that they have only to plunder and murder sufficiently to be entitled to all that they please to ask. Could we expect that the English rough would not take the hint ? "

"5 ONSLOW GARDENS, *Jan.* 30 [1886].

" *Blackwood* came duly, and the *Scottish Church* this morning. Of course we recognised your hand in the first. You have been a true friend to me through evil and good in this world. Everybody is civil enough now ; but the gold sovereign is one thing, and the farthing gilt is another. . . . It is interesting to see how the weighty opinions of our wisest men, so many of which we have heard and read in the last three months, pass for *absolutely nothing*. They considered only the welfare of the country, and therefore shot entirely beside the mark. In the rigging of parties at Westminster the welfare of the country is the last matter that any one thinks about. Some day or other the country will find this out, and will wring the necks of the Parliamentary vermin. But it will be a long day yet. John Bull will be an attenuated animal when the fever leaves him, with barely strength to do justice to his misleaders."

[While the fate of the Home Rule Bill hung in the balance, Froude was keenly interested. "The question," he wrote, "is whether there is still stuff enough in the English and Scotch people to recover themselves when they get their senses again." In the meantime they appeared to him to be bewitched. Across the Atlantic, too, the weather-signals indicated storm. "Though all wise men there think as wise men do here, these are the days of the mad majorities" (May 2, 1886).]

"SALCOMBE, *September* 14 [1886?].

"I had seen the advertisement, and was minding to get a *Blackwood* for myself the first time I was at a railway station. The post this morning brings me the number from yourself, and of course I set to work on *Liddington* with eager appetite. You are perfectly right in taking a good large piece of canvas, and filling in the surroundings with a free pen. . . . The imaginary dialogue and Knox's part in it is new to me, and very amusing. I do not recollect seeing it either in Banna-

tyne or Calderwood. We are leaving Salcombe early
this year. Ruskin has been ill, and would like to see
me. . . . I have not been very well this summer. I
had undertaken to write a sixpenny *History of Ireland*.
Lord —— was anxious about it, and I fully meant to
make it my summer work; but when I tried, it was
like trying to walk with a ' sleeping' leg, which doubles
up under one. I must get myself into condition somehow, but my stomach has gone wrong, and refuses to
be comforted. The world outside looks wild; but I
hope we shall do our proper work in setting that
wretched island in order before we meddle with Turk
or Russian."

"KNOWSLEY, PRESCOT, *October* 17 [1886].

" Elphinstone could not have us till the end of the
month, and by that time my holiday will have run out.
We shall probably be at Naworth in January, and
again within your reach. Inexorable fate now insists
on taking us home. We have been dropping about
in various houses. We spent four delightful days with
Ruskin, and four more with my cousins in Bassen-
thwaite. Since then we have been at Castle Howard,
and now we are with the Derbies, where I like to come
from time to time to learn the inner side of the working of political parties. I for my part have some kind
of a book beginning to grow up in me—happily *not*
about politics. I do not know whether it will come
to anything; but I am anxious to get settled at home,
and see what I can do."

"HIGHCLERE CASTLE, NEWBURY, *Nov.* 14 [1886].

" I am doing nothing; but I am thinking of spending the winter in the West Indies.   I want to see Crown Colonies, niggers, &c., &c., and I am still capable of getting intense enjoyment out of climate and scenery. You won't get leave of absence and come with me ? "

"5 ONSLOW GARDENS, *December* 21 [1886].

" Yes ; I am going to the west Indies.

' Mich wundert wenn Ich winderkomme.'

I wish to use what remains of strength in me for some purpose which I know to be disinterested, and may, if carried out, have a value. . . . The dinner was pleasant enough.   The Lord Chancellor, whom I did not know, said pleasant things about me, and my entertainers were all kind and gracious.   Your glen will be looking beautiful in the frost.   My best regards to Mrs Skelton and the *Water-hens*."

"ONSLOW GARDENS, *April* 23 [1887].

" I have come home, and the first thing which I have done (after looking round me, and at a few West India books) has been to read your *Lethington*.[1] . . . You will have left behind a genuine portrait of a remarkable man, to take its place in the Scotch His- torical Gallery.   Thank you warmly for your kind

---

[1] Vol. i. of *Maitland of Lethington and the Scotland of Mary Stuart.* W. Blackwood & Sons, 1887.

words about myself. Had I written about Charles
the Fifth, it would have been to do for his memory
very much what you are doing, and to show that the
Protestant pictures, both of him and Philip and Alva,
are absurd caricatures. I hope you have passed the
winter as pleasantly as I have done. The climate out
there is delicious, the islands are beautiful beyond
imagination. The sugar-planters are almost all ruined.
The whites everywhere are selling their properties for
less than the value of the *stock* upon them. In Domenica, Rodney's Island, there are but twenty English
left. A French boat from Martinique, with a corporal's
guard, might take Domenica, and not a man there
would fire a shot to keep them off. Grenada, the most
charming and fertile of the Windward Antilles, is already a black island. The planters have disappeared,
and the whole island is divided among black free-
holders,—a gold mine to the Attorney-General, for
every nigger is at law with his neighbour. The state
of things is absurd, yet not past mending if we have
any sense left. The old days of the sugar millionaires
are gone, and black freeholds are inevitable; but the
poor children of darkness are not without sense, and
will respond well to rational government. I must try
to get something said about it."

"THE MOLT, SALCOMBE, *October* 1 [1887].

"I have heard nothing of you for a weary long day.
. . . Tell me also what you think of *The Bow of Ulysses*
as a title for my West India book. Once upon a time

we did grand things out there, as we did in other places. Now all is going to the Devil. All our white people there flung overboard like the Protestants in Ireland, and the islands becoming Nigger Warrens. I don't believe that we are any more degenerate than Ulysses' bow was rotten. The bow was all right, but there was no Ulysses to string it. Penelope's suitors were not unlike the sort of fellows who court Britannia now at the hustings. I have used the illustration any-how, and I mended my pen to describe what came to the said suitors with Pallas Athene looking on approv-ing. The country will wake up some day, but I fear not speedily. . . . The book is done now, and I register many vows that I will never undertake another. Indeed I believe I cannot if I would, for my eyes are giving out at last, and as I don't want to go blind before I die, I must save and spare what remains of them."

"5 ONSLOW GARDENS, *November* 11 [1887].

" I sent you the sheets of *Occana*, and your report was like the blessing of Abraham upon it. Bless my West India book, even bless this also. Whether you bless it or not, I despatch you a set of proofs (a very few mistakes left uncorrected). They may amuse you or put you to sleep; or at worst you can make them into pipe-matches."

[Many of the letters of 1887-88 refer to the Mary Stuart controversy, which had again been opened by the publication of my *Maitland of Lethington*. As the substance of these letters subsequently appeared in the sumptuous volume on *Mary Stuart* published in 1892 by Messrs Boussod, Valladon, & Co., I need not refer to them now. "The West India book," he wrote, "is doing very well—much better than I expected. There *is* a public even for sentiments so extravagantly heterodox." And in another,—"I have been at work now for a month, and have been very busy with an Irish *Novel* of the last century. I can't tell yet whether it will do to publish. Off one's regular lines one is curiously unable to judge of the merits of one's own work" —September 23. And again,—"I look eagerly for the continuation of *Maitland*. . . . I am myself reading De Thou with great interest. There are details of Mary's history in France,—some especially connected with the conspiracy at Amboise."]

"5 ONSLOW GARDENS, *December* 28 [1887].

"I have read *Blackwood*.[1] You are more than fulfilling all that I hoped and looked for when you took Maitland up. You show him to be just what I conceived; a modern man of the highest intellect and finest purpose—just answering politically, as you say, to Erasmus—trying to steer the vessel of humanity in a storm. I miss only what I suppose will come in the next number—his Scotch pride and patriotism, and his desire, above all things (in which he carried Murray with him), to secure the English succession

---

[1] Several chapters of both volumes of my *Maitland of Lethington* originally appeared in *Maga*.

and Mary's recognition as heir-apparent. This it was, and the assumption of the English arms by Mary, which made the real difficulty in any agreement between her and Elizabeth. Whether Maitland could have carried Mary with him into real tolerance, and the adoption of the English system, is a question on which you and I will think differently. I believe her to have been too distinctly Guisian, too well satisfied with the burning of the French heretics, which she had witnessed before she came home. The passions on both sides lay too deep, in my opinion, to be controlled by reason and moderation. Even now I see that actual work in the world only gets done by intense and narrow people. The water spread over the ground makes a morass; gathered into a channel, it is a running stream and drives a mill. Smooth glass transmits the sun's rays as it finds them. The lens gathers the rays into a focus and lights a fire. I myself think as Maitland did, and as Erasmus did; but I think they would have been nowhere in their own age (however circumstances had favoured them), and but for the fighting sort, the Luthers and Knoxes, you and I would have been less comfortable to-day than we find ourselves. I am not sure even that, with our toleration of exploded LIES, which, if they recover power, will not tolerate us, our grandchildren may not have to fight the old battle over again with the old weapons. I am none the less grateful to you for giving us the other side so skilfully, and with so much appreciation of what in itself you dislike. For the first time you will have

made the story of the Scotch Reformation intelligible.
. . . My *West Indies* will appear in a fortnight. . . .
The next summer we are thinking of Scotland, and if
you hear of any place near a lake where there is fishing
and decent accommodation, kindly let me know."

"5 ONSLOW GARDENS, *April* 6 [1888].

" Norway will be agreeable enough, and there is a
splendid river for us to catch salmon in ; but you would
have been in Mull; we would have come there; and
that would have been best of all.   The summers
which I at least will be able to enjoy are growing few,
and should be made the most of.   Perhaps next year
we may manage better.   Already I feel past shooting.
I have a curious dislike to hunting warm - blooded
creatures.   Fish don't count.   I look eagerly for the
continuation of your *Maitland*.   I would be grateful to
Blackwood if he would kindly send me the numbers
when they come out.   I will repay him if he likes by
a little sketch or two of our life in the Fiords."

"THE MOLT, SALCOMBE, *April* 15 [1889].

" I had so bothered myself over the book [*The Two
Chiefs of Dunboy*] that I could not tell whether it was
good or bad, and was humbly prepared to hear that it
was a dead failure.   Now I can at least feel that you
(and Lord Derby, for he says the same as you do) can
find amusement in it, and what you feel may perhaps
be felt by a few other people.   I wanted comfort, for I
have been out of condition all the spring—ever since

Christmas indeed; and when one can't sleep, and lies tumbling about all night, the Devil has one at advantage. I wonder whether there is any chance of your coming down here in the summer. You know how heartily we shall welcome you if you can, or either of your young ones if you like to send them down. . . . I may say that the Morty of the *Two Chiefs* is nearer the real article than the Morty of *The English in Ireland*. I am almost certain that he actually was with the Pretender. There were Irish officers on his staff—one Sir Edward [Thomas ?] Sheridan, another a Colonel *Sullivan*. This is historical; as also their capture and escape. There was no other Sullivan living of sufficient representative rank to have held the place by the Prince which a certain Sullivan undoubtedly had. Irish officers in the Continental armies did uncommonly well, and, of course, acquired a different way of looking at things from their countrymen."

"About the Calvinists. Whatever was the cause, they were the only fighting Protestants. It was they whose faith gave them courage to stand up for the Reformation. In England, Scotland, France, Holland, they and only they did the work, and but for them the Reformation would have been crushed. This is why I admire them, and feel that there was something in their Creed which made them what they were. In a high transcendental sense I believe Calvinism to be true—*i.e.*, I believe Free Will to be an illusion, and that all is as it is ordered to be.   But leaving this, which belongs to abstruse philosophy, the Calvinists practically, like the early Christians, abhorred lies, especially in matters of religion, and would have nothing to do with them.   An idol, an image of Jupiter, or the Mass, if it is not true, is a damnable imposture, which men degrade themselves by affecting to respect.   Knox was the embodiment of this feeling, and I think Knox was right.   It has all gone to squash now, and likely enough, in fifty years, we shall have Romanism back again when we have rotted out the old stuff sufficiently.   But it remains in the English nature in other forms.   The two English sailors who refused to kiss a mandarin's toe in China, and let themselves be killed sooner, had the same mind in them.   What was kissing a Chinaman's toe but a mark of respect, a custom of the country, a form of reverence for established authority?   Yet one feels it was better for the poor men to die than do so.   I entirely agree with Knox in his horror of that one Mass.   If it had not been for Calvinists, Huguenots, Puritans, or whatever you like to call them, the Pope and Philip would have won, and we should either be Papists or Socialists.   Erasmus and Maitland saw more clearly than any of their contemporaries; but intellect fights no battle, Reason is no match for Superstition, and one emotion can only be conquered by another.

"... I hope at last I have got a subject when I shall tread on nobody's corns: you alone of all my friends have been able hitherto to differ from me without flying into a passion.   But, indeed, I care little

what people say,—unless it be you and one or two
others.   The pleasure to me is in writing the book.
We are counting on you for next summer, and I am
busy making plans for a boat which I intend to have
built for me—a large open rowing galley with a couple
of big lug-sails.   That is, on the whole, the most useful
craft when there is both river and sea, and one does
not want to be out at night or in bad weather."

[During the winter of 1888-89 Froude was more or
less of an invalid, and left London in the early spring
for The Molt: "I had to give up Norway.   I was told
that wet or cold might play mischief with me, and I was
afraid of spoiling Ducie's enjoyment.   I had a constant
pain in my side, and unexplained aches which had no
visible cause suggested disagreeable possibilities."   But
by November he had completely recovered.]

"THE MOLT, *November* 10 [1889].

"Your kind letter reproaches me with the long time
which I have let pass without communicating with you
—you who have always been the truest of my friends.
I suppose it is for that reason—as the country farmer
excused himself for sleeping under the Rector's sermons.
"Lord, sir, when you are in the pulpit, we know it is
all right."   The newspapers as usual are better aware
of our doings than we are ourselves.   I now feel better
than I have done for years; and I am going back to
London next week into the old round of things, saving
that I have registered a vow to go to no more dinners.

I don't know that I should have gone back after all. Perhaps I should have stayed here, except for this Beaconsfield undertaking.   Ralph Disraeli promises to help me,—indeed has already done so.   The Duke of Rutland will help me, and I must see and talk to a good many people.   I hesitated a long time before I agreed to do the thing. . . . But it will give me an opportunity of saying many things which I wish to say about modern Liberalism and the universal disintegration which Lord B. saw *clearer than any one* was certain to come of it.   I admired him in spite of his affectation and coxcombry, which I discovered to have been itself affected, and to have been no more than a very valuable suit of armour.   I did and do entirely disagree with his views on Russia, &c.   I consider that we ought to be good friends with Russia, and that a war between us will shake Asia from the Dardanelles to the Wall of China, and cause infinite misery to half the human race.   But I think he understood the social and political condition of England more clearly than any other living man (not excepting Carlyle), and *Lothair* I regard as one of the most instructive and remarkable books that has appeared in our time.   This is what I mean to dwell on.   The Peace with Honour, and all that, I shall pass over as lightly as I may.

"So there you have an account of this adventure of mine which, if I continue able to work, I hope to achieve in the course of the winter.   If I break down again, why I do, and there will be an end, and I shall not achieve it.   The world will not be much the worse.

"In April I am due in Edinburgh, when the University is to give me a degree, and once more I shall offer myself to Mrs Skelton's hospitality. The Philosophical Society has petitioned for a lecture or lectures. I said I would make no engagement, so uncertain I was of my condition; but if I was well, and if they would give me an extra night, I would talk to them for an hour about Carlyle.

"The summer here has been beautiful, and has hardly yet left us. The orange-trees are in blossom; begonias brilliant; geranium, heliotrope, and fuchsias bright as they were two months ago. The winter at Salcombe is winter only in name, and we are hardly conscious of it except in the short days. Only the sea is wild. The cutter lies in the mud dismantled, and I am driven to walking (which I am now better up to) or lounging about the garden. In July and August we had yacht visitors in plenty,—dukes, earls, &c., very sumptuous and splendid, but subdued in mind compared to what they used to be. The last who appeared was W. H. Smith in the Pandora, recruiting from the session. He, I think it was, who finally decided me to undertake Lord B., though I do not think that he will be of much service to me.

"I suppose you know (I don't) who wrote that most feeble and unintelligent article about Maitland in the *Edinburgh*. It had a North-Country flavour, stupid as it was, and came, I am sure, from your side of the Tweed. He entirely fails to see that the ruling principle in all the Scotch statesmen of all sides, Murray,

Maitland, Morton (even Knox to a degree), was to secure the English succession to the Scotch line. This is the single and simple explanation of all their inconsistencies. Patriotism, Scotch vanity, whatever you like to call it, was the strongest passion of their lives.

"It will be very pleasant to see you and Mrs S. in London. My friends that are left are few, and I am grown too old to interest myself about acquaintances. Let me know when to look for you. You must stay with us, and nowhere else. — Ever with warmest remembrances, your affect.,

"J. A. FROUDE."

[The *Life of Lord Beaconsfield* was the last book Mr Froude wrote before he went to Oxford. It is a lively political sketch; but the subject as a whole was hardly congenial. It cannot compare with *Oceana*, which for scholarly finish ranks with the inimitable *Eōthen* of Kinglake. In *Oceana*, Mr Froude as a man of letters is seen at his best; and at his best Mr Froude had few rivals. No other writer of our day, not Cardinal Newman hinself, had, as I think, such an easy mastery of our mother tongue, — in no other writer were masculine vigour and feminine delicacy so blended in the expression of, what may be called, intellectual emotion. The thought was personal; the personality was unique. From the purely literary point of view *Oceana* is indeed a masterpiece. Froude complained in it, as he complained in his letters (as we have seen),

of being an old man: but there is no trace of age in
the book.   On the contrary — brimful of keen and
ardent life — it hurries us along from cape to cape
and from sea to sea, with brilliant dash and more
than youthful vivacity.   And in it the rarer qualities
of Froude's genius were as manifest as in any of his
earlier writings — the imaginative light, the brilliant
definition, the play of Jacques-like humour, the touch
of latent tenderness, the severe ideal.   It is vivid,
it is picturesque, it is immensely interesting—bringing
us into closer contact with the people on the other
side of the globe than any realistic romance could
do.   And yet, after all is said of its literary excellence,
it remains in substance and pre-eminently a long,
eloquent, and impassioned plea for Imperial Unity.
Froude was a patriot to the core.   He never forgot
that he was a citizen of no mean country.   He loved
England and Englishmen; and he never wearied of
praising her great statesmen and her great sailors and
soldiers.   And if he spoke bitterly of the men who had
led her astray (as he fancied), it was out of the love
he bore her.

Froude had intended to be in Edinburgh for a week
in April 1890 to receive his degree, but he was prevented by illness from coming.   "I find that at sev-
enty-two one does not entirely recover from these things.
If I am to hang on at all, it will only be by resigning
myself to the conditions, and by henceforth living
under doctor's instructions.   I have written to Muir
and charged him with my acknowledgments and apol-

ogics to the Senatus; but I had looked forward for
many years to the honours of Edinburgh, and I cannot
reconcile myself to the loss. I fear 'my inward parts'
are full of wickedness,—liver and all the rest of it"
(April 8, 1890). But during July and August he was
again fishing with Lord Ducie in Norwegian rivers—
"fishing from morning to midnight in the wettest
season ever known in Norway."]

"5 ONSLOW GARDENS, *April* 12 [1890].

"I am indeed sorry at the news which you send.
I will still hope to see the Hermitage once more under
happier auspices. The University generously offer to
give me the Degree *in absentiâ*. *Cæsar* has been brought
out again, and is doing very well. Carlyle's Life is to
follow. A Yankee asked me which of all my books I
thought most valuable. I said beyond doubt the *Life
of Carlyle*. If value be measured by the cost to myself
it ought to be worth something."

"YACHT MONARCH, *August* 3 [1890].

"We live in great luxury; a steam-yacht of 360 tons,
with a crew of eighteen, and only our two selves to enjoy
it all. But I am too old for the work. The river mon-
sters are too many for me. I cannot any longer run
along the banks, and plunge among rocks, and wade
in deep stream to save fish which put their heads down
these furious streams. I lost one as big as a porpoise
only the day before yesterday, because in desperation
and confidence in my tackle I resolved to hold on and

kill him in mid-stream, when of course the hook came
away, breaking the hold in his gills. I console myself
on these occasions by reflecting that he is better off
and I am no worse; and meanwhile I wonder at myself at what I am still able to do. All my ailments
have disappeared, and I am extraordinarily well.
Work enough waits for me when I get back. My
own sketch of Dizzy was done and printed before I
came away. . . . Another edition of Carlyle's Life
is going through the press, of which I shall have things
to tell you which I need not write. That done, I have
to revise my *History of England*—a big job which will
see out the rest of my working powers. I am glad to
hear that you have had such a good time in the En-
chantress."

"5 ONSLOW GARDENS, *November* 3 [1890].

"Of course I sent my book to you. To whom else
in the world should I send it?—but I was especially
anxious that you should have this, because I knew
you suspected me of not sufficiently valuing Dizzy;
and that you did not wholly understand what I thought
of him. . . . The interesting part of the business
has been the relation in which I found myself with D.'s
friends, who, as you may have concluded, have helped
me a good deal, specially Lord Rothschild. Lord R.
has the Brydges-Willyams correspondence. I wish
he would publish it. . . . We are in—I see plainly
—for an ultra-Democratic Parliament at the next election. It must have come sooner or later; and better

sooner than later while the old traditions are not
hopelessly dead. I remain pretty well. I cannot
cure the incurable disease. I am seventy-three years
old, and have to avoid dinners and all kinds of follies
of similar kind. . . . I was particularly delighted with
the Orkneys,—the sight of which has made a whole
chapter of Norse history intelligible to me. The Western Islands were very interesting too; but our weather
was wild, wet, and cold.—Ever yours affly.,

"J. A. FROUDE."

[1890 ends with a letter of good wishes (December
19), in which, after remarking that speaking is not in
his line,—"I have been brought up to another trade,"
—he goes on to relate how an old Protestant Irish-
woman, on hearing some one say that an eminent
politician of another generation deserved to be hanged,
replied, "Ah no; lave him to the Lard, and the Lard
will play the Divil with him."

I may add here that the type of mind most distasteful to Froude was what may be called the evasive
or casuistic. He loved candour. His friends could
not be too frank and outspoken. I remember an
application being made to him to subscribe to a
memorial to an eminent Catholic dignitary. "They
ask me to contribute," he exclaimed, "though they
know that I think he did more to hurt the English
regard for truth than any other man." Of the Newman - Kingsley controversy, too, he did not hesitate
to speak with perfect plainness. Newman had made

mince-meat of Kingsley; and yet in substance Kingsley was right; though the emotional fervour of the
English Churchman was no match for the deft dia-
lectic of the Catholic Priest.   There were lay leaders
too whose beguiling words were false as Vivien's, but
which were accepted as Gospel by the enfranchised
democracy.   Yet—after all—the subtle logical formulas
of medieval monks and schoolmen were arrows shot in
the air.   They might perplex the unlearned and em-
barrass the timid for the moment; but they failed
to secure the assent of the really influential class whose
verdict, if long delayed, was final.   When the con-
juring trick was detected, as it always was in the end,
the conjuror was sent to jail,—if he did not abscond
in the interval.   The interval, unhappily, was sometimes considerable.   These were lessons, I presume,
that Froude had learnt at Chelsea; but he had made
them his own.   Between the "fatally supple and persuasive rhetorician," and the pupil of Carlyle who had
been "brought up to another trade," there could be no
fellowship.]

"5 ONSLOW GARDENS, *December* 19 [1890].

"My useless little life of Lord B—— has done well
enough.   It is worth nothing, and I cared little about
it when I was doing the thing.   Still I had a real
admiration of *Lothair* and *Sybil*, and for the man too,
who in all his life never condescended to cant.   Also,
I bore him genuine good-will for having offered the
G.C.B. to Carlyle."

[We spent a week at Onslow Gardens early in 1891. Save for a few hours later on, it was our last meeting. Froude was well and happy. I had sent him a little Christmas reminder of cloudless days among the Summer Isles. " I was myself over much of the same water in August. We left the Sound of Hoy in a storm, and forced our way against head-wind and sea all the way to Cape Wrath. We can talk it all over when you come" (January 17, 1891). It was a delightful visit; and the letters that followed made it still more memorable. By-and-by, but still in the early year, he went back to The Molt.]

"THE MOLT, SALCOMBE, *April* 3 [1891].

" All is very quiet here, and would be pleasant if it were not so unnaturally cold. The air has not recovered from the great snow-storm of the first week of March, which buried all this part of the country in drifts 20 feet deep, and are not yet gone. Four ships were wrecked almost in sight of our windows, and fifty or sixty poor fellows drowned, or lost in the snow after they had struggled ashore. The bodies are even now being discovered as it melts off. Life is very tragic— in spite of political economy and a reformed House of Commons. The storm played wild pranks with our garden. The great elm-trees are gone in front of the house. Shrubs of all kinds torn up by the roots. M—— used to say she could not breathe. She can breathe well enough now when the South-Westers come sweeping in. . . . My little yacht has been in Medea's

Caldron ; has been cut in pieces and been restored to life, larger and more beautiful. I told the builder I wished he could do as much for me. I wonder whether you and Mrs S. will ever come here again and let me take you out sailing in her.—Yours ever affectly.,

"J. A. FROUDE."

"5 ONSLOW GARDENS, *November* 17 [1891].

" The political pendulum is going far and fast on the backward swing. Democracies always worship some one leading individual, and Gladstone is the imposing figure just now with the British voter."

["We may look out for a spell of storms, with real peace to follow," he wrote about the same time. Then in January 1892 came a letter of congratulation. " One of the pleasantest features in old age is the seeing such of our friends as are not dead promoted to the honours which they deserve" (20th January). Two months later Lord Salisbury offered him the Chair of Modern History at Oxford. After some hesitation the offer was accepted.]

"5 ONSLOW GARDENS, *April* 8 [1892].

" In the tumult into which I have let myself be thrown, the kind words and wishes of my *real* friends are my best comfort. ' I was well, I would be better, and here I am.' Good-bye to quiet days and quiet work at my own fireside. The temptation of going back to Oxford in a respectable way was too much for me. I must just do the best I can, and trust that I shall not be haunted by Freeman's ghost."

"CHERWELL EDGE, OXFORD, *November* 5 [1892].

"So far the new element in which I find myself floats me very comfortably. The old Dons are civil, and the undergraduates come to my lectures in large numbers. This will pass off with the novelty of the thing. The pace generally is not hard, and I shall do well enough: when the spring comes round, you and Mrs S. will pay us a visit. Boyd had told me of your Orkney adventures. I was there two years ago with Lord Ducie. We were at Kirkwall, and then went round to Stornoway (I think). We saw Maeshowe and the Stones of Stennis. We drove along a lake on our way there which was possibly Scapa Flow—anyway it answers your description. Maeshowe interested me immensely, and never shall I forget the merits of the cod and haddock from the Pentland."

"CHERWELL EDGE, OXFORD, *Jan.* 30 [1893].

"The Master of Gray never interested me particularly, though I had to study and describe the outside of him. You have let in daylight upon him, but not much to his advantage.[1] . . . I am sorry that Lord Elphinstone is dead. I had promised him a visit at Carberry to see the 'Holy Places,' and now I suppose I shall never see them. I did once stand on the spot

---

[1] Froude alludes to a sketch which appeared in *Maga—Queen Mary's Holdfast*—February 1893.

where Mary and Bothwell parted; but it was in a
storm of rain and mist, and I could make little of
it. . . . If you don't come here, I think I shall run
up to you in the Easter vacation."

"CHERWELL EDGE, OXFORD, *February* 28 [1893].

"The sight of your handwriting is always welcome,
specially here where, from the associations of the place,
all the long years' interval since I left Oxford seem as
if they belonged to another person, and as if I, like the
Seven Sleepers, had taken up the threads of my old
existence. When I left in 1849, I had never seen *you;*
I had never even seen Scotland. My time has since
been all my own. Now I have to fall into regulation
terms and vacations. Easter vacation comes near, and
I have various plans, one of which might bring me
down to the Hermitage. I want, if possible, to see
Ruskin again—at Coniston. I shall then be near the
Border, and may easily run on. . . . What a time we
live in! It is like the breaking up of the ice on the
Neva,—great cracks opening, preliminary to the general
split up. Carlyle always said that the catastrophe
of the Constitution was very near; and perhaps it is
well that it should come now before the character of
the people is further demoralised. But there will be a
fine shaking of the nations when the big central mass
bursts up."

[We were now on the eve of the second Home Rule
Bill, and the country was growing keenly excited.

"The Protestants," Froude wrote, "will no more stand it than they did in Tyrconnell's time. But beyond this all is dark." Then he recurred to a favourite topic. The supporters of Home Rule on either side of the Channel were "equally unable to understand the *dour* Calvinism of Ulster. Calvinism at its highest was only a savage determination not to be crushed by *lies* and Tyranny; and in Ireland now there is just the same feeling."]

"You have filled out the figure of the Master of Gray —I daresay correctly. I could never make him out very clearly. I have been, and am, reading De Thou with immense interest. He lived through all that time. He was greatly interested in Scotland, and lets us see the feeling in France—very passionate and very mixed as it was. I wish somebody would write a good book on the House of Guise. All the Guises had immense personality. They would be splendid subjects."

"CHERWELL EDGE, OXFORD, *April* 22 [1893].

"On the whole, I am tolerably happy here—a great deal better in health than I was in London; and I really like a few very young men who have come about me. Some of the old Dons, too, have been rather touchingly kind. . . . Lord Derby is a real loss. He has been more than a kind friend to me. . . . There are consolations—not in *this*, for the dead do not come back, and cannot be replaced — but in Home Rule Second Readings and other political madnesses. Let

them do as they will with Ireland, it will be crushed
down again before ten years are out, and I shall not be
surprised if our Parliamentary System goes down along
with it.   Lord Derby once said to me that kings and
aristocracies can govern empires, but one people cannot govern another people.   If we have to choose
between the Empire and the Constitution, I think I
know which way it will be."

"WOODCOT, KINGSBRIDGE, SOUTH DEVON, *August* 31 [1893].

" I ought to have written to you weeks ago to thank
you for your Mary Stuart book. . . . I do not know
why I have neglected so long what is both a duty and
a pleasure.   Perhaps because on the rare occasions
when a duty and a pleasure go together, the sense of
duty interferes with the pleasure, and the sense of
pleasure diminishes the authoritative order of duty.
. . . I am old, obstinate, and unconvinced; but you
undoubtedly make a strong case out of Crawford's
Deposition.   If it could be proved that Crawford's
Deposition was *made before the letter was discovered* in
the Casket, I should agree with you that the letter must
have been made up out of what Crawford had said.
But as well as I know, the Deposition was made afterwards. . . . However that be, the book is charming
in itself, and excellently illustrated.   Goupil[1] brought
it to me himself, and urged me to write a companion volume on Elizabeth, taking the opposite side.   I

[1] Or rather, I should imagine, the English representative of the French
house.

absolutely refused, however, to get into any kind of
controversy with so old and dear a friend as yourself;
and, besides, you were generous enough to print such
objections as I had made to your view in writing to you,
so that really I had no more to say, except that, according to all the evidence that I met with, *Seton* did
accompany the Queen to his castle, and so did Bothwell.   I wonder where you are this summer.   I myself
drift lazily along at Salcombe, preparing lectures for
the undergraduates, and sailing when winds and waves
will let me.   The professorship answers in providing
me with just so much occupation as keeps me from
being a plague to my family, and not too much for
my years."

"CHERWELL EDGE, OXFORD, *November* 9 [1893].

"I have to lecture on Tuesdays and Fridays.   To
my sorrow I am popular, and my room is crowded.   I
know not who they are, and have no means of knowing.
So it is not satisfactory.   I must alter things somehow
—I can't yet tell how.   But anyway we can have a
day to talk and enjoy ourselves.   It will be 'a Good
Joy.'"

[Looking last night through the bundle of letters
belonging.to the year now rapidly drawing to a close, I
came upon the last which I received from Froude,—
the last letter of a correspondence extending without a
break over five-and-thirty years.   He had more than
once asked me to visit him at Oxford; and being in

London during June, I offered to spend a night at
Cherwell Edge.   This letter was in reply.   I was
struck at the time by its despondent tone; but I had
no apprehension that I was not to see him again.]

"WOODCOT, KINGSBRIDGE, SOUTH DEVON, *June* 22 [1894].

"MY DEAR SKELTON,—Alas! I have few chances of
ever seeing you, and when a chance offers I cannot get
the good of it.   I left Cherwell Edge a month ago,
having wound up my year's lecturing, and being myself
much the worse for the work.

"The teaching business at Oxford goes at high
pressure — in itself utterly absurd, and unsuited altogether to an old stager like myself.   Education, like so
much else in these days, has gone mad, and is turned
into a mere examination Mill.   The undergraduates
come about me in large numbers, and I have asserted
in some sense my own freedom; but one cannot escape
the tyranny of the system.   I have been out of health
with it all for a good many months.   I had hoped to
get right when I could go sailing, &c.; but since we
came here it has been as cold as mid-winter.   Fires
still and thick clothes, and we still shiver; while outside there is nothing but rain, wind, and fog.

"I have more than half a mind to accept an invitation from Sir George Grey, and go back with
him in the autumn to the Antipodes.   At least one
could get a baking in the tropics again.   Ducie wanted
me to go to Norway with him—salmon-fishing; but
I didn't feel that I could do justice to the opportunity.

In the debased state to which I am reduced, if I hooked a 30-lb salmon, I should only pray him to get off.

"Is there no chance of your paying us a visit with Mrs Skelton again, either here or in the winter at Oxford? I have the start of you in the world; but we have neither of us a very long spell to look forward to, and we ought to use the time when we have it. When, if ever, shall I see the Hermitage again?

"Yours ever, with warmest remembrances to Mrs Skelton, J. A. FROUDE."

"When, if ever, shall I see the Hermitage again?" Coming from the tried friend of the better part of a lifetime, the simple, wistful words of farewell (for as such I read them now) have acquired a touching significance. *Sunt lacrymæ rerum;* or (as he phrased it in one of the letters I have quoted), "Life is very tragic—in spite of Political Economy and a Reformed House of Commons." Seldom more tragic, perhaps, than when a strong, ardent, eager spirit leaves us, with little warning, to go out into the darkness alone. It was Edmund Burke who exclaimed the other day— "What shadows we are, and what shadows we pursue!" but the burden of the complaint—*All flesh is as grass, and all the glory of man as the flower of grass!* —is as old as Hebrew sage and psalmist,—as old indeed as Death itself.

Had Arthur Stanley lived, a corner would have been

found for Anthony Froude within the walls of the
Abbey; but probably it is better as it is. This son
of Devon will sleep the sounder "upon the beachèd
verge of the salt flood," within hearing of the surf
that beats upon Bolt Head and the Start. And possibly no more fitting inscription for his gravestone
could be chosen than the tersely monumental lines
which I take from the *St James's Gazette* :—

> " Now, when heroic memories pass
> Like sunset shadows from the grass,
> When England's children cry and stir,
> Each for himself, and few for her ;
>
> We may think tenderly of one
> Who told, like no unworthy son,
> Her history, and who loved to draw
> Champions a younger England saw.
>
> We act no critic's part, and when
> They rate him less than lesser men,
> We feel the golden thread that goes
> To link the periods of his prose.
>
> Perhaps our busy breathless age,
> That leaves unopened history's page,
> Hath need of work like his to strike
> Imperial chords, Tyrtæan-like."

X.

MAINLY ABOUT THOSE WHO FAILED.

THEY are burying him to-day, while the snowflakes fall silently on the tombs, in the old churchyard of St Andrews which overhangs the sea ; he has returned in this fashion to his first and last love. Nor can I, who knew St Andrews in the old time as a boy, marvel at his constancy.

* *
*

St Andrews was in those days a real academic city, —a dark, sombre, ruinous, ill-lighted, badly-paved, old-fashioned, old-mannered, secluded place. Then came the era of Sir Hugh Playfair, who destroyed its scholastic repose and wiped away its classic dust. But in those early ages a few noble fragments of ancient ruin, which had resisted the fury of the Puritan iconoclasts, —the massive walls of a feudal castle, the great tower of St Rule, the lovely windows and arches of the cathedral,—rose above an old-fashioned street, not inconveniently crowded with old-fashioned houses, in which old-fashioned professors and old-fashioned ladies looked after keen-eyed threadbare students, who here, in red and ragged gowns, like the early Edinburgh Reviewers, cultivated the Muses upon a little oatmeal. Very cheerful and homely was the life thus led,—a life through which the shrill sea-wind blew healthfully, and to which the daily round of "golf" on the links, and the evening rubber of long whist in the parlour, added the keen zest of physical and intellectual ex-citement. Death has swept them all clean away,— wonderful old Scotch ladies, wonderful old Scotch pro-fessors; and new streets, new terraces, new men, and new manners have transformed modern St Andrews— during the summer months at least—into a fashionable watering-place for the lawyers of Edinburgh and the traders of Dundee. But go to it during winter or early spring, before the College session is over, before the students in their red gowns have deserted the streets, before the sociable academic society has taken flight, before the links are crowded by golfers who cannot handle a club, before the wild east wind has abated, before the hoarse complaints of a sea often vexed by storm are silenced, before the snow has melted away from the distant Grampian range, and you may even to-day understand the bleak charm that thirty, or forty, or fifty years ago endeared this sea-girt seat of early learning and piety, — this severe mother of the intellectual Graces, *Mater sæva Cupid-inum*,—to the most apathetic of her sons.

* * *

Of all the denizens of a quite innocent Bohemia, Pat,[1] for sheer original force, was among (if not) the foremost. As a young fellow, his physique was magnificent; he positively towered above the other golfers on the links of St Andrews (where he was born); and in the remote ages when I knew him first, few of the professionals even were better players all round. He fell away from his game, indeed, more quickly than most; late sittings over metaphysics, whisky, and tobacco are not favourable to steady play. As the years went by he kept more and more to his den in Broad Street, where any night he might be discovered, dimly visible like an Olympian deity, through the cloud of negrohead or cavendish. He was not exactly sluggish by nature; but he did not care for fame, and he grew indolent as he grew old. His most incisive and brilliant hits were either too abstruse or too tart and bitter to suit the popular taste. He would send a scrap of verse worthy of Clough or Matthew Arnold to a provincial paper—and there an end. Though at heart a man of the finest courtesy, he was in certain superficial aspects a rough diamond; and as he sauntered along Broad Street in threadbare

---

[1] "Pat," I may say in a footnote, was the familiar and affectionate abbreviation for "Patrick Proctor Alexander."

Inverness cape and battered old wide - awake, his closest friends were shy to recognise him. The general air of seediness was pronounced and undeniable. He was careless of the proprieties and conventions; and as the conventions and proprieties are the gospel of our West End, he had no place in its society. Pat was the dreadful sort of creature who could quite calmly dine in a shooting-jacket; I am by no means sure, indeed, that he owned a dress-coat. Then at times he could be savage and Swiftian. He could tolerate no insincerity; in art, in letters, in life, he demanded in highly peremptory terms that a man should be neither hypocrite nor pharisee, neither sneak nor toady. But the sardonic cynicism of this humorous philosopher was entirely on the outside; the nature underneath, as I have said, was singularly simple and tender. We all knew, those of us who were his friends, that he had a genuine gift of humour: but we hardly any of us, I think, recognised that his poetical faculty was as genuine as his humorous. If these waifs and strays of his muse are ever brought together from the poet's corner of obscure country newspapers, it will be found, I think, that few poems more finished in form, more original in suggestion, more charming in expression, have been written in our time. The comparison is somewhat trite; but I venture to assert that those short swallow flights of song have the brightness, simplicity, unexpectedness, and bird-like music of the Elizabethan masters. In the latest there is, moreover, a pathetic hopelessness

—the pathetic hopelessness of a wasted life.   Some of
the lines once read haunt the memory ever afterwards.

"OUR POET.

" I wander where the river strays
    Through woods asleep in pearly haze,
    With quiet nooks where earliest peer
    The firstlings of the dawning year.
I feel, but scarcely seem to share,
This sense which haunts the happy air,
Of young life stirring everywhere ;
    For ever at my heart of hearts
    A pulse of nameless trouble starts.
I watch this tender April sky ;
I see its aimless clouds go by ;
I gaze, and gaze, and only think—
It would have pleased our poet's eye.

From his low nest the glad lark springs
And soars, and soaring ever, flings
Blythe music from the restless wings.
Though all the air be trembling pleased,
The unquiet soul is nothing eased ;
I hear with scarce the heart to hear
That carol ringing quick and clear;
I hear, and hearing, only think—
It would have pleased our poet's ear.

His ears are shut from happy sound ;
His eyes are softly sealed ;
The oft-trod old familiar ground,
    The hill, the wood, the field,
This path, which most he loved, that runs
    Far up the shining river,
Through all the course of summer suns
    He treads no more for ever."

*   *
  *

"The pity of it, the pity of it, Iago!" Here was a man of the most perfect and scrupulous veracity, who had outgrown all formulas, whose life had become aimless, whose lucid intellectual force had failed to find any desirable or fitting "outgait." He sat in his Olympian garret, with clouds of tobacco-smoke about him, revolving many things. Thus occupied, though his nature was as sweet and sociable as ever, a fine scorn for the coin that passes current in the busy world, for the impostor and the charlatan, took possession of him. One saw latterly that he was dying. The finely cut face showed worn and weather-beaten; he still walked firmly enough, but with a slow, measured, deliberate gait; the ragged Inverness cape hung limply about him; it was all too clear that the splendid constitution had failed, and that life had become a weariness to him.

I had known him more or less since I was a boy at St Andrews—about the '43. He was then twenty or thereby—just the age of the "Principal," whose lifelong friendship he enjoyed. He was never, they said, exactly the same man after the Principal's death; he had lost the friend who was closer than a brother, who knew, as no one else did, his genuine and sterling worth, who resented with large-hearted scorn any allegation of moral or spiritual decline, and remained to the end as frank and cordial and appreciative as when they had been lads at college, with the future all before them. We used to regard "Pat" in my school-days with boyish curiosity and wonder,—this

stalwart giant, this handsomest of a handsome race,
who carried all before him on the links, and who
could swim from the harbour-mouth to the Witch's
lake.   All his life his heart was in St Andrews; it
was the playground to which he constantly returned
from his somewhat dreary lodgings, from the drudgery
of commerce, from the monotony of literature.   Between the two periods when I remember him best,
he could not truly be said to have done much.
People in general, the outside public, would say that
he was a failure; those who knew him best recognised
dimly that one who had retained, in spite of all superficial reverses, the courage, the unblemished rectitude,
the fine courtesy, the modest reticence of the boy—
"the white flower of a blameless life"—could not in
the highest sense be said to have been born in vain.
He had lived a true life; and such a life, under whatever forlorn conditions or unpropitious eclipse, cannot
be quite valueless.

> " Men must endure
> Their going hence, even as their coming hither;
> *Ripeness is all.*"

Pat had little to show, indeed, in the way either of
worldly prosperity or of fairly accomplished work.
He had failed in smoky commercial St Mungo; it
was a pity, indeed, that he had adventured on a
career for which he had no aptitude.   But he made
one or two fast friends in the West,—notably Alexander Smith, the most amiable and modest of poets;

and the two came east about the same time, and a
queer, happy, healthy, humorous, grotesque intimacy
sprang up between them, which continued, growing
always warmer and warmer, till Smith's untimely
death.   Then what he had done in literature was for
the most part carefully hidden away.   He did not
write very much at any time, and much of what he
did write could not now be recovered.   But his serious
encounter with Stuart Mill (there is nothing in English
controversial literature quite equal to Pat's rapier-like
lunge, except, perhaps, Goldwin Smith's in the famous
assault on Mansel), and his exquisite mimicry of the
philosopher of Cheyne Row, are too inimitable to be
quite forgotten.

Around the cloudy Olympus where for ten years Pat,
the cloud-compeller, smoked his grimy churchwarden
and wielded his editorial sceptre, many notable men
gathered at intervals.   Among them was the Principal
to whom I have referred,—the Principal of a Venerable Academy, who often came at the end of a week
with one or other of the Professors or Men of Letters
of that secluded seat of learning to spend the Sunday
with Pat.   Two or three of the visitors were known
by name to a bigger world; they made a pleasant
addition to the select society of our innocent Bohemia;
and the Principal at least, divested of hood and gown,
enjoyed himself with boyish *abandon*.

Sometimes but not always, for, alas! it was sometimes otherwise.   This ruddy Apollo, who belonged,
as the blue eyes, the fair skin, the yellow locks unmis-

takably declared, to the wholesome north-country folk who have a dash of Norse blood in their veins, as broad-shouldered as he was large-hearted, with the great, hearty, uproarious, almost convulsive laugh that shook him to the centre, and simplified so many problems, ecclesiastical and other,—the stalwart golfer, the expert swimmer, the devout Christian, the tolerant and statesmanlike churchman, the gracious and courtly man of the world,—was on one side the healthiest of human souls. Yet this fine, bright, frank, candid intelligence was occasionally overshadowed and darkened by a mysterious cloud which made him unutterably miserable, even though he was sustained through its deepest gloom by a high spiritual outlook, by a real faith in the Divine goodness, and by the unwearied ministrations of one of the sweetest of women. The pitiful tremor in the voice, the pitiful entreaty, like that of a dumb animal, in the eyes, were inexpressibly sad, yet somehow not uncharacteristic of a man in whom the physical and the spiritual had been unequally yoked.

Even when at his moodiest, however, it did him good to be with Pat; and the Sunday stroll down the glen was better than doctor's drugs. An occasional Professor—Baynes for choice—would come across with the Principal, and then, in the upper chamber over the writer's office, there were Noctes Ambrosianæ and Suppers of the Gods! The fame of the punch, the savour of the finnan-haddies, spread far and wide; and though of that good company but one remains,

the traditions of the logical sword-play, and the metaphysical high-jinks that grew more and more abstruse
as the night waned, still linger among us.

*   *
*

Pat's letters, as a rule, were extremely idiomatic and
quite unconventional; one I remember descriptive of
a Border Meeting of Dandy Dinmonts at a rustic
hostelry on Tweedside where Pat had been fishing—
Dandies who would either fight with you or drink with
you; but the bundle has been mislaid. Here, however,
is a scrap sufficiently characteristic : — "Something
which mayhap may interest you *apropos* of the main
incident in *Nancy's Tryste*—on the whole, I think, my
favourite of the Romance Studies or what you will.
An incident nearly identical happened this last spring
at Galashiels. A shepherd from the neighbourhood
of Stow had gone over to Galashiels; got drunk as
is the manner of such; and blundering towards midnight into the Gala, been treated to rather more water
than he needed for the purposes of grog. His dog
went in to save him; and failing to do so presently
rushed up to a policeman dripping wet, and in such
a state of doggish agitation as you can imagine (the
thing has often happened). The policeman was impressed to the effect that something was wrong; one
or two people gathered; and following the brute they
very soon came upon the poor devil drowned past
revival. Meantime his wife, seven or eight miles off,

had been sitting up waiting for her husband; not in any anxiety about him; thinking only—as is like—'Jamie, puir man's got *fou* again'; when suddenly she heard his voice outside crying as if in some distress,—'Jeanie! Jeanie! Jeanie!' Not doubting to find him she opened the door, and found only night and darkness. Naturally much troubled, at streak of dawn she was afoot and over to Galashiels, where she found Jamie waiting for her as before said. The dog marked the time on the one side, she on the other; and so far as could be made out they almost exactly tallied. Telling this to a friend the other day who has a turn for such things, I was assured by him that the story is current and believed all about Stow, where in autumn he had been fishing for a week or two. In order to your belief and mine, it might have been desirable that some competent person should have been on the spot to make very strict inquisition; but taking the story as it stands, I certainly cannot say I *dis*-believe it. Do you?"

* * *

Another of the *Infanti Perduti* who from the beginning was bound to fail—failure was written upon garb and gait—was Henry Westerley. I did not know him till he was well on in life; but up to the time we met he had been failing with cheerful pertinacity. He came to edit our Nonconformist *Chronicle;* and from the day he entered the editor's sanctum the health of the

Chronicle declined. Though well on in life, as I have
said, he always looked like a boy, and somehow we
treated him as such; we could not help it; he was
so frank, so impulsive, so delightfully foolish and irresponsible. His Nonconformity was kept for the office;
when with the Doctor, or the Principal, or myself he
was a staunch Tory and Churchman. They gave him
a fair salary I believe; but he was perennially impecunious. He delighted, like Fakredeen, in his debts;
his creditors interested him keenly; he would entertain
us with narratives of monetary adventures and moonlight flittings without the least reserve. He had a
marvellous faculty of borrowing,—his success in that
far from profitable calling being phenomenal; but
whoever lent him a five-pound note might better have
cast it into the sea. It melted like snow in summer;
and on his oath he could not have told how or where
it had gone. But in spite of squint and stutter, which
were trying to his friends if not to himself, he was
blest with the sunniest temper. Persistent ill-luck
could not sour it; he took to the Court of Bankruptcy
as ducks take to the water; and when he came out of
the Sanctuary for his Sunday dinner with us, he was
the gayest and least embarrassed of the company.
Though utterly irresponsible—irresponsible as faun or
satyr—he was yet—strange conjunction!—the soul of
honour. He did not understand what meanness or
double-dealing meant. To save his life he could not
have lied. It was not in his nature. It never occurred
to him. He would have been the last indeed to claim

any merit for his transparent and guileless simplicity; and indeed I claim no merit for it; seeing that it had no moral basis, nor any connection, however remote or accidental, with ethics.

* *
*

Hope Leslie was another of the perennially impecunious. When I first knew him (about 1850 it would be) he was living in a corner house in Westmorland Street—a delicate, emaciated, olive-skinned, secluded student—very tall and very thin—with eyes and hair black as jet—who just managed to crawl between his bedroom and his study. He had not been out of the house for months. No one expected him to recover,— he looked at times the image of Death. All this time, however, he was working away at *Acrostics*,—a wonderfully bright, clever, and yet intrinsically fantastic and unsubstantial book, which was published by a London firm about 1852. There was a good deal of the hothouse about both the book and its author,— it had the tone of the sick-room and of the shy student who had mixed little with men. And at that time Hope was as innocent as a baby. He and his mother and sister—all more or less invalids—had always lived together very quietly—plain living and high thinking— the thinking, a curious cross between Aristotle and Sir William Hamilton, with a dash of the speculative frivolities which occupied the Schoolmen thrown in for condiment. Judge then of our surprise when his

health suddenly mended ; when he ceased to be gaunt
and cadaverous; when he became the sporting oracle
of the *Tomahawk*, and fell in love with a not too coy
or reluctant Hebe, who was twice his age and long
past her prime. He wrote in the *Tomahawk* the most
subtle delicate refined fastidious criticism of her more
than robust art ; went to see her every night; and
finally in mere foolishness and virginal ignorance
married her.   Then he settled in London, where
suddenly, as the literary critic of the *Morning Star*
(at a time when a notice in its columns was worth
a moderate fortune), he became a celebrity.   The
extravagance of that household knew no bounds.   His
little dinners, his little suppers (in certain social circles,
artistic and theatrical), were all the vogue.   He soon
tired of his wife; his eyes were opened, as was perhaps
inevitable ; and he turned away to less lawful diversions.   Once or twice, on urgent entreaty, his old
friends gave him a helping hand — the money was
always to be repaid within the year !—at his death
it was still outstanding.   He was lavish in promises
to pay—a true Oriental magnificence of Castles in the
Air—when he was editing the *Evening Star* (just before
it set) he offered Dizzy (so it was said) ten thousand
pounds for a serial romance, and another eminent story-
teller was very sore about a princely bargain the Editor
had made with him, which of course never came off ;
for Hope by this time was borrowing quite shamelessly
right and left, and the *Evening Star* was *in articulo
mortis*.   He had determined to make a palace of his

house in Randolph Square, and the contractor he employed brought it down about his ears. This was the beginning of the end—an enormous loss—a blow from which he never recovered. Then he left the *Star* and started the *Bugle* (or the *Big Drum*), for which an ecclesiastical publisher found the money. The *Bugle* might have succeeded; but there was something in the third number which frightened the publisher out of his wits, and he threw it up in a theological panic. Then there were constant household bickerings about a Lady Somebody, then Divorce, then deep and ever deeper waters, and death at forty-five. It was all very tragical; but in spite of his fine-spun theories about the true, the beautiful, and the good, there was a lack in Hope of downright honest manliness; a leaven of charlatanism which was bound, sooner or later, to spread and infect the whole lump. We may or we may not extract a moral from his paradoxical career; *that* depends upon the individual taste; but this at least may be said with confidence, that few men of such parts, of such undoubted attainments, have gone to the bad with more startling rapidity.

*   *
*

I have been working all night at an ethical conundrum—the *Infanti Perduti !*—which somehow will not come right; if I put it away now I may find the answer to-morrow—or rather to-day. For the candle which has been flickering for some time has at length gone out

with a final splutter, and I am writing by the uncertain
light of the dawn, in which one twinkling star looks
faint and pallid—like a belated ghost. Everything is
quiet and still; the heavy dew lies thickly upon the
yellow bent; and the sea—so motionless that it mir-
rors the phantom sickle of the waning moon—is dotted
here and there with the dark forms of fishing-boats waiting lazily with outspread sails for the morning breeze.
The world is asleep—all save myself and an adventurous
rabbit who is nibbling the grass upon the lawn. Wasp,
who is curled up at the foot of the bed, growls in his
sleep—he sees a foumart in his dream no doubt—opens
a drowsy eye for a moment, and then expresses his
disapprobation of my untimely proceedings by turning
his back upon me. You are right, sir, — to bed, to
bed.

And so into dreamland,—with the haunting music of
the deep for lullaby or—dirge. It is a song without
words. Only Heine could have written them; and
Heine is dead.

XI.

MAINLY ABOUT DISRAELI.

FROUDE, I see, disrespectfully alludes to a wild parliamentary hurricane as "a storm in a slop-basin"; and many of us are beginning to think that in this, as in other respects, Froude was not so far wrong. So that I do not anticipate that our modest Table-Talk will be sensibly agitated by the winds of doctrine that stir the political duck-pond at St Stephen's. But this bright and clever little book on Pitt—Lord Rosebery's eulogy of the great Tory Minister—is one indication of a remarkable change in popular feeling which is really interesting, and ought not to be overlooked.

The great electoral contest at Liverpool, which took place soon after Pitt's death between Mr Canning and Mr Brougham, is still remembered by those who write and by those who read political biographies. "To one man while he lived," Canning declared, "I was devoted with all my heart and all my soul. Since the death of Mr Pitt I acknowledge no leader; my political allegi-

ance lies buried in his grave." To which Brougham
replied : " Gentlemen, I stand up in this contest against
the friends and followers of Mr Pitt, or, as they partially
designate him, the immortal statesman now no more.
Immortal in the miseries of his devoted country ! Immortal in the wounds of her bleeding liberties ! Immortal in the cruel wars which sprang from his cold miscal-
culating ambition ! Immortal in the intolerable taxes,
the countless loads of debt, which these wars have flung
upon us—which the youngest man among us will not
live to see the end of ! Immortal in the triumphs of
our enemies and the ruin of our allies—the costly purchase of so much blood and treasure ! Immortal in the
afflictions of England, and the humiliation of her
friends, through the whole results of his twenty years'
reign, from the first rays of favour with which a delighted Court gilded his early apostacy, to the deadly
glare which is at this moment cast upon his name by
the burning metropolis of our last ally ! But may no
such immortality ever fall to my lot ; let me rather live
innocent and inglorious ; and when at last I cease to
serve you and to feel for your wrongs, may I have a
humble monument in some nameless stone, to tell that
beneath it there rests from his labours in your service
*an enemy of the immortal statesman—a friend of peace and
of the people.*"

Mr Stapleton informs us that when riding one day
with Mr Canning near Brighton, they heard that
Brougham was dangerously ill. " Poor fellow ! "
said Canning, " I am sorry to hear it ; " and then

MAINLY ABOUT DISRAELI.   243

added,—" If he should be taken from the House of
Commons, there will be no one left *to pound and
mash.*" Canning's satiric touch, like Disraeli's, was
much lighter, much more deft and dexterous than
Brougham's; but the passage I have quoted is a fair
specimen of the elaborate invective—the pounding and
mashing—which was much esteemed in its day.

What may be called the Brougham - Jeffrey - John
Russell estimate of Pitt held the field for long.
Through the pages of the *Edinburgh Review*, a score
of brilliant essayists continued to give it a wide circulation. The vehemence of their dislike indeed made
them at times not only grotesquely unscrupulous, but
insanely unpatriotic. While they damned Pitt, they
canonised Napoleon. Blessing the one, they banned
the other. Even the victorious progress of Wellington,
the triumphal march from Torres Vedras to the
Pyrenees, was either coldly condemned or bitterly de-
rided. About the year 1850, when Lord John Russell's
' Memorials' appeared, the Whig tradition of a desperately wicked and incapable Minister was flourishing
vigorously. At the same time the Holland House
legend—the cult of a quite fabulous Fox, who was not
only the most charming of companions, but the most
sagacious of statesmen, and the most trusted of
leaders—met with very general acceptance. The dissent of a few obstinate and obsolete Tories did not
count; and Lord John Russell concluded his memorial
volumes with the portenous intimation,—" It will be
my business, if I should be able to continue this work,

to point out *the utter want of foresight by which the con-*
duct of Mr Pitt was marked when he led the people of Eng-
land into a crusade against the people of France."

Edinburgh was at that time one of the shrines of
the Whig faith; and it was "Shirley's" good fortune
as a lad (through James Syme, Andrew Coventry, and
other true believers who hailed from Fife and Kinross)
to see something of the priests who ministered at its
altars. It is pardonable sometimes to be generous as
well as just; and even in a company of Tories I may
venture to say that, during the closing years of his life,
Jeffrey, at his pleasant villa of Craigcrook, with his
granddaughter at his knee, presented as charming a
picture of a serene but vigilant old age as one could
wish to see. Sydney Smith years before had said of
him when he went on the bench: "His robes, God
knows, will cost him little; one buck-rabbit will clothe
him to the heels;" and during the interval the wonderful little man had grown even more transparently delicate and fragile. His boyhood had been earnest and
passionate, his manhood energetic and distinguished;
but there was a peculiar mellowness about his age. The
enthusiasm and the passion had not died out, nor the
keen and finely discriminating intellect been dimmed.
But now, besides and beyond the fastidious taste, the
playful irony, the dignified reserve, there was added
an admirable grace and simplicity, a peculiar sweetness and gentleness, which it was difficult to associate with one who had been an unsparing critic and
a formidable foe. "A man," Goethe said the year

before he died, " has only to become old to become tolerant ; " and Jeffrey was a notable example of the mellowing catholicity of advancing years. It was no wonder that such a man should have retained his influence to the last. Outsiders who had found his collected essays rather thin and jejune, might fail to understand wherein the charm consisted ; but then, as Pitt once said of his rival, " they had not been under the wand of the magician."

It was about the year 1850—the year of Jeffrey's death—that some of us who were then preparing for active life began to rebel against the prevailing superstition. The Whig tradition was still all-powerful in the city where so many of its high-priests had been bred, and from whence its sacred writings had issued ; and John Wilson and his jovial companions of the ' Noctes ' were regarded as outlaws and banditti by the select and privileged caste to whom the true faith had been revealed. *Maga* was then as ever true to her colours ; but *Maga* appealed to a wider than a provincial audience. Might not something be done, we inquired tentatively, to mitigate the severity of the sentence which a rather narrow, if austerely virtuous, tribunal had pronounced against those who like ourselves were outside the pale ? It was then that a highly speculative friend, whose resources were as slender as his projects were vast, audaciously declared that he was prepared, if properly supported, to give the Dissenters, the rebels, the despised minority, a chance of being heard. " We shall have a weekly paper from which the Whig, and the Whig only, shall be severely excluded. The lion shall lie down with the lamb; ultra - Tories and ultra - Radicals shall work harmoniously together; and in fact, gentlemen, you are welcome to ventilate any paradoxes, or heresies, or superstitions you like, so long as you vigorously assail the common enemy."

On the basis of this elastic confession of faith the *Edinburgh Guardian* was established about the year 1852. It was published every Saturday, and it lived for four or five years. There was certainly some admirable writing in its columns — Dallas's critical and artistic articles, and Baynes's weekly "Diary of Juniper Agate" being really first-rate. To "Shirley" the department entitled "Things in General" was intrusted, and in the audacity of one-and-twenty he hit so hard all round that more than once the coach threatened to upset. Edinburgh was then a stronghold of the Free Kirk as well as of the Whigs; and when, in addition to defending Disraeli from the onslaughts of the *Saturday*, and Currer Bell from the insults of the *Quarterly*, and Bribery and Corruption (on the ground that if the franchise was an inalienable natural right, a man was entitled to do what he liked with his own) from the political purists, we took to recommending the incomprehensible heresies of Maurice and the muscular latitudinarianism of Kingsley, the paper and its editor began to get into deep water. When even a pacific John Brown—the dear and delightful friend of after-years

—was moved to warn us that it was positively sinful to excuse or condone the political peccadilloes of a "splendid scamp" like Dizzy, what mercy could we expect from the successors of John Knox and Balfour of Burley? But I suspect that the direst offence we committed against the code then of binding force in the northern metropolis was a series of semi-historical, semi-political articles designed to show that Fox was from the beginning to the end of his career a persistent failure, and that Pitt, on the other hand, was the Pilot who weathered the Storm, and brought the labouring vessel into port.

It was Disraeli himself who first pointed out that the imposing figure of the Constitutional Whig— a figure which had filled so large a place in the popular imagination — was stuffed with sawdust. Until *Coningsby* appeared, the Whigs had used the parliamentary history of England for the glorification of their own political virtue. Hampden had died on the field and Sidney on the scaffold to enable Mr Macaulay[1] to write a series of brilliant essays in the

---

[1] It is the fashion at present to belittle Lord Macaulay; but I adhere to the opinion I expressed long ago in *Nugæ Criticæ* that at a time when we were going to revolutionise our politics, our theology, and our morals, it was an immense advantage to have at the head of our literature a man who thought calmly, who spoke moderately, who wrote fastidiously, whose enthusiam was never intemperate, whose judgment was never disturbed. As a lad, I heard him deliver the Glasgow Rectorial Address in 1849, and the impression of high and lucid intellectual force I then received was never effaced. Again, in later life, I heard him deliver his last great speech. It was when Edinburgh had repaired the wrong it had done him. Already disease had begun its work. The burly figure was bent and at-

Edinburgh. The Whigs ever since the glorious Revolution of '88 had been the consistent and persistent
advocates of civil and religious liberty; whereas Bolingbroke and Chatham and Pitt had no claim, in respect
of the public services they had rendered, to the regard
of any enlightened patriot. *Coningsby,* which was
published in the Forties, pricked this "radiant
bubble." It then appeared that during the whole
or nearly the whole of last century England had
been governed by a Venetian oligarchy as unprin-
cipled as it was corrupt. The great Whig houses
had usurped the powers of the Crown and invaded
the liberties of the people. The monopoly of public
virtue on which they had prided themselves turned
out to be the merest sham. This novel version of
history was at first received with derision; but it
made way—slowly but surely; and the claim of the
Whig to have been in evil times the one disinterested
guardian of civil and religious liberty has ceased to
be recognised — is in most quarters, indeed, flatly
denied.

The old superstition, however, died hard, and those
of us who had taken Mr Disraeli's view from the

tenuated; but the eye was still full of light, and the silver voice, though
feeble, had lost none of its persuasive charm. He was visibly affected
when he rose; and when he alluded to the men of Edinburgh who had
been taken away since he last stood among them, to the friendly faces and
voices that would greet him no more, the strain was almost painful. "And
Jeffrey too," he added, with a suppressed sob, as he finished the enumera-
tion. There he faltered and stopped short. The simple pause of feeling
was better than any rhetoric,—more touching and impressive than the most
laboured panegyric could have been.

beginning found considerable difficulty in laying its
ghost. As late as 1864, indeed, I was moved to
write a reply to an article which appeared, I think,
in the *Edinburgh Review* of that summer. The *Edinburgh* held that the history of our legislation during
a hundred and fifty years proved, and proved con-
clusively, that the Whig Walpoles had always been
right, and that the Tory Pitts had always been wrong.
Any "liberal" measure passed by a Tory had, of
course, been stolen from a Whig. Mr Disraeli's
sarcasm against Sir Robert Peel was turned against
his own friends. They had found the Whigs bath-
ing and had run away with their clothes. This,
indeed, had been a favourite thesis with Macaulay,
who had ridiculed the opposite view on the occasion
of a controversy with Lord Mahon, afterwards Earl
Stanhope,—a sound if not a brilliant historian. As
the fallacy has still a certain currency, it may not be
amiss to restate as briefly as may be the substance
of the argument, more especially as two of the letters
which the discussion elicited—one from Mr Disraeli
and one from Lord Stanhope—were (and are) not
without interest.

The fallacy rests upon the assumption that politics
is one of the exact sciences. "I cannot but pause
to observe," Lord Mahon wrote, "how much the
course of a century has inverted the meaning of our
party nicknames—how much a modern Tory resembles
a Whig of Queen Anne's reign, and a Tory of Queen
Anne's reign a modern Whig." Mr Macaulay prompt-

ly retorted. The modern Tories resembled the Whigs of Queen Anne's reign, because the principles which the Whigs recommended had been accepted by the Tories. The Whig had remained consistent ; the Tory had gone over to the enemy. The retort cannot be regarded as conclusive. Is it fair to assume that a party must be inconsistent because it adopts a policy which ten or twenty or fifty years before it had opposed ? During these fifty years the world has changed. The conditions have altered. Truth, in a political sense, is a relative term. Lord Bolingbroke said quite truly to Sir William Windham, " It is as much a mistake to depend upon that which is true but impracticable at a certain time, as to depend on that which is neither true nor practicable at any time." Thus the party which votes against an extension of the franchise during one century, and which votes in favour of its extension during the next, may be acting consistently as well as sagaciously. *Everything depends upon the surroundings. It is right to resist until it is time to give way.* It would have been folly for Somers or Walpole to have extended the suffrage during the first half of the eighteenth century. Had they done so, it is more than probable that the Stuarts would have been restored. Until we recognise that in the political world there is no absolute right or wrong, and that the duty of a legislator is to consider only whether it will be for the general advantage of the community that secret voting (say) or universal suffrage should be introduced under the conditions that exist at the moment, we shall fail to preserve the partition which separates, and ought to separate, the province of politics from the province of ethics.

Moreover, it was positively incorrect to affirm, as Macaulay did, that during the early part of the eighteenth century the Whigs represented an advanced and the Tories a stationary policy. "The absolute position of the parties has been altered; the relative position remains the same." But as matter of fact the Tories of the first half of the century were the *advanced* party. At least they advocated comprehensive measures of reform which the other side refused to adopt. And the anomaly, if it be an anomaly, is easily explained. There is a great deal of human nature in man. The Tories wanted power; the Whigs possessed it. The Whigs had attacked the prerogative when it was directed against themselves; the Tories, when the Elector of Hanover was "brought across in a storm," were willing to impose limitations on the authority of a sovereign whom they detested. So also with regard to the question of electoral reform. As long as the Whigs corrupted the electoral bodies, the Tories clamoured for change; while the Whigs did not become reformers until the electoral bodies, under the second Pitt, had gone over by tens and fifties to the Tories.

The comments of Mr Disraeli and Lord Stanhope are, as I have said, interesting and characteristic :—

"GROSVENOR GATE, *May* 16, 1864.

"DEAR SIR,—I thank you for your article, which I read this morning. I read your criticisms always with interest, because they are discriminative, and are founded on knowledge and thought.

"These qualities are rarer in the present day than the world imagines. Everybody writes in a hurry, and the past seems quite obliterated from public memory.

"I need not remind you that Parliamentary Reform was a burning question with the Tories for the quarter of a century at least that followed the Revolution of 1688. Not only Sir William Windham and his friends were in favour of annual Parliaments and universal suffrage, but Sir John Hinde Cotton even advocated the ballot. These were desperate remedies against Whig supremacy. It appeared to me in 1832 that the Reform Act was another 1688, and that influenced my conduct when I entered public life. I don't say this to vindicate my course, but to explain it.

"So also I looked then — as I look now — to a reconciliation between the Tory party and the Roman Catholic subjects of the Queen. This led, thirty years ago and more, to the O'Connell affair; but I have never relinquished my purpose, and have now, I hope, nearly accomplished it.

"If the Tory party is not a national party, it is nothing.

"Pardon this egotism, which I trust, however, is

not my wont; and believe me, dear sir, with respect, faithfully yours, B. DISRAELI."

"GROSVENOR PLACE, *March* 18, 1868.

"SIR,—I thank you for the address upon Lord Bolingbroke which you have had the goodness to send me, and which I have had much pleasure in reading. It gives, I think, a very accurate sketch of that 'all-accomplished' man.

"Allow me also to assure you of the gratification with which a year or two since I read the *Campaigner at Home*. I was only sorry that you had omitted from that interesting series of chapters the one which I had read as an article in *Fraser* as to the transmutation of the Whig and Tory parties—the controversy carried on now thirty-five years ago between my lamented friend Lord Macaulay and myself. Your discussion of it was, I thought, very good, and it would have been better still if you had followed it to its final close. For if you will now refer to Lord Macaulay's second article on Lord Chatham, as published in the *Edinburgh Review*, October 1841, and since collected in his Essays, you will find from the opening passage—enforced by a most ingenious illustration from Dante's Malebolge—that Lord Macaulay's opinion of the point at issue had come to be very nearly the same as mine.

"I ask pardon for having so long detained you; and I am, sir, your very faithful servant, STANHOPE."

I have said enough to show that the political

horizon has sensibly widened during the past thirty
or forty years. We live in a new world. The old
landmarks have been removed. Hampden has ceased
to die on the field, and Sidney on the scaffold. Fox
and Brougham and Jeffrey and Holland House and
the *Edinburgh Review* have fallen quite into the background; while out of the mists of controversy, and
above the babble of the crowd, rise the great figures
of Pitt and Canning and Disraeli. And nothing can
bring the change more vividly home to us than to
compare the narrow and conventional prejudices of
Lord John Russell in his *Fox* with the manly and
vigorous independence of Lord Rosebery in his *Pitt*.

*   *
*

There has as yet been no complete biography of
Benjamin Disraeli, though Mr Froude's rapid summary
of his career was not ineffective as a sketch. I suppose that when Lord Rowton (the indispensable
"Monty Corry" that was) has leisure to revise his
reminiscences those of us who survive will know all
about it. The letter which I have had occasion to
quote reminds me that in various old Note - Books
there are not a few passages in which my first and
fresh impressions of the most striking personality of
our time are recorded; and as certain features of
which the public knew little then, and knows less now,
are faithfully reflected in these contemporary memor-
anda, they may not be without interest in the meantime. A few pages at least can hardly come amiss,—

though indeed the notion that Disraeli was a cynically reticent and repellent " Sphinx" is already wearing away.

* * *

"*January* 1863.—Old Parker writes me that *Thalatta* has already done very well; the edition is nearly sold out, and a Frenchman wants to translate it. The hero is a cross between Canning and Disraeli; and the words in the preface to the effect that had dedications been still in fashion I would have dedicated it to the one English statesman of the day to whom the conception of imperial duties to a world-wide Empire appeals, brought me on the same morning two curiously contrasted letters,—an amazing contrast indeed, for the old leaven of the judicious Whig (which Dizzy hates like poison) is still strong in ' Dr John.' This is Dizzy's :—

"'Torquay, *Dec.* 28, 1862.

"'Dear Sir,—I am honoured and I am gratified by the dedication of *Thalatta*. I entirely sympathise with the object of the work, which gracefully develops a tone of thought and sentiment on which the continued greatness of this country depends.—Believe me, your obedient servant, B. Disraeli.'

"This is Dr John's :—

"'23 Rutland Street, Edinburgh, *Sunday.*

"'My dear Skelton and Shirley,—*Thalatta* has come, and I am sure I will get much enjoyment from it. Whaur gat ye that style? and how I envy you

your bits of verse, which seem to have had for their
final cause and end their being so embedded! But
I don't envy you your worship of Benjamin. Do you
really and truly look upon that splendid scamp as
either a patriot or a politician. I think you must
lash yourself into all your Tory fury in some unknown
cavern, and thence issue into your besmoken room
in Alva Street. I admire Benjamin too, as a man
of genius and audacity and the author of *Henrietta
Temple* and of his own fortunes; but as an English
Minister and the mouthpiece of the British will and
power it amazes me that with your bumps of causality
and comparison you can believe in him. Thanks
again for this beautiful book. I wish I were younger
and happier, and away in Rannoch in the Black Wood
with it at the end of June.—Yours ever truly,

"'J. BROWN.'"[1]

*   *
*

"*July* 1867.—Since he became Chancellor, Dizzy
has been cordially helpful; his anxiety to do his old
allies a good turn has certainly been very marked.
People will not believe that behind that impassive

---

[1] I had fancied that this poor little political trifle—which Sir William
Fraser, I see, attributes to an unknown author—had been long ago forgotten; and it was a very pleasant surprise to learn the other day, from
one of the most capable members of the Unionist Administration, that
"many years ago my heart was charmed, and my ambition stirred and
quickened, by *Thalatta*." One cannot but prize such testimony; it is a
"good joy," as Mrs Carlyle would have said, to know that the seed you
have sown has not fallen on stony ground.

mask there can be any warmth of feeling; but they are much mistaken, as I have good reason to know, and as indeed all the young fellows about him without any exception or reservation are eager to acknowledge."[1]

* * *

"1 *November* 1867.—We have had Dizzy here in splendid form. I found a note from the Advocate when I got home after the great speech,—'Come and meet Dizzy to-morrow.' So I went. Old Lady Ruthven was there—a miraculous old woman. She and Mrs Disraeli, sitting over the fire with their feet on the fender, made between them the funniest pair, —the witches in *Macbeth*, or what you will. And the potent Wizard himself!—with his olive complexion, and coal-black eyes, and the mighty dome of his forehead (no Christian temple, be sure)—is unlike any living creature one ever met. I had never seen him in the daylight before, and the daylight accentuates his strangeness. The face is more like a mask than ever, and the division between him and mere mortals more marked. I would as soon have thought of sitting down at table with Hamlet or Lear or the Wan-

---

[1] Here is a later extract which may go in as a footnote. The date is "March 10, 1868." "Dizzy has been indefatigable, and yesterday the conclusive letter came from the House of Commons. It was Lord Advocate Gordon who wrote : 'This evening Hardy told me that he was ready to approve of your appointment. We spoke of it to Dizzy, who was next us on the bench, and he said he was very glad to hear of it. You had better however say nothing about it till you get the official intimation.'"

R

dering Jew.   He was more than cordial,—specially appreciative of the Scotch allies—*rari nantes in gurgite
vasto*—who had stood by him through thick and thin.
' I fancied indeed till last night that north of the Border
I was not loved ; but last night made amends for much.
We were so delighted with our reception—Mrs Disraeli
and I — that after we got back we actually danced
a jig (or was it a hornpipe ?) in our bedroom.'

   " They say, and say truly enough, What an actor the
man is !—and yet the ultimate impression is of absolute sincerity and unreserve.   Grant Duff will have
it that he is an alien.   What's England to him or
he to England ?   There is just where they are wrong.
Whig or Radical or Tory don't matter much perhaps ;
but this mightier Venice—this Imperial Republic on
which the sun never sets—that vision fascinates him,
or I am much mistaken.   England is the Israel of
his imagination, and he will be the Imperial Minister
before he dies—if he gets the chance."

                    *   *
                      *

   " 10*th June* 1868.—It is certainly a very remarkable
alliance.   That her heart, however, is as kind as her
taste is queer, everybody admits ; and she has splendid
pluck and illimitable faith in Dizzy.   To this curious
old lady—'the severest of critics, but a perfect wife '
— the great man is apparently devoted ; but after
seeing her a little one cannot but wonder a little
what his feeling for her really may be.   Is it true

chivalry? or gratitude? or what? I am told that
he gallantly refers and defers to her critical judgment
whenever opportunity offers. 'Mrs Disraeli is reading
your *Campaigner at Home*, and gave me last evening
a most charming description of it.' Such references,
I believe, are frequent in his correspondence; and
when visiting at the big houses, where the big ladies
fight a little shy of her, he won't stand any nonsense.
' Love me, love my Mary-Anne.' People will laugh
no doubt when he is not looking; but to my mind
there is something distinctly fine in this jealous
and watchful regard."

* * *

"*April* 1881.—There is a common impression that
Dizzy was not particularly anxious to acknowledge
literary service, or to maintain friendly relations with
his brethren of the pen. My own experience (and I
believe the experience of others) does not confirm
this impression, — on the contrary, tends to refute
it. The cordial little notes continued to be deftly
worded,—even when the ' B. Disraeli' of the earlier
had later on been exchanged for ' Beaconsfield.' Only
a month or two before the rout of last year, a political *jeu d'esprit* appeared in *Maga* which pleased him
mightily. He made a guess at the writer, and next
morning a line of flattering appreciation arrived. ' It
is capital, and worthy of the good old days of the
Rolliad and the Anti-Jacobin.' This was the last letter :

I did not see or hear from him again. I was told
that—after the blow fell—he aged rapidly : and though
he bore himself in public with characteristic calmness
and intrepidity he must have felt, I fear, that it was
hard to be beaten at the end.   We had all hoped—
not his friends only — that he would have lived to
come back to Downing Street.   But it has been
otherwise ordered ; and (though he would not be
laid in the Abbey) I keep repeating to myself Pope's
splendid compliment to Mansfield :—

> ' Conspicuous scene ! another yet is nigh,
>   More silent far, where Kings and Poets lie;
>   Where Murray long enough his country's pride
>   Shall be no more than Tully or than Hyde.'

The last line is inimitable ; ' shall be no more than '—
the Immortals ; no finer eulogy was ever penned.''

XII.

MAINLY ABOUT THE STORY-TELLERS.

THERE can be no doubt that what is called the "*grotesque*" has obtained a recognised and definitive position in art and literature. I fancy that it was originally the form in which the grim humour of the medieval architect found expression. I do not know that it had any place in classical art or literature. I cannot at the moment recall any Greek or Roman work where we meet with it (except perhaps the Faun of Praxiteles); and indeed one feels that the men who built the Parthenon would have regarded it with a dislike from which contempt was not absent. Now that it is accepted as a legitimate factor in letters as in art, it is very necessary to discriminate between the true and the false or bastard grotesque. Which is the coin from the Royal Mint, and which the counterfeit? The supremacy of a master of the craft like Heine and Charles Lamb is willingly admitted; but the claims of the mob of modern "humourists" to enter the Calendar will, no doubt, now or hereafter, be strenuously resisted

by the *advocatus diaboli*. And justly? Of how many
of them indeed can it be said with truth that their use
of the grotesque is not ignoble? We have exchanged
the mellow irony of *Tancred* for the boisterous horse-
play of *The Innocents Abroad*, and the ballads of Bon
Gaultier have been eclipsed by the *Bab*.

* * *

It may be asserted with confidence that, in the highest walk of the imagination, the personality of the
worker is never obtruded. We do not detect Shakespeare in *The Midsummer Night's Dream*, nor Scott in
The Heart of Mid-Lothian; for the medium in which they
work is colourless. In other words, they have no
mannerism. Mannerism infers limitation—the limitations of caprice or eccentricity—and is therefore easily
recognised; but the Masters are inscrutable.

"Others abide our question ; *Thou* art free."

It is true of course, at the same time, that there is a
certain class of writers of whom it may be said that their
mannerism is their main attraction. But few, if any, of
these writers are in the first rank. It is not their intrinsic merit that keeps the *Religio Medici* and the *Urn-
Burial* alive; it is because they were written by Sir
Thomas Browne. The perennial charm of his quaint
and engaging personality is impressed upon every line.
Hence their vitality. But a mannerism is not neces-

sarily attractive ; sometimes it repels ; indeed, as often as not it is a positive drawback. If *The Ring and the Book* survive, it will be in spite of its mannerism. And the same may be said of more than one of our prose writers —especially of those, as it happens, in whom the imagination is most active. Meredith, Blackmore, Hardy —each has his mannerism. In some cases it is more pronounced than in others, affecting the substance as well as the style. Where in Wessex will we meet with those curious peasants of whom Mr Hardy dreams, and whose dialect at least he so faithfully reproduces ? They are not inventions, but they belong to "worlds not realised " ; we see them through the stained glass of a whimsical imagination. And it is to be observed that in the case of each of the writers the mannerism has grown. What was at first little more, it may be, than a casual inadvertence, has become, as the years passed, a confirmed and inveterate habit. George Meredith's earlier works (*Evan Harrington* for choice) are to my mind examples of the true grotesque in some of its finest moods ; but of late years the eccentricity has ceased to be artistic, or even intelligible. Blackmore's *Lorna Doone*, and Hardy's *A Pair of Blue Eyes*, are absolutely faultless when compared with some of their successors. Of these, as of *The Ring and the Book*, it is true that if they live it will be in spite of their mannerism. The mannerism itself is a dead weight ; the vitalising element must be sought elsewhere.

* *
*

I sometimes fancy that in these waning years of the Victorian era we have overdone, or are overdoing, the freakish and the whimsical ; that a reaction is at hand ; and that the simple transcript of life which we get from a born story-teller like Mrs Oliphant will by-and-by recover its high place in our regard.

* * *

Each of us has his pet ambition and his pet hero— his Napoleon, his Goethe, his William the Silent, his Cromwell, his Shakespeare.   As we grow older our tastes become simpler, and I sometimes fancy now that the fame of Izaak Walton is that which I would most covet.   What a safe immortality his innocent prattle enjoys !   Such fame as his is altogether pure and lovely.   One cannot perhaps entirely understand its persistent vitality,—this fragile Nautilus on the stormy boundless Atlantic ; but the conviction that it would be a thousand pities if so much mildness, and sweetness, and ineffable content with trifles were to be ship-wrecked on the shore of oblivion, and lost to living men, may possibly explain it more or less.   *Grata quies.*   The turbid restless world is soothed and mollified by this simple picture of goodness which never changes.   It is like those rustic pictures on the Urn which Keats must have seen somewhere,—what would that Urn bring at Christie's to-day, I wonder, if it could be found in Borghese Palace or elsewhere ?

> " Fair youth, beneath the trees, thou canst not leave
> Thy song, nor ever can those trees be bare ;
> Bold Lover, never, never canst thou kiss,
> Though winning near the goal—yet, do not grieve ;
> She cannot fade, though thou hast not thy bliss,
> For ever wilt thou love, and she be fair ? "

But if Izaak Walton's is something unique and out of
reach, the fame of a writer like Mrs Oliphant, who has
done much in her long day's work to make our common
life brighter and sweeter, is surely very enviable.   Just
think of the millions she has made happy—if for an
hour only !   I declare to you in all honesty, that the
reputation of the great Captains who have marched
with conquering banners across a continent seems to
me poor and shabby in comparison.   Soldiers, like Poor
Laws and Prisons and the Hangman, are necessary
evils : but this is the finest bloom and blossom of life,
which suffices in itself and needs no justification.
What a debt we owe her !   How much pure pleasure
she has given us !   When we talk of the great benefac-
tors of our race, let not the poor story-teller be forgotten.
And during these many years of eager activity in our
service, how loyal and constant she has been to truth
and beauty and goodness.   I do not suppose that Mrs
Oliphant is one of the writers who consciously entertain
or profess, what is called in the jargon of the day,
"high views of the literary *calling*;" but it may certainly be said of her that she has never written a page which
she would wish unwritten, and which is not perfectly
sweet and clean and wholesome.   The *nastiness* of some

of our female novelists is simply amazing; it sins
against art as much as against good morals and good
manners; it leaves a bad taste in the mouth for weeks
afterwards; yet the most prolific and the most brilliant
of the Sisterhood, who has had the widest experience
and shows the clearest insight, never once fails to preserve her womanly reticence, never hurts the most
shrinking modesty, never violates the finest code of
honour.   The value of such an example is incalculable,
—it is to the England of letters what Queen Victoria
(might I not add Lord Beaconsfield?) has been to that
other England which, in spite of craven counsels and
infatuation in high places, is still strong and of a good
courage.

* *
*

Mrs Oliphant is of course specifically a story-teller,
—as Walter Scott and the Homer who wrote the
Odyssey were story-tellers.   There is an air of almost
garrulous ease about her best work which is highly
characteristic.   She is not a " painful" preacher; she
does not care overmuch for that curious felicity in the
construction of sentences to which the Thackerays and
the Matthew Arnolds attain; she does not polish her
periods till they shine like old silver.   We are told
nowadays that Scott was no poet, and that his prose
style was abominably ungrammatical.   Mrs Oliphant
is never so slovenly as Scott can be when he likes;
but we learn when we read her books, as we do when
we read his, that there is something better than style.

The man who is sensitively and finically fastidious about the arrangement of words is generally good for little else. He grows weary before he gets to real business. There are whole pages of *The Antiquary* and *Quentin Durward* where not a single erasure or correction appears on the manuscript. Would *The Antiquary* and *Quentin Durward* have been what they are if the writer had been harder to please? I doubt it; and even the style would have lost something. It would have lost not merely its easy unstudied charm, but something more—something that recalls the sough of the wind, the murmur of the sea, the plash of the waves. The *Lord of the Isles* is said by one eminent critic to be no better than a big blunder; but the breeze blows all about it; it sparkles as the waves sparkle; and through its spontaneous unsystematic natural music there breathes the true spirit of the stormy Hebrides. Mrs Oliphant's style at its best has something of the same outdoor charm. It belongs to the conservatory and the hothouse as little as Sir Walter's. It does not surprise us therefore that in particular her description of natural scenery should be brightly picturesque. She does not know much of our brilliant West, with its orange and purple sunsets across the wide Atlantic; but the bleak charm of the east of Scotland, of breezy headlands and level links, is dwelt upon and emphasised with the true artist feeling. An *édition de luxe* of *Katie Stewart* with cuts by George Reid would be a book to prize. Her English landscape too is admirable,—the gracious wealth and richness of the midland summer—

> "The moan of doves in immemorial elms
> And murmur of innumerable bees"—

has seldom been rendered with more genuine joy and
sympathy.

All this of course belongs more or less to the outside;
but in the essential elements of her craft, Mrs Oliphant
has few rivals. When we remember that, for at least
thirty years, not a summer has passed without its
romance in three volumes, its thrilling ghost-story, its
seaside ramble, we get some measure of the amazing
fertility of her invention. And take them all in all,
how good they are !   There may be no Uncle Toby or
Jonathan Oldbuck among the characters; but what
variety, what delicate discrimination, what a keen sense
of the subtler lights and shades of human nature !   She
treats the male sex, it must be admitted, with habitual
tolerant good-humoured contempt,—these big unwieldy
awkward creatures, who are so much in the way, who
don't know what to do with themselves of a wet morning, but stand about with their hands in their pockets
before the fire and yawn in your face, are apt to pro-
voke a soft breezy laughter, that after all has no malice
in it,—but the girls are invariably attractive.   The
estimable Miss Marjoribanks (why not spell it March-
banks at once ?) who is so resolved to do her duty to
her dear papa, is in many ways, to be sure, little better
than a man, and is therefore regarded at first with a
certain implicit suspicion; but Mrs Oliphant cannot
harden her heart for long against a woman, and even
Miss Marjoribanks is ultimately allowed to escape.

They are none of them by any means faultless; they
practise the engaging ruses, and are not superior to the
charming foibles of their sex; but yet with infinite
diversity of superficial trait, how tender and gracious
and womanly they are. Mrs Oliphant's ideal of
English girlhood, kept constantly before us for so long,
has done a world of good to our girls, who begin to see
that to be loud and fast and *risqué* is essentially bad
style.   And the *talk*—how unaffected and natural it is
—no one saying what he ought not to say, but just the
right thing—never strained or rhetorical, though often
nervous and sparkling, and rising at a tragic crisis to
an almost monumental simplicity.   There are whole
passages of dialogue in the more intense and dramatic
situations which for close sustained excellence of mere
writing could hardly be surpassed.

* *
*

Love must always be, as it has always been (from
Helen of Troy to Hetty Sorrel), the main theme of the
story-teller.

> "Of all the follies that I know,
> The sweetest folly in the world is love,"

says an old singer; and though Mrs Oliphant sometimes treats the complaint more seriously, I fancy she
is half inclined to agree with him.   She has hardly
ventured at least, except once and again, to touch
its deeper chords.   On the other hand it must be

admitted that Love with her, even at its slightest, is always a fine and noble pastime.   It is never materialised into mere animal instinct,—never made cynical sport of, as even a Thackeray could make cynical sport of it.   It may be fooling ; but it is tender and gracious fooling—such as befits pure maidens and wholesome lads.   For none of her works appeal to the moody satirist or the cynic whose text is *Vanitas !* or only to the very gentlest of the craft ; they are addressed to a simpler audience—*virginibus puerisque !*

* *
*

While I cheerfully recognise that the imaginative force of Charlotte Brontë and George Eliot is in certain respects inimitable, I am often inclined to maintain that Mrs Oliphant is the most remarkable woman of her time.   Charlotte Brontë wrote three novels before she died ; a long interval separated *Silas Marner* from *Middlemarch*, and *Middlemarch* from *Daniel Deronda*. Each of these great romance writers concentrated all her faculties for months (I might say for years) upon a single work.   Mrs Oliphant has never had leisure for this absorbing devotion, this almost fierce concentration.   Many a year she has written three or four novels at least, to say nothing of Essay, History, and Criticism — the mere trifles of an unfrequent holiday.   Yet Tozer is not far below Mrs Poyser, and pretty Rosa Elsworthy is just as naively natural and foolish as Hetty Sorrel.   Had Mrs Oliphant con-

centrated her powers, what might she not have done ?
We might have had another Charlotte Brontë or
another George Eliot, with something added which
neither of them quite attained,—the soft gracious and
winning charm of mature and happy womanhood.
And this leads me to say that the pitiless and searching anatomy of *Adam Bede* and *Romola*—of Hetty in
the one, and Tito in the other—is not so much beyond
Mrs Oliphant's power, as outside her inclination.   We
feel that she might try it—not without fair hope of
success ; but that she does not care to try it.   I
hesitate to affirm that this modest restraint — the
womanly reticence and delicacy which refuses to probe
the festering sores of humanity—is, even from the exclusively artistic point of view, an error to be condemned, though in the serene impartiality of a Goethe
or a Shakespeare, there is, I suppose, something of
the moral insensibility of the great surgeon who does
not shrink from vivisection.

* *
*

The sustained and serious interest of *The Chronicles
of Carlingford* entitles them to a foremost place in the
long catalogue of Mrs Oliphant's writings ; but considered merely as the story-teller, she is at her best,
I think, in her shorter tales ; and among these *The
Curate in Charge* is one of the simplest but most
perfect.   There is only the slightest scrap of narrative ;
but how fresh, how tender, how true to nature it is—

a village idyl, in which the simple English life and the
simple English landscape are touched with a softly
pathetic light.   It is a distinct conception—absolutely
graceful because absolutely simple—like a soap-bubble
or a Greek play or a Raphael.   There is nothing by
the way or out of the way; nothing that does not
lend itself to the progressive development of the
history.   If life could record itself as on a photog-
rapher's glass we know that this is the record which
it would leave; there is the unambitious exactness,
the homely sincerity, the inevitableness.   And yet
there is something more,—there is the imagination
which realises the immense pathos of human life,—
of life, that is to say, into which no special adventure
or misadventure enters, but which simply as *life* is so
fundamentally sad, so intrinsically a tragedy.   *For
what is your life ?   It is even a vapour, that appeareth for
a little time, and then vanisheth away.*

XIII.

MAINLY ABOUT THE WORD IN SEASON.

I N a letter from Thackeray to John Brown, which I
have had occasion to quote, the writer says: " I
see Mr Skelton has been saying kind things of me in
Fraser." To have said things which were deemed
kind by a great man is a lasting gratification; and,
indeed, at the close of life (when the shadows at least
are beginning to gather) there is nothing on which a
writer of books can look back with more entire satisfaction than the "kind words" which have helped
others on. I suppose we must be bitter at times, and
it is, of course, a public duty to expose the quack and
the mountebank. But one is never quite sure in such
cases where public duty begins and private feeling
ends; and the executioner is not a popular function-
ary nor an acceptable companion. On the other hand,
the appreciation of excellence is twice blessed; it
blesses him that gives and him that takes. A work of
true genius is stimulating; there is a certain inspiration about it which affects the critic while he reads,

S

as well as the author while he wrote. Some of the pleasantest intimacies, some of the most valued friend-ships, we make in this world are effected through the relations thus established. The critic picks up at a railway bookstall a volume which no one is inclined to buy; finds, as he is hurried along, that it has a dis-tinctive flavour which suits his palate; and thereupon writes a notice, long or short, in which he gives ex-pression to the enjoyment he has felt, and which is perhaps quickened by the sense of discovery. The Word in Season, let us call it. The author, on his side, is gratified by the reception accorded him; it is possibly the earliest recognition he has received; and a mutual regard springs up which, thus begun, may last a lifetime.

* *
*

He must deem himself fortunate who has had a fair opportunity of speaking his mind freely and honestly on what he holds to be excellent; and I cannot but feel that in this respect (if not in others) my friend " Shirley " has been exceptionally favoured. To have had in " beginning life " two such friendly editors as Thomas Spencer Baynes and John William Parker does not fall to the lot of many. Of Baynes I have spoken more at large in connection with the volume of his essays which has been lately published by the Longmans; here let me say that it is difficult for those of his friends who survive—" the gleanings of hostile spears "—to express without an air of exaggeration the debt of gratitude they owe to Parker. Oblivion scattereth her poppies; it is five-and-thirty years now since the editor of *Fraser* died; yet I venture to say that not one of us has forgotten him. We keep his memory green in our hearts; and when, at long intervals, we meet, it is of him that we speak.

*   *
*

Like the Apostle, his bodily presence was weak. Yet though one of the most fragile of human creatures, he could hold his own with the best. Alertness, restless energy, unflinching loyalty, true courage, immense tenacity—these are the qualities we associate with his memory. The pale, worn, delicate, spectacled face— how well one remembers it, and the rooms in the Strand where he lived *en garçon*, and where one's earliest and pleasantest hours in the vast solitude of the great city were spent. Such pleasant days! and then such hospitable nights! when round the homely but well-appointed table, the "lad from the country" met the famous men of whom he had been dreaming. And yet life with Parker was always somewhat sad; as the little girl said of her relations with the clamorous turkey-cock, he was "sair hauden down by the bubblyjock"; sometimes oppressed, often depressed, it was only at rare intervals that he escaped into the freer and sweeter air that he loved.

*   *
*

Many of the best men of his time loved Parker as they loved no one else. *He was so loyal.* A few veterans still living, whose testimony would be accepted all over the world, might be cited as witnesses; and in old letters I find emphatic evidence to the same effect. " Didn't you know John Parker? " acted for years as a spell; and when one was able to reply, " I met you at his rooms," an offensive and defensive alliance against all comers was forthwith concluded. Thus, Arthur Helps, recalling those pleasant dinners in the upper chamber overlooking the Strand, "where so many good fellows used to meet who will now perhaps never see each other again," adds, " Poor John Parker! Your letter naturally reminds me of him; not that I need to be reminded, for who that rejoiced in his friendship can ever forget him?" And in one of those eagerly friendly epistles which Charles Kingsley would dash off in frantic and fervent haste (when he was making up his arrears of correspondence, or had recovered the letter he had carefully mislaid—as was his way), there is the glow of a still warmer regard. "I trust that if you come to London," he writes, "you will take courage to come forty miles further to Eversley. You will meet here, not only for your own sake, but for Parker's, a most cordial welcome. Before our windows lies the grave of one whom he adored—Mrs Kingsley's favourite sister. He was at her funeral; the next funeral which her widowed husband and I attended was his; and Froude (her husband) nursed him like a brother till the moment of

death. He was a great soul in a pigmy body; and
those who know how I loved him, know what a
calumny it is to say that I preach 'muscular Chris-
tianity.' "

* *
*

I have ventured to unloose, after many years, the
red tape which has kept together a packet of old
letters. The tape has lost its colour, being now of a
dingy yellow. So to a certain extent have the letters.
But it is a packet which has been jealously guarded—
as a lover keeps those of his mistress written in the
springtime of his wooing. For it is labelled, as you
see, " With thanks"; and it is made up of the letters
which came from men and women (some of them
little known at the time) whom I had been permitted
by friendly editors to welcome. They go back a long
way; 1849 brings a letter from Longfellow, and this is
1894. It is the earliest, I see; the first volumes of his
prose had only recently crossed the Atlantic; and
Hyperion (*Hyperion*, I think it was) had fascinated us
all, and we were eager to greet its author. So with
considerable perturbation (for it was a liberty we would
not have taken with a countryman) a congratulatory
letter was penned and duly despatched. I noticed in
his *Life* the other day that the receipt of the letter—
coming as it did from this side of the water — had
pleased the poet; but I am certain that when the
gracious answer arrived—the message from a new and

unknown world, as it seemed to us—our gratification was incomparably keener.

"CAMBRIDGE, *October* 3, 1849.

"DEAR SIR,—Your most friendly letter has deeply moved me. From time to time there have come to me voices out of the dark—from persons before unknown—but never one that has spoken so truly to my heart. I thank God if I have been able to write anything which can console and strengthen others! The poem you particularly allude to was produced in a state of mind not unlike that which you describe, and came from my inmost being, not from my brain ; and it is, indeed, a very great satisfaction to know that many accept it as a faithful expression and transcript of their own deepest convictions.

"I sincerely thank you for writing to me. Too often these feelings of sympathy perish where they were born, and the writer of a song remains for ever ignorant that far away in another country he has an unknown friend, who listens with pleasure to his words, and would fain say it, and yet does not.

"May I beg you to accept a small volume which I published a few months ago, entitled *Kavanagh.* I will send it by an early opportunity; and in the winter, if an opportunity offers, will send you also a new volume of poems now in the press. I do not know that you will find anything in these books which will particularly please you, but it will be gratifying to me to know that you have them.

"Your name is an old name in the history of English poetry. Are you descended from the Oxford Laureate of Henry VIII.'s time? or do you disavow any kindred with so fantastic a gentleman?

"With sentiments of true regard and sympathy, I remain, dear sir, yours faithfully,

"HENRY W. LONGFELLOW."

The poet promised to visit me if ever he came to Scotland; but when he did come—years afterwards—I was unluckily abroad, and I only got his card, and a little note which he had left for me, on my return. Long-fellow, I understand, is quite out of date now—as much out of date as *The Traveller* or *The Deserted Village;* and I must admit that though *Hyperion* and *Evangeline* are still as delightful to me as ever, I never venture to read them, except when perfectly certain that I am not ob-served.

* * *

The letter that follows—the ink, you see, of the Haworth stationer was not of the best, and has faded almost into illegibility — was written by Charlotte Brontë. The acutely malignant article in the *Quar-terly*, and its ponderously jocular rival in the *North British*, had been taken as a personal insult by those of us to whom *Jane Eyre*, *Shirley*, and *Villette* revealed a force it was difficult to measure; and an indignant paper in the *Edinburgh Guardian* (then edited by Baynes) was written to prove that "Currer Bell" had

been foully slandered.   Dallas, who at the time was
our theatrical critic, sent a copy of the paper to
Messrs Smith and Elder, by whom it was forwarded
to Miss Brontë.   You may be sure that what Jane
Welsh Carlyle would have called a "good joy" was
ours when we found that the vindication had served
to "refresh and cheer" the wonderful little woman—
"the austere little Joan of Arc" (as Thackeray called
her), who had been so wantonly assailed.

"HAWORTH, KEIGHLEY, YORKS, December 9th.

"SIR—If you know the writer of the article on
Villette in the Edinburgh Guardian for December 3d,
will you offer to my kind critic the grateful thanks of
Currer Bell.

"A few words at once so friendly and so discriminating refresh and cheer inexpressibly.—Believe me,
yours sincerely,   C. BRONTË.

"E. S. DALLAS, Esq."

* * *

"Rab and his Friends" are now known all over the
world; but for a season the volume in which they
appeared hung fire.   "Doctor John" was nervous
about its reception; I don't think he was quite certain
that it was strictly professional; and I suspect that he
introduced the medical biographies (which in truth
were a trifle dull) to appease the scruples of himself
and his brethren.   "Rab" was the gem of the book;

and "Rab" was the eldest of a large and increasing family.   It was unquestionably the first of those sketches of rustic life where (as in Mr Barrie's *Auld Licht Idylls*, and Mr Crockett's *A Stickit Minister*[1]) pawky humour and homely pathos are happily blended. How "Rab" was to be introduced to English friends had been the subject of much discussion; Parker had been consulted, but Parker had doubts; until at last the suggestion that the *Horæ* might be made the text of a discourse on "Professional Sectarianism" secured his assent and co-operation.   My impression is that the article in *Fraser* was Doctor John's earliest recognition on the other side of the Border; and it was greeted accordingly.   He carried it off to Syme; he read selected scraps as he drove from patient to patient; before the day was over he had filled more than one sheet with cordial thanks.   There were only two or three monthly magazines in existence at the time; and possibly the good word of *Fraser* (which under John Parker had become a power in the critical world) may have been useful.   So at least Doctor John thought, and it is pleasant to look again at the old letters.

---

[1] Here again the first is the best; nothing that Mr Crockett has since done can compare with the earlier work.   The reader is now constantly tempted to inquire, Is this a direct transcript from nature, or the copy of a copy?   Faint reminiscences, pale reflections, of Sir Walter are possibly inevitable in a Scottish story-teller's story; but what are we to think when we find one of the most august passages in all literature incorporated in the confession of a Marrow Minister?   "One day they held a book together till they heard their own hearts beat audibly, *and in the book read no more that day.*"   This is not theft only; it is sacrilege.

"MY DEAR 'SHIRLEY,'—Many thanks for all your great kindness. I am not a little pleased at Mr Parker being pleased; and you may be sure few things will gratify me more than having Shirley's word in *Fraser*. The objection to reviewing the *Horæ* substantively is only half an one—nearly the half of the book is quite new. However, this matters little, so that it be spoken of, and you could give me no better companion than the old Knight of Norwich. There is a very readable and somewhat germane book by old Ferrier of Manchester, *Medical Histories and Reflections*, which, if you care to see, I can let you have. Are you the author of the very neat *mot* about the words *Horæ Subsecivæ?* A little girl asks her father what is the meaning of these Latin words at the top of Dr Brown's book, and he replies, ' Brown studies, my dear!' If there is anything else you would like to learn, or to know, in reference to the Bye Hours of the Doctors, let me know, or come and see me any day between one and two; but not till next week, as I am hoping to get off for two days to the Mearns.— Yours ever truly, J. BROWN."

"23 RUTLAND STREET, *Friday morning.* [I *April* 1859.]

"MY DEAR 'SHIRLEY,'—My very best thanks for yours of this morning. It has made me very, perhaps *too* happy; praise such as this is always sweet, even though known to be overpaid. In my small way I

have sent it off instantly to Mrs Brown, who is at
Ben Rhydding; it will please her not less than
'Brown' himself; and I mean to purchase a copy
to-day and present it to Syme. That is capital what
you say of him, and will rejoice his great and modest
(for he *is* modest) heart. Thanks again. I hope you
have seen Thackeray. Thank Parker also, for his
valuable kindness in this matter.—Yours ever,

" J. BROWN."

Later in the same day :—

" 1 *April*, 2 P.M.

"Of course when I wrote you, a few hours ago, I
had read merely my own bit; what other mortal man
could have done otherwise? I have now read *your*
bit, and it will be a pleasant thing for me to remember
that such an honest, hearty, telling bit of sense and
spiritual virtue, ἀρετὴ — *vir-tus*, was read by me in
Princes Street, and down through the other streets to
Inverleith Row, &c., *en route* to my clients. It is
admirable, and there is one sentence, *sententiola vibrans*,
which I will assuredly print in my 2d edition among
my *jacula prudentum*,—'In proportion to the power of
the *whole* mind is the power of its constituents; narrow
the mind and we narrow its members.' It is full of
vital and strong truth, and much needed in these latter
days. So good-bye. I daresay you have had enough
of me to-day, but you know what day it is!"

* *
*

Some day I may put together a few of the bright,
cordial, picturesquely idiomatic letters which Doctor
John was constantly writing about the men and
women and dogs and books he liked. Nothing made
him happier indeed than hearty appreciation of a
favourite. Here, for instance, is a little note of thanks
which the *éloge* on *The Scottish Probationer* in *Blackwood*
elicited. He took the whole family of the " Browns "
under his wing; but the dear and delightful Dr James
of Paisley, whose loss we never cease to deplore (the
Fates were unkind to us that autumn; William Sellar
had died only a month before), occupied of later years
a first place in his regard :—

"23 RUTLAND STREET, 31 Jan. 1878.

"MY DEAR 'SHIRLEY,'—You are excellent on the
Probationer. Poor fellow, your words would have
been nuts to him were he here; who knows but
that he may take in *Maga* where he is? One faithful
heart you will delight; the homely-faced sweetheart's
in Brunswick Street to whom that (almost) Shake-
spearian sonnet was written. I am glad to get a
pleasant account of you and Placens from John.—
Ever yours and hers, J. B."

In another strain how entirely admirable is this
incisive sketch of an old Scottish gentlewoman (widow
of Lord Cunninghame, a Scottish Judge, and by birth
a Trotter of Mortonhall), whose kindly and caustic use
of the vernacular none who knew her are likely to

forget.   The date is "Wednesday" only; but Mrs
Cunninghame died on 19th December 1877 :—

"MY DEAR 'SHIRLEY,'—It is good of you to think
of telling me.   I needed it; for I have been in such a
state of mental torpor all this year that I never thought
of putting the two things together. . . . Our great old
friend at Morton is gone—at seven this morning—the
last of the great race who were the meet companions
of our older gods; no such women now.   She was a
true Autochthon, a child of the soil; Scotch in face, in
voice, in nature, in figure, in shrewdness, in humour,
in heart.   All are going now.   I have far more dead
friends than living.—With best regards and thanks,
(my love to *mater pulchra*), yours ever truly,

"J. BROWN."

*   *
*

It was through Parker's good offices also that
Principal Tulloch's fine volume on the Reformers
was introduced to the readers of *Fraser*.   Kingsley
had an unusual liking for Scotsmen: "I am afraid
I am a bad Englishman, for I like you Scots far
better than I do my own countrymen," he wrote me
once; and Parker shared this curious and rather
unaccountable predilection.   The owner of many well-
known initials had possibly opened his eyes to the
intrinsic superiority of the North Briton; and when
a eulogium on the youthful Principal was proposed he
cordially responded.   Tulloch, like Doctor John, was

pleased, and with fine frankness thanked Parker and Parker's henchman :—

"ST MARY'S COLLEGE, ST ANDREWS, *Dec.* 1, '59.

"MY DEAR S.,—Parker has kindly sent me *Fraser*, with your article.   After reading it I cannot help saying that you are a good fellow, and feeling as if I were a bit of a swell.   'Such a certificate,' Sellar says, ' I have nowhere got.'—Yours always,

"JOHN TULLOCH."

"Sellar says"—the words summon up a Past which few of the survivors can recall without smiles and—tears.   In 1859 the Society of St Andrews was at its best, as were its links.   Then it was possible for even a duffer (like—what eminent man of letters shall I name?) to play the round with comfort.   I remember going over one spring—it was the early spring of 1857, I think—and finding only George Condie (the younger) and Lord Charles Kerr at the club.   Condie had brought his "caddie" with him from Perth; he gave me "The Rook" for partner in a foursome which lasted from Monday till Saturday; and during the whole of the week we had the links absolutely to ourselves.   One or two old gentlemen played "pool" at the club in the afternoon; Tom Morris looked at us from afar, occasionally descending to see us off; otherwise the isolation was complete.   But after the play was over, and we had got back to South Street, where we lodged with the baker, there was no lack of good company.   So far as gaiety and high spirits went, it was the *Noctes Ambrosianæ* over again. Most of us were young at the time; the world was all before us where to choose; meanwhile the men were brilliant and the women witty and well-favoured. It was admirable while it lasted; the pity was that it did not last long enough. Ferrier was the luminary round which these bright particular stars revolved, and with Ferrier's death much of the glory departed. Tulloch, to be sure, was left; and by-and-by a circle of not undistinguished men and women met at St Mary's (is it not written in the *Chronicles of the Country Parson?*); but the ardour of youth was dulled, and the high-jinks of the Fifties had ceased to be possible.

*   *
*

The same freedom in the expression of opinion which (within certain well-defined limits) Parker had encouraged, was sanctioned by his illustrious successor. So "Shirley" was permitted to fight the battles of more than one eminent man to whom, as he fancied, rightly or wrongly, fair play had not been accorded. Our new Chief had prejudices—may I venture to call them?—of his own; but he was ready to give a hearing to those of the other side; and whether it was Disraeli, or Mary Stuart, or Rossetti, or Swinburne, or Robert Browning, the virtue of unfettered discussion was frankly recognised. Browning, I think, was the main difficulty. In 1860, he was comparatively unknown. It was the fashion to ridicule his uncouthness and to resent his obscurity. The prolonged unpopularity of our sincerest and most masculine poet may perhaps admit of explanation; and it is easy to understand how to a master of "our English," whose style is limpid as the mountain stream and lucid as the dawn, the roughness of Browning may have been a rock of offence; yet the elaborate and protracted defence was listened to with patience, and ultimately, I believe, with some measure of assent; and Browning himself was satisfied that it had not been without effect. Among these old letters none is more valued than this:—

"19 WARWICK CRESCENT,
UPPER WESTBOURNE TERRACE, W., *March* 31*st*, '63.

"MY DEAR SIR,—I find your note, on returning to London after a fortnight's absence; you will have guessed the reason of any delay in answering it. I read your article last month. I am glad indeed of the opportunity your kindness gives me of saying that I do not think it 'weak' or 'inadequate'—but assuredly generous, and in that respect not unworthy of you, however it may be undeserved by me. I do not often speak about myself, but I think I feel your sympathy as gratefully as you could desire.

"I am settled here for some years superintending the education of my son; if you ever come to London, and care to call on me, I shall have great pleasure in seeing you, face to face.

"In any case, I am yours very faithfully and obligedly, ROBERT BROWNING."

Many years afterwards Sir Noël Paton sent me the copy of a letter from the poet which a friend had made for him that it might be forwarded to me. (The "friend" was the late J. M. Gray, the curator of the Scottish National Portrait Gallery, who died the other day—a sad loss to us, and to Scottish art and letters.) "It will not displease you," Sir Noël wrote: as indeed it did not. It was plain that the cordiality of the early greeting had left a pleasant warmth behind it. "I think it a very generous piece of criticism," the poet wrote, referring to the *Fraser* article, "and have no doubt that it exercised much influence on the fortunes of my poetry." With such kindly words before me, I thought that I might venture to ask him to accept a volume of Sketches at Home and Abroad which the Blackwoods had recently published.

"19 WARWICK CRESCENT, *Nov.* 15, 1878.

"DEAR DR SKELTON, — Your letter manages to understate the truth on nearly every point. I was not simply 'interested' in the book which Mr Gray so kindly sent me, but rendered abundantly grateful for the notice of myself which it contained. I cannot generally bring my mind to thank a judge when he lays down the law, and it favours me; but I may say that the points wherein you pronounced for my poetry were precisely those which I should wish made conspicuous. I must naturally desire acquaintance with all you have written or shall write; consequently I more than coldly 'accept '—warmly welcome the present gift—which I

T

thankfully acknowledge now that I can cordially praise it—having finished my first reading. The paper concerning Venice comes at the proper time to me who renewed my love for her a few weeks ago ; but many other matters have been a true delight to one who has seen God's country as well as man's town—and still enjoys both.—Pray believe me, dear Dr Skelton, yours very sincerely,   ROBERT BROWNING."

The *Fraser* paper, I may add, is referred to in the exhaustive Browning Bibliography prepared by Mr Furnival (1881), where the reader will also learn (possibly to his surprise) that " Shirley " is no other than " Charles Lever." We know what we are, but we know not what we shall be ; nor for that matter—what we have been.

*   *
*

I have spoken of two of the editors to whose good offices I owed much when I began to write ; I were ungrateful if I failed to acknowledge my obligations in later life to one possibly more widely known than either of the others—John Blackwood. It is a good many years now since he died ; but the pleasant Sunday afternoons when among the woods of Braid we discoursed of golf and politics and the forthcoming number of *Maga* are not like to be forgotten. They are very pleasant in the retrospect, they were very pleasant at the time,—not least so to the poor Cabby who thus got a whiff of country air, good for him after

his long hours of waiting at ball or theatre, and a
generously refreshing "tip" into the bargain.

* *
*

Of John Blackwood's conduct of the Magazine, I
need hardly speak.   He was its guiding spirit for
thirty years, and his unwearied interest and delight in
its wellbeing continued to the end.   He had inherited
the traditions of " 45 "; his very terriers—Ticklers and
the like—revived memories of the " Noctes "; but
though never without a redeeming spice of devilry
(reminiscences of its earlier Bohemian or rather
Chaldean days), *Maga* under his rule became decorous.
It could never indeed, even when best behaved, abide
prigs and snobs; but it ceased to *flay* them, as it had
done in the consulship of Plancus.   Except his contributors (with whom he maintained closely confidential relations) not many know how much of unity and
distinct personality the Magazine owed to its Editor,—
to his fine mother wit and native shrewdness.   His
marginal notes on the *proofs* of articles—suggestive,
anecdotical, brightly conversational — were altogether
admirable.   He did not, like Jeffrey, rewrite articles,
so that their authors did not know them again; but
every article was so assimilated by him that anything out of keeping or character, anything inconsistent with the traditions of the Magazine, was at once
detected by the practised eye and the fine sense of what
was fit.   For though neither bigot in politics nor zealot

in religion, he stuck to his convictions as a limpet sticks
to its rock.   He was the great Tory editor, as Russel
of the *Scotsman* was the great Whig editor; and the
two had a good deal in common.   Both were sports-
men; both were humourists; both lived much in the
open air—one on the links, the other by the river-side;
both were given to hospitality; both were endeared
to their friends.   But Blackwood's Toryism was indel-
ible—bred in the bone; whereas Russel's Whiggism
was more or less accidental.

* * *

He bore discouragement and bad luck well—almost
gaily.   From 1845 to 1874 he was almost constantly in
Opposition; but he had a stout conviction that things
would mend before he died.   It was somewhat late in
the day perhaps before he recognised the masterful
genius of Disraeli — some of whose moves in the
political game were distasteful to him; but he came
ultimately to feel that the true determining forces of
Toryism—its devotion especially to a high ideal of
Government, of Empire—were safe in his hands.

* * *

A true simplicity (even to homeliness of speech and
gesture) characterised John Blackwood.   None of the
men I have known, not even Professor Sellar, was
more simple and unaffected.   He never resorted to

finesse; but on the other hand he detested swagger. He saw through rogues and charlatans; and though by no means "glib at the gab," he could hold his own against the noisiest pretender,—his quiet backhanders being remarkably effective; the slow deliberate utterance, the pause, the hesitation, giving emphasis and unexpectedness to the retort when it came at last. (This was after the manner of Dizzy; but what in Dizzy was art, in John Blackwood was nature.) The most distinguished men of his time were proud of his steady friendship; but he never lost his head, his respect for his calling, his friendliness for smaller men, his delight in doing a good turn to a young fellow. Neither in play nor in business did any one find him at any time mean or base or small or petty; his very hatred of Radicalism had in it a sort of jocular breadth which kept it from becoming mere bitterness. There was in all his pictures of his political foes what art-critics call "atmosphere," — the lines were not hard or obtrusive, but mellowed in a soft light of humour and good fellowship.

* * *

As he reached middle life, the old circle dropped off. His brothers, to whom he was warmly attached, died early. One after the other, Wilson, and Aytoun, and George Moir, and Lord Neaves, and Lord Lytton were taken away. He began to feel lonely at times. Younger men came about him: but he lived more

and more within the family circle.   Yet, in spite of
failing health, the ineradicable habit of hospitality
survived to the last.   Only the month before his death,
a set of young fellows—some of whom he had trained
to letters—were gathered round the cheery Strathtyrum
hearth.   Then came a brief period of restlessness and
disquietude, and he passed away from those whom he
had loved in the quiet, undemonstrative, loyal, constant
way that was natural to him.   To him, indeed, *loyalty*
was everything,—loyalty to the political faith in which
he had been bred, loyalty to the good cause as he held
it, loyalty to his friends, loyalty to his own convictions,
loyalty to honesty, and fair dealing, and manliness.

*   *
*

Even while these last sheets are going through the
press, I hear with profound sorrow of the death of my
dear and admirable friend, Professor Huxley,—to the
whole world a thinker of brilliant faculty and immense
force, to his friends one of the brightest, bravest, and
cheeriest of men.

Huxley had probably the most trenchant intellect of
the time; yet, on the emotional side he was extraordinarily tender and sympathetic,—no woman more so.
He was one of the best talkers, if not the best talker,
I have known,—alert, swift at repartee, apt to respond
to badinage of any kind in kind.   Yet his constancy to
his convictions, to his serious convictions, was pro-
verbial,—he was at all times honest as the day.   The

John Knox of Agnosticism, it might be said of him
as Morton said of the Scotch Reformer,—"He never
feared the face of man." His letters, like his talk,
were delightful; a mine of gay wisdom; the wisdom
never pedantic; the gaiety never forced or frivolous.
A score of those lying beside me are so characteristic
of the writer in his graver as in his lighter vein, that
I venture to string together a few sentences, taken
almost at random from their pages.

* * *

"Being the most procrastinating letter-writer in
existence, I thought or pretended to think that it
would not be decent to thank you until I had read
the book. And when I had done myself that pleasure,
I further pretended to think that it would be much
better to wait till I could send you my Hume book,
which, as it contains a biography, is the nearest
approach to a work of fiction of which I have yet
been guilty. The 'Hume' was sent, and I hope
reached you a week ago; and as my conscience just
now inquired in a very sneering and unpleasant tone
whether I had any further pretence for not writing
on hand, I thought I might as well stop her mouth
at once." [*London, January* 1879.]

"I am not quite sure about giving up work—but
I am giving up pay, which is more serious. Not
that I have anything to complain of—H.M. Treasury

having acted as generously as could be expected. Age, bad health, and anxiety came arm in arm, and marched straight over me this time last year — so that there was nothing for me but to bolt to Italy according to doctor's orders and try to get better.

"But all the king's horses and all the king's men have not put Humpty Dumpty exactly where he was before. I cannot stand the racket of the last twenty years any longer; and the only thing was to get out of all official burthens. So I am absolutely relieved; but I have retained a certain connexion with my old school at S. Kensington, and I have not yet renounced the Presidency of the Royal Society. What I shall do by-and-bye depends very much on what happens here. We came ten days ago; and I have so distinctly improved that I hope by-and-bye to be fit for something."—[*Filey, Yorkshire, August* 16, 1885.]

"There is a paragraph in your preface which I meant to have charged you with having plagiarised from an article of mine, which had not appeared when I got your book. In that Hermitage of yours you are up to any codesicobuddhistotelespathic dodge! It is about the value of practical discipline to historians. Half of them know nothing of life, and still less of government and the ways of men. I am at present engaged on a series of experiments on the thickness of skin of that wonderful little windbag —— ——. The way that second-rate amateur poses as a man of science really 'rouses my corruption.' What a good phrase that is. I am cussed with a lot of it, and any fool can strike ile." [*London, March* 7, 1887.]

"I am going to read your vindication of Mary Stuart as soon as I can. Hitherto I am sorry to say I have classed her with Eve, Helen, Cleopatra, Delilah, and sundry other glorious —— who have lured men to their destruction. But I am open to conviction, and ready to believe that she blew up her husband only a little more thoroughly than other women do— by reason of her keener perception of logic." [*London, December* 31, 1881.]

"I have been in the Engadine for the last four months trying to repair the crazy old 'house I live in,' and meeting with more success than I hoped for when I left home. . . . I have been much interested in your argument about the 'Casket Letters.' The comparison of Crawfurd's deposition with the Queen's letter leaves no sort of doubt that the writer of one had the other before him; and under the circumstances I do not see how it can be doubted that the Queen's letter is forged. But though wholly agreeing with you in substance, I cannot help thinking that your language on p. 341 may be seriously pecked at. My experience of reporters leads me to think that there would be no discrepancy at all comparable to that between the two accounts; and I speak from the woful memories of the many Royal Commissions I have wearied over. The accuracy of a good modern reporter is really wonderful.   And I do not think that 'the two documents were drawn by the same hand.'   I should say that the writer of the letter had Crawfurd's deposition before him, and made what he considered improvements here and there."   [*London, November 2, 1888.*]

"I took a thought and began to mend (as Burns's friend, and *my* prototype (G.O.M.) is not yet reported to have done) about a couple of months ago, and then Gladstone's first article caused such a flow of bile that I have been the better for it ever since.   I need not tell you I am entirely crushed by his reply—still the worm will turn, and there is a faint squeak (as of a rat in the mouth of a terrier) about to be heard in the next '*XIX.*'"   [*London, January 21, 1886.*]

"Yes.   I am sorry to say I know—nobody better— 'what it is to be unfit for work.'   I have been trying to emerge from that condition first at Bournemouth and then at Ilkley for the last five months with such small success that I find a few days in London knocks me up, and I go back to the Yorkshire moors next week.   We have no water-hens—nothing but peewits, larks, and occasional grouse ; but the air and water are of the best, and the hills quite high enough to bring one's muscles into play.   I suppose that Nebuchadnezzar was quite happy so long as he grazed and kept clear of Babylon,—if so I can hold him up for my Scriptural parallel."   [*London, June 4, 1886.*]

"Seriously it is to me a grave thing that the des-

tinies of this country should at present be seriously
influenced by a man who, whatever he may be in the
affairs of which I am no judge, is nothing but a
copious shuffler in those which I do understand."
[*London, February* 20, 1886.]

"Many thanks to you for reminding me that there
are such things as 'Summer Isles' in the Universe.
The memory of them has been pretty well blotted
out here for the last seven weeks. You see some
people can retire to 'Hermitages' as well as other
people; and though even Argyll *cum* Gladstone powers
of self-deception could not persuade me that the view
from my window is as good as that from yours, yet
I do see a fine wavy chalk down and soft turfy ridges
over which an old fellow can stride as far as his legs
are good to carry him. The fact is that I discovered
that staying in London any longer meant for me a
very short life and by no means a merry one. So
I got my son-in-law to build me a cottage here where
my wife and I may go down-hill quietly together,
and 'make our sowls' as the Irish say—solaced by
an occasional visit from children and grandchildren.
The deuce of it is that, however much the weary want
to be at rest, the wicked won't cease from troubling.
Hence the occasional skirmishes and alarms which
may lead my friends to misdoubt my absolute detach-
ment from sublunary affairs.—Perhaps peace dwells
only among the forked-tailed Petrels!" [*Hodislea,
Eastbourne, January* 13, 1891.]

" I am happy to say I got the screws fairly tightened
up at the Maloija, and I hope the rickety old machine
will jog through the winter.   But I must have done
with such escapades as that at Oxford.   If ever there
was an egg dance, that was.   Imagine having to talk
about Ethics when ' Religion and Politics ' are for-
bidden by the terms of the endowment !—and to talk
about Evolution when good manners obliged one to
abstain from dotting one's i's, and crossing one's t's.
Ask your Old Man of Hoy to be so good as to suspend
judgment until the Lecture appears again with an
appendix in that collection of volumes the bulk of which
appals me.   Didn't I see somewhere that you had been
made Poor Law Pope or something of the sort ?   I
congratulate the poor more than I do you, for it must
be a weary business trying to mend the irremediable.
(No.   I am *not* glancing at the whitewashing of Mary.) "
[*Hodislea, Eastbourne, Oct.* 17, 1893.]

* * *

One letter I may be permitted to quote entire, seeing
that I have somehow come to associate it with that
noble passage (one of the most perfect in our literature)
in which, vindicating himself from the charge of feeling satisfied with a merely negative philosophy, Huxley
wrote,—" I venture to count it an improbable suggestion that any such person—a man, let us say, who has
wellnigh reached his threescore years and ten, and
has graduated in all the faculties of human relation-

ships; who has taken his share in all the deep joys
and deeper anxieties which cling about them; who
has felt the burden of young lives intrusted to his care,
and has stood alone with his dead before the abyss of
the Eternal,—has never had a thought beyond negative
criticism.   It seems to me incredible that such an one
can have done his day's work, always with a light
heart, with no sense of responsibility, no terror of that
which may appear when the fictitious veil of Isis—the
thick web of fiction man has woven round Nature—is
stripped off."

"4 MARLBOROUGH PLACE, LONDON, N.W.,
May 20, 1878.

"MY DEAR SKELTON,—I would give a great deal
on all grounds to be able to welcome Mrs Skelton and
you here next Monday; but I must be inhospitable,
and straitly forbid you the house.

"Last Monday evening my youngest child was
attacked by diphtheria. On Monday my eldest followed, and on Thursday my son who came home for
his holiday from St Andrews to his sister's wedding
a fortnight ago.

"He and my youngest child have had the horrible
disease very mildly, and they are practically well.
But my poor Madge, the light of my house, has given
us a week of terrible anxiety. On Tuesday I did
not leave home, not knowing what the issue of the
day might be. On Saturday I hoped she was safe;
but yesterday there was a relapse, and we had a

weary night of anxiety.   This morning I am glad to
say she is a little better, and I am hopeful again.
But her condition is very critical.

"Under these circumstances the house is tabooed
and our friends come no further than the gate.   I am
sure I need not say how glad we should have been to
welcome Mrs Skelton and yourself, and I hope Froude
would have come with you as he sometimes does.

"You have children and will understand what life
is under these conditions.   One sets one's back hard,
and lives from day to day.—Ever yours very truly,

"T. H. HUXLEY.

"Fanny Bruce was to have been with us, but of
course is not.   Let us have another chance of seeing
you on your way back."

Here is the last letter I had from him—written in
January of this year, during the terrible frost which
none of us is like to forget :—

"HODISLEA, *Jan.* 12, 1895.

"MY DEAR SKELTON,—I do not wonder that between my essays and the weather you are driven to
fly your home.   Only the notion of bettering yourself
by coming here into the jaws (or at any rate jaw) of
the essayist — with the thermometer below freezing
all day on a south wall, and down to 20° or even 19°
at night, and with a violent N.E. gale, which brings
vividly to my recollection a 'coorse day' in Edinburgh
—savours to my mind of eccentricity.

"But a wilful man must have his way, and if you like you shall feel how much reason you have to envy our 'South Coast winter.' I don't wish to write 'sarkastic,' but I should think there are plenty of vacant houses just now. If we had not a son and his wife and a couple of grandchildren filling up our cottage at present, and if my poor wife were not laid up with a complication of rheumatism and sore throat from the horrid cold of last week, we could gladly find room for you and Mrs Skelton here. But send me word what accommodation you want, and I have not the least doubt you may be suited. I am confoundedly honest, considering how glad we should be to see you, in warning you that our glacier may be as bad as your snow-field. With kindest remembrances and good wishes to Mrs Skelton,—Ever yours very truly,   T. H. HUXLEY."

*　*　*

There are some fine lines by Heine (admirably translated into English by Mr Leland, who has indeed a real genius for translating Heine) which, with suitable modification, might have been written by Huxley; for, in the prolonged struggle for intellectual freedom, Huxley was in the foremost rank, and fought with the best. Would it be permissible to inscribe these lines under the bust we are to have in the Abbey ?—

"*I really do not know whether I deserve that a laurel wreath be laid on my coffin. Poetry, dearly as I have loved it, has always been to me only a holy plaything, or a conse-*

crated means whereby to attain a heavenly end. I have never attached much value to a poetic reputation, and I care little whether my songs are praised or blamed. But ye may lay a sword on my coffin, for I was a brave soldier in the War of Freedom for Mankind."

* * *

It is past midnight. The moon is high in heaven, but on the wane. It casts a dim mystical twilight—the twilight of the night—upon the land; but on the brow of the sea it brightens for a space, and strikes keen and clear. "They cuist the glamour o'er her," says the old ballad of the stricken maiden; and a dark barque, with drooping sails, lies listless and becalmed, upon the enchanted water. Down below here, among the lesser planets, it is very still; yet aloft in the heavenly places and near the eternal stars one hears the rustling murmur of the wingèd hosts, who speed through the noiseless night. On what mission are they bent—what behests do they carry? Very sad in this waning light—so sad that one has scarcely heart to enjoy its strange beauty—sad with the menace of the Death which approaches. The earth is dead already; and even the heavenly lights begin to fail. What, then, remains? We will go down to the moonlighted shore, and wash our hands and feet in the incoming tide, and wait on the beach there for the black-stoled weeping queens, who will take us with them to the land that is very far off beyond the sea.

Ah, well! the sea and the stars are fine things no doubt ; but the night grows cold, and the winter breeze shivers among the bulrushes on the bank.   Very grand are the infinite spaces, and the pale armies that marshal their visionary banners along the northern sky ; but right beneath Orion lies a little cosy nest.   The nestlings are asleep ; their twitterings have ceased ; the peace of dreams is about them.   A rosy fragrant cheek presses the snowy pillow—a smile of sweet content rests upon the parted lips—one nut-brown curl has escaped from the braided hair.   Yes—the night is cold.   We will go HOME.

XIV.

MAINLY ABOUT A SCOTCH
PROFESSOR AND AN OXFORD DON.

HERE these rambling reminiscences might have closed. I am reminded, however, that two eminently characteristic figures have been omitted— one as typically English as the other was typically Scotch. But the notes made at the moment having been mislaid, anything I could now recall would fail in freshness and vivacity. Yet without them the gathering is incomplete! So I am fain to turn to the two little "chap-books" by my old acquaintance Mr Andrew Lyell—*Our New Candidate* and *The Sergeant in the Hielans*—which in their day and generation (1880-81) ran through many editions. I do not know that they crossed the Border, and they will probably be new to the audience I am addressing. Looking over them in 1895, one is startled to find how the world has changed in less than fifteen years. Oblivion scattereth her poppies. The men who were associated either

officially or personally with the Great Heresy Hunt—
the Beggs, the Wilsons, the Macaulays—are already
wellnigh forgotten ; the Gaelic Chair is still occupied
(not by the Sergeant, alas ! who has been gathered to
his fathers), but where are the kilted Gaels who were
to sit at the Master's feet, listening intently to the
" hollow oes and aes " of Celtic chronicle and bard?
and even the mighty shades of an Arnold and a Blackie
grow dim in the distance.   I do not believe that there
was any malice in Mr Lyell ; he did not mean to be unkind ; and his narratives, we may be sure, were not
conceived in a satirical spirit.   Than the Scottish Professor and the Oxford Don no two men could be more
unlike : and yet they had this in common,—a perennial vivacity, an insistent and excessive vitality, which
readily lent itself to caricature.   Caricature is not
necessarily misleading ; without a touch of exaggeration
it is often impossible indeed to convey a true impression ; Richard Doyle and Tenniel have sometimes succeeded when Watts and Millais have failed.   Let us
hope that any exaggeration of which Mr Lyell may
have been guilty was at least artistic.   The same, I
trust, may be said of his Doric.   The Doric has of late
become a weariness to the flesh ; but for Mr Lyell's
I offer neither apology nor glossary.   He who runs
can read.

* * *

OUR NEW CANDIDATE.

AN ADVENTURE IN THE WINTER OF '79.

So you see, Mr Drumly, that oor place is a bit lonesome in the winter-time; and tho' this has been a rare winter, wi' snaw and ice and skatin' and curlin' and beef and greens at the Royal, we began to tire o' the weary thud-thud o' the sea upon the rocks, and the everlastin' skirl o' the sea-maws. A veecious clood o' sleet drove day after day across the loch; and the wind roared in the chimley a' nicht as if Hornie himsel' were lowse. The Captain wad pit on his blue pea-jacket, and warstle doun to the pier thro' the drift; but the rest o' us keepit mainly to the Langate, where there was aye a cheery blink in Mrs Catto's parlour ahint the bar. Then the Captain wud come back in the gloamin', wi' his face shining like a brass kettle, and clash wi' us aboot the brig that was fechtin' wi' the storm ootside the skerry; and Mrs Catto wud bring ben the Glendronoch and the het water and the rizzared haddies. There was the Doctor and the Minister and the Captain and the Souter and the Shirra and a wheen mair; and there was Sergeant Duncan MacTavish o' the Fit Guards, wha is the stootest man in the coonty; and there was mysel', Andrew Lyell, head maister in the grammar-school o' the burgh, and Inspector o' Nuisance under the Act o' Victoria, chapter wan hundred and wan, section nine.

It was wan nicht aboot the end o' the year that we were toastin' oorsels at the parlour fire whan the Captain walks in wi' the Journal in his han' (and the snaw in his beard), and says he, as he took his ain seat—

"Duncan," says he to the Sergeant, "here's your chance." And he pinted to an adverteezment in the first page o' the paper :—

"WANTED,

"A PROFESSOR OF GAELIC."

"There's not one man in one thoosand, Duncan," says the Captain, "who can beat you at the Gaelic,—not one man in

Cawmeltoun, and it is known that the best Gaelic is spoken in Cawmeltoun.   So it is right that you should become a Candidate, and, by George, you shall, sir, this very night, as sure as my name is Dochandorris."

"It is ferry goot of you, Dochandorris," the Sergeant replied modestly, polishin' his wooden leg as he spoke, "it is ferry goot of you to speak so: and indeed it has occurred to my own mind that it would be improbable to get one who knows the Gaelic petter: but there are deeficulties in the way.   I am not so young or so soople as I wass, Dochandorris."

"Come now, Duncan, that's arrant nonsense.   You are fresh as paint.   Why, man, the girls are all setting their caps at you, and the pretty lass up-stairs would take you to-morrow, I believe,—wooden leg and all."

"You will be having your fun, Dochandorris," said the Sergeant with a modest blush, "but I pelieve you might not be so far wrong, if it wass not that I am a poor man, having peen in the army."

"A poor man!" shouted the Captain.   "Bless my soul, they will give you six hundred pounds to start on, and Plackie will put you in his will, and leave you his kilt and his claymore.   And—to be sure,—I'll write you a letter to the Professor— the Professor is my very good friend.   What say you, Mr Lyell?   Will you take the Sergeant up to town, and lend him a helping hand with the big-wigs?"

The schule had scaled for the holydays, and the smells in the back-yairds which I had been direckit to inspec' by the Boord were in the meantime keepit doun by the black frost; so I was free to accompany my freen, and moreover the change o' air micht benefit my osecophagus, which is naterally somewhat weak.   So it was sattled that we sud leave by the neist boat,—which was due on the Friday mornin'.

Indeed, Mr Drumly, we had a weary time or ever we gat to Auld Reekie.   The wind rose to a gale, and we ran to Loch Ranza for the nicht; and later the engine gaed aff the line into a snaw-drift at Lenzie, and the Sergeant lost his leg, which had been tied up wi' the rugs.   We had designed to ludge at a tavern in the Fishmercat Close, whar I had been in use to ludge whan attendin' the sittin's o' the General Assembly as ruling elder for Drumwhacket ; but deil a close cud we find ; it had been clean sweepit awa' by the Ceety Improvements—so they said—and whan we knocked at the door of what used to be the auld "Crappit Heads," we were certified by a puir-looking body on the stair that it was *The Scotsman* Offisch.

"Might it be convenient to speak to the yeditor?" asked the Sergeant, who had got his leg back at the lost-luggage place, and was steppin' alang verra blithely.

"Na, na," I interrupit, "dinna fash him.   He's a desperate Radical, and he'll be for pittin' some young chiel into the chair wha swears by Gledstane and Roseberry and the Rooshians and the Society for the Iceberation o' releegion frae kirks and schoolmaisters; and wha kens nae mair o' the Gaelic than oor new Oxford Inspector kens, that canna read Burns and Allan Ramsay in the vernacular, and disna like a gude auld Scots tune whan he hears it; but blethers aboot Jowatt an' Swineburrin an' Max Miller an' comparative pheelology an' the evolution o' the species an' the emawncipation o' the intellec'.   Na, na, Sergeant,—we'll get beds at the Temperance Hotel roun' the corner whar they keep gude whusky,—an' the new water frae Muirfoot wi' its taste o' moss is jist famous for punch—they tell me."

"Is it Ferintosh?" said the Sergeant to the waiter a little later, when we were seated cozily roun' the fire, wi' a Lammermuir farmer an' a brace o' bagmen frae Hawick an' Galashiels, wha had been during the day at Mr Gledstane's fecht wi' the faggots in the Corn Mercat.

O they weary politics ! For my ain pairt, I hould wi' the side that's up : for it's only nateral to believe that Providence jidges best ; but at the end o' the year, what wi' the Eerish and Cawbuul and Gledstane, it was clean impossible to guess which side was up and which was doun.

But the Lammermuir man wud na tak a freen'ly hint ; an' aboot wan in the mornin' he an' the bagmen were fechtin' vecciously ; for the whusky—it *was* Ferintosh, Mr Drumly, and Ferintosh is not a safe speerit except the water is good.

The bagmen waxed boastfu' an' opeenionative aboot the policy o' the great Leebral pairty, and how the Leebral pairty wud dae this, that, and the ither thing: but Tap o' North, as they caed him in spite, was dour an' swear an' sateerical, an' wud na lat a word they said pass him.

"The policy o' the great Leebral pairty at hame an' abroad —that's it, is it?   And what's the policy o' the great Leebral pairty at hame, Mr Pedlar?"

"The abolcction—o' Kirk an'—State—on the bassis o'—releegion an'—pheelosophy," says the first bagman, wha had been drinkin' varra steady throughout the evenin'.

"Ay, ay! To be sure! And what's the policy o' the great Leebral pairty abroad?"

"The policy o' maisterly inac-teevity," says the second bagman, wi' a hiccup, for he had mixed his drink, and was far gone.

"Ay, ay! To be sure! And what's maisterly inacteevity, ye doited body?" says Tap o' North, wha was jist able to speak, an', savin' the Socratic interrogatory, had lost a' poo'r o' argument.

"Steakin' the stable-door when the steed's stown," says I to the Sergeant, in a jocose aside, as we slippet awa.

We were onquestionably somewhat declatory at breakfast the neist mornin'—at least I was—for the Sergeant declared that he had been roun' Arthur Seat and the Blackfurd Hill afore I was up.   Indeed, Mr Drumly, I was no jist mysel' for twa-three hours, and I began to enterteen some doobts aboot the quality o' the Muirfoot water,—there was a peaty flavour in my mouth for which it was impossible to accoont by ony ither hypothesis.   Nevertheless a strang cup o' tea and the least taste o' speerits at startin' pued us thegither, and whan we left to veesit the Professor we were crouse as twa corbies— suppin' on sheep's-head.   But the discreet and decent lass wha opened the door (for he canna thole a man-flunkey, Mr Drumly) tell't us fairly that it was clean impossible to say whar the Maister micht be.   If he wus na at the Hielan' Society he micht be in the Parliament Hoose; and if he wus na in the Parliament Hoose he micht be at the Advocates'

Library, or at the Colledge, or at the Pier o' Leith, or in Mr Blackwud's back parlour, or in the pu'pit at the Tron, or on boord the man-o'-war at the ferry.

"Noo, Sergeant," says I, "tho' I'm thinkin' we micht as weel be chasin' Spunkie"—which is the vulgar, Mr Drumly, for the ignis fatuus o' antiquity—"my opeenion is that we should veesit the Parliament Hoose. Angus MacCraw o' Kilberry is ane o' the Macers, and he'll be pleased to forgather wi' an auld freen', specially frae Cawmeltoun,—for the Cawmeltoun whusky is weel liket by the Lords. He kens a' the inns and oots o' the place, and ye may depen' upon it that a gude word from Angus MacCraw wull hae wecht wi' the Electors."

Weel, Mr Drumly, there's nae disputin' that it's a gran' Ha', wi' its auld aik rafters, and its pented windows, and its picters o' sharp-nosed lawyers, and its figures in plaister o' Paris, and the lads wi' their horse-hair weegs. But as Angus said while the Sergeant was inspecin' the pentins,—Icabod, Icabod, the glory is departed!

"They're puir, fushionless, feckless bodies," he continued, lookin' roun' him wi' his nose in the air. "There's a great fa'in' awa. Whar's Jaffrey and Cowburn and Rutherfurd and Moncreiff and Colonsay and Peter Robertson? Na, na, I ken my place, and I mak' a pint o' being ceevil to the Bench; but it's God's truth I'm tellin' you—the College o' Justice is far through. The Justice,[1] to be sure, is a too'r o' strength; and aften and aften, when on his road to the gowf, he'll turn and say,—'There's a kittle pint o' practice, Mr MacCraw, on which I wud like to hear your opeenion. There's not a man in Coort has your experience,'—and sae on. But to come to your business, Sergeant MacTavish. I'm not to be a cawn-di-date mysel', — tho' I've been sair pressed to gang furrit by some o' the lads here. But as the Justice said whan I spoke to him,—What could we do wi'oot you, Mr MacCraw? And what's mair to the pint, Mr Lyell, I have not much of the Gaelic now, for it is fifty-wan years since I left Drum-whacket. But indeed there's nae wale o' cawn-di-dates—jist

---

[1] "The Justice,"—John Inglis, of course, Lord Justice-General, the most famous of Scottish Jurists and Judges.

a wheen doited gillies an' chairmen an' sic like—savin' auld Doctor MacCloskie o' the Lews and a lad frae Skye. The Skye man, they tell me, has a wechty backin'. But as you know, Mr Lyell, the Skye Gaelic has not the purity o' the Cawmeltoun, tho' I have heard it said at times by the young Whig chiels in the hoose that the whisky is better."

"Neither the Gaelic nor the whisky is petter," the Sergeant interposed decidedly.

"That is my ain opeenion, Sergeant MacTavish, and it should be a great pint in your favour wi' the Electors. Noo, as to what you should be doin'. You maun see the lecterary Professors,—Dawvid Mawson is verra thrang wi' his Three Deils, and Siller is ane o' the useless bodies that attend to ae thing at a time,—but Plackie—that's of coorse. He's aff to Hunter's Bog wi' his Volunteer corpse o' riflemen : but he wull be in the College at wan. You maun be there in time, and whan you have fand him you maun grip him siccar—like the Leddy Jean wi' her sweetheart in the auld sang. Speak him hooly and fairly,—he has a kind heart as weel as a glib tongue, and if you could say a word or twa discreetly aboot Homer and Ossian and John Knox and the Apocrapha and the Egyptian mummies and his ain contributions to creeticism and pottery, it might not come amiss. But the Kirk as weel as the Professors maun be considered. Hech, sirs, the black coats hae their fingers in maist pies—het or cauld—that are cooked in oor toun. So you maun see Dr Giles o' the Laigh Kirk wha wrote Tober-snore" — ("Whist, man, whist," said I, for I kent the Doctor wudna like it—and indeed, tho' the buik is maist divertin', yet it canna be conseedered a solid contribution to deeveenity)—"ay, ay—to be sure,—and if you come across the lad they ca' Hugh Jeames (wha sees to the bawbees at the 'Piscopal), he micht get you a word wi' the Bishop—mind ye ca' him My Lud,—for it's weel to hae freens on baith sides o' the bar ; and then there's Doctor Bagg,——Gude be here ! you maunna forget the Doctor. He'll mak' a spune or spile a horn, you may be sure. But—be frank wi' me, Andrew Lyell—is the Sergeant soun' in the essentials? Is he safe on Moses? And what aboot instrumental moosic and human hymns and the doxology and the Te Deum ludamos? And does he sit under a judicious expounder o' the Word, wha follows the beaten track, and disna loup ower the dyke, like a camsteerie tup, at ilka turn o' the road?—Troth, Mr Lyell, I'm rejoiced to hear it, —Sergeant MacTavish, you have my best wishes on your behalf.—But you'll prent your certeeficates and testimonials? —that maun be seen to.—Oh, jist a wheen lines frae your freens—a scrape o' the pen from the Minister and the Doctor and the Shirra and Mr Lyell here. 'It is Mr MacTavish who has the good Gaelic.' 'It is Mr MacTavish who is soun' in the essentials.' 'It is Mr MacTavish who knows the whisky that is pest.' And noo, my freens, there's the Deeveesion bell,—his Lordship wants a word wi' me i' the robing-room, —it's that kittle case o' the Hielan' stot they are preparin' to advise—but come back at three, and tak pot-luck wi' Mailie and me,—Mrs MacCraw will be prood to see ye."

We gaed roun' the Colledge Square, and into the empty class-rooms: but the Professor was inveesible. At the far corner we heard a strange bummin' soun', that seemed to rise from the grun', and the Sergeant, after listenin' a bit, was clear that we should depart quam primum; for he had heard the same soun', he said, at Balmawhapple, before the great earthquak o' saxty-wan. But a Colledge lad that met us at the door tellt us that the manifestation was due to nateral causes.

"It's moosic," says he; "it's Sir Herbert at the organ or the piany. He plays the organ and he plays the piany. He's trying desperate hard to catch the tune o' 'Scots wha hae' (the Colledge porter, tho' a stoot lad, is fairly oot o' wind blawin' the bellows), for Plackie has sworn by a' the thieves that ever crosst the Scottish border——"

"The Professor himsel'?" I interjected.

"Her nain sel'?" said the Sergeant.

"The verra man," responded the Colledger wi' a suppressed wink; "Plackie has sworn by the bones o' a' his ancestors, from Fin-ma-coul to Donald Bane——"

"Angels and ministers of grace defend us!" I exclaimed, while the Sergeant (bein' Hielan' by birth) shook in his shoes at the deadly poo'r o' the incantation.

"——— that if Yokeley canna play a gude Scots tune—
'Scots wha hae,' or 'The Bush aboon Traquair'—by New
Year's Day, he'll ding the kist o' whistles aboot his lugs!"

"And does the puir man no apply to the Shirra for a
caption or an interdict?" I asked after a pause. "I wonner
if he kens Angus MacCraw?"

"Weel, you see he's not sure aboot his locus standi. The
Professor will pit in a plea o' justification, and he'll mak a
speech on Aristotle and the Game Laws, and he'll cross-
examine the Plaintiff aboot the lectures on the science and
practice o' Moosic which were lost in the Flying Scotsman on
the road frae Lonnon (and were never recovered), and the
hail business o' the coort will be stoppit, and the Shirra, wha
comes from Aberdeen, is verra freenly with the Professor, and
so—and so———"

"I understan'," says I, noddin' my head after the similitude
o' Lord Burleigh. "But Sergeant MacTavish, my freen here,"
—wi' a boo—"to say naething o' mysel' (Andrew Lyell, Head
Maister and Inspector o' Nuisance frae Cawmeltoun)"—anither
boo—"is verra anxious to consult wi' the Professor on a bit
business o' a private nature. Would you be pleased to tell us
whar we micht find him?"

"It's nae gude," our freen replied, "nae gude ava; his
head's jist fu' o' maggots—I mean, o' manure. He's leased
a farm o' a thoosand acres in East Lothian, near Dunse; for
you see he's in favour o' freedom o' agriculture; and he says
the rotation o' crops is an interference wi' the leeberty o' the
subjec', and to pit dung in the grun' a reflection on the
boontiful care o' the Almichty. Cincinnatus at the pleugh—
ye'll mind Cincinnatus, Mr Lyell—Cincinnatus at the pleugh
canna compare wi' Plackie at the Chaummer o' Agriculture.—
But try him in Hill Street,—he had posted his letter to the
papers on the acceleration o' the Greek Kalends in Leap Year
when I parted wi' him on the Mund."

Noo, wud you believe it, Mr Drumly, as we gaed doun the
Bridges whom should we meet but Doctor Bagg himsel'—the
Doctor in propria persona? He was elbowin' his way thro'
the crood, like an honest man wha had as gude richt as the

Duke to the public causeway ; and indeed, apart from superficial distinctions o' rank an' breedin', as Mr Gledstane has
weel remarked, the hail sons o' Adam are wan flesh and
blood,—tho' some o' us, to be sure, are maistly skin and bone.

"Hoo are you, Doctor?" I observed agreeably, for I had
met him in Cawmeltoun at Mr MacWhistler's Ordination
Soiree. "This is my freen Sergeant MacTavish,—the great
Celtic scholar an' pheelologer—of whom you have doobtless
heard.   He's a cawn-di-date for the Gaelic Chair."

The Sergeant lifted his bannet, an' made ane o' his gran'
boos.

The Doctor regairded him suspiciously—as a toon cat
might regaird a foumart.

"A scholar? A pheelologer? I am sorry, Mr Lyell, to
find a decent body like you consortin' wi' scholars an' pheelologers. It is your scholars an' pheelologers that have brought
dispeace into oor Zion. It is your scholars an' pheelologers
that have dung doon the battlements o' Jerusalem. It is
your scholars an' pheelologers wha are infeckit wi' the de-
structive an' rationalistic speerit o' modern creeticism.   It
is your scholars and creetics and pheelologers wha have
disowned the legislation o' Moses, the chronology o' the
Pentateuch, the morality of Dawvid, and the weesdom of
Solomon ! "

The Doctor paused oot o' breath. He spoke in a loud
vice : so that a crood o' students and idle limmers gathered
aboot us.

I explained to him, Mr Drumly, that Sergeant Duncan
MacTavish, late o' the Fit Guards, was ruling elder in Kil-
calmonell and Kilberry, as weel as deacon in the kirk at
Cawmeltoun ; that he had nae acquaintance wi' Strass, and
Renan, and Colenso, and the yeditor o' the *Cyclopædia Britannica*, but spak the purest Gaelic, and was the best judge
of whusky, of any man in Mull.

"And he is not a comparative pheelologer?" said the
Doctor, beginning to melt.

"Comparative pheelologer!" I exclaimed, wi' mair heat
than was seemly.   "We hae nae comparative pheelologers in

Cawmeltoun. Every word o' English that's spoken in the broch is translated straight oot o' the Gaelic. Na, na, Doctor —the Sergeant is soun' in the essentials."

He turned to the Sergeant, and took him by the han'— "You may coont on my vote," says he, with tears in his eyes. "I have been over-hasty. But the backslidin' even amang oor ain folk is fearsome, and it is weel-nigh impossible noo wi' ony certainty to divide a sheep from a goat. But rejoice, my freens," he continued, wi' the inspired air o' an auld prophet cursin' the Caananites, "the day o' judgment is at hand. We shall hew Agag in pieces before the Lord in Gilgal, and burn the infeckit thing wi' fire upon the altar."

Then he dived into the crood, and as I looked anxiously after him, the Colledger, wha had followed us doon the North Bridge, advised me, in a confidential whisper, no to mind,— it was jist the new complaint that Sir Hairy had invented— it was only "Smith on the Brain."

"Sergeant," says I, pinting to the lad, "I begin to doobt if that young man is in bona feedy."

Nevertheless he gaed alang Princes Street in oor company, an' made himsel' verra agreeable and enterteenin'.

"Ye'll be a great eddition to Edinboro society, Professor MacTavish (for between oorsels the appintment's as gude as made), which is dreich, verra dreich. There used to be constant high-jinks, they say, when Moir and Aytoun and Russel and Neaves and Doctor John were to the fore : but an Edinboro denner-pairty noo, wi' the flunkies, an' the heat, and the gas, and the mock turtle, and the mixed drinks, and the everlastin' Parliament Hoose hash, and Lord Fozey's jokes, —a surgical operation, Mr Lyell ?—faith, it needs naething less than a steam-crane to get a joke a yaird lang into the head, —wi' a' this an Edinboro denner-pairty o' the preesent day is a perfec' Black Hole o' Calcutta. And then the moosical re-union,—the moosical reunion, wi' the sanwiches an' the sherry negus an' the cauld tea, an' the Baarenet at the piany, an' Miss This an' Miss That skirlin' like a demented solan at the Bass, an' the deaf auld Cornel layin' doun the laa at the tap o' his vice, an' the young leddies jammed into corners, an' the young lads sittin' on the stairs,—a moosical reunion, Mr Lyell, is jist incredible meesery.—Yes, sir, ye'll be a welcome eddition to the society o' the place : but tak my advice and keep the length o' the table between yersel' and ane o' Lord Fozie's jokes.—But here's the door o' his den,—see that ye pit your pest fit foremost, Mr Sergeant," says he, winkin' wickedly at the wooden leg, as he vanished roun' the corner.

Never, Mr Drumly, never to my dying day shall I forget the pecooliar sensation I experienced when the curtain was lifted, and we stood within the Sanctum Sanctorum.   It was a scene weel calclate to thrill the heart an' confoon' the imagination.   We had past at wan step, like Tammas o' Ercildoune, from the mire and muck o' Auld Reckie into the twilicht o' an enchanted lan'.

A forest o' dirks darkened the wa's.   Claymores by the dizzen were heaped upon the rug.   The carpet was littered wi' spleuchans.   A hail kist o' kilts stood in a corner.   A sporran made from the crest o' the Gowden Eagle served as a pen-wiper, while the pen itsel' had been seleckit frae the tail-feathers o' the same royal bird.   A gran' speeritual an' meethological pentin' by Dawvid Scott, in which Ossian was fechtin' wi' Fingal for the preevilege o' crooning wi' the thorny symbol o' Scottish independence his gifted godson, hung aboon the hearth,—before which a meeserable "West-ender" (an abortive creature, hateful to gods and men) was slowly roasting,—a muckle pair o' self-acting bagpipes being used as bellows to keep the fire *het*.   And there, Mr Drumly—there, amid the coontless trophies of a mair than mortal acteevity, —stood the kilted chief o' Hielan' sang and fable and romance ;—

> " He stood in simple Lincoln green—
> The centre of the glittering ring
> And Snowdoun's knight is Scotland's king ! "

"Stood," did I say, Mr Drumly?—he was pacing back an' furrit—skeelfully avoidin' the spleuchans nevertheless—like a Numidian Lioness that has tint her cubs.

"He's in a dwam," said the Sergeant, reverently liftin' his bannet. "Disturb him not."

It was indeed a maist interestin' and instructive exhibeetion o' that mysterious faculty (weel kent to this day in the Hielan's as the second sight) which the illustrious Bard had inherited from a barbawric ancestry—that irrepressible hoose o' primeval Titans to which Modern Royalty is a Mushroom.

I canna deny, Mr Drumly, that I was affeckit; but I lookt in vain for my pocket-nepkin. Could the Doctor have onconsciously appropriated it in the pressure o' the crood? The idea crossed my mind; but it was instantly dismissed. I drew the back of my han' across my nose, and murmured wi' the Great Lexicographer—"Far from me and my freens be such freegid pheelosophy as may conduct us indifferent and unmuved over any grun' that has been deegnified by bravery, virtue, or weesdom, et cetera, et cetera."

As he paced back and furrit, Mr Drumly,—seatin' himsel' noo an' again in the agony o' composition on the aite suidhe Fhin which occupied the centre of the apairtment—we becam' involuntary spectators, so to speak, o' the veesion an' faculty divine in wan o' its sublimest ootbraks.

"Aye, my Lords, upon the rugged ribs of Ben Macdhui, amang the cloods and corries o' the Grampians, we shall invest our Professor and anoint our Bard. The Lion will be there, as weel as the original Scots eagle, wha will flap her wings above our laurelled broos wi' a passion unfamiliar to the degenerate eagle o' the democracy. Every piper in broad Scotland, from the Minsh to the Mull, is summoned to oor revel: and the music of ten thoosand bagpipes shall wauken, wi' their roar, the virgin echoes o' Cairngorum. Seat yourselves, my Lords, upon our primeval boulders, and,—Ho! Heralds! bring furrit the Cawn-di-dates. They shall toss the caber—they shall rin wi' the red deer—they shall loup wi' the wild cats—they shall recite the Sagas o' Fin-Mac-Dhui and Ben-Mac-Nevis—and finally, my Lords, they shall translate into oor Mountain tongue wan o' the gran' national covenantin' hymns which was prented in the first an' only edition o' my leerical pottery." (So far he had spoken in prose ; but, as his thoughts reverted to the Past, he munted Pegasus, and, in a vice tremblin' wi' retrospective emotion, proceeded—)

> "There's lads that lo'e Queen Mary,
>   And lads that lo'e Queen Bess,
> And ithers lo'e Aspasia,
>   The quean o' Pericles.
> But o'er a' the warld's braw hizzies
>   There's ane that bears the rule,—
> The lass that stood the session,
>   And cuist the cutty stool.
> Wi' a row-dow—at them now—
>   Jenny ————

WHENCE COME THESE CAITIFFS ?"

Glowerin' veeciously, like a verra bŭl o' Bashan, at the intruders, he paused a mument ⏝   ⏝   ⏝

⏝   ⏝   ⏝   ⏝   ⏝   ⏝   ⏝

"Hon hoi theoi philousin apothneskei neos," he exclaimed in the purest Gaelic, an' then — then seizing his claymore, an' swingin' it aboon his head, he cam stracht at the Sergeant.

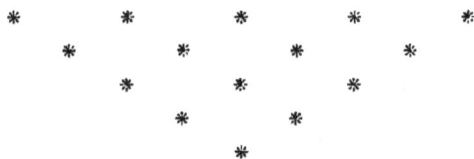

*   *   *   *   *
*   *   *   *
*   *   *
*   *
*

We gat hame neist day ; and, as the Professor is awa for a week's pleasurin' in the Hielan's o' Abyssinia wi' the Queen o' Sheba an' King John, the Election has been postponed in the meantime, an' wull not be decided until he returns. But the Sergeant—honest man !—is verra hopefu'.

*   *
*

Paradise Regained does not rise to the height of *Paradise Lost*. But though part two is as a rule a rather risky experiment, the second part of Mr Lyell's adventure is quite equal to the first. The School-master's hand had not lost its cunning. If there be greater breadth and freedom in the portrait of the Scotch Professor, there are mellower lights and shades in that of the Oxford Don. The reader who has leisure may now proceed to compare them.

*   *
*

X

THE SERGEANT IN THE HIELANS.

DEAR JOHN DRUMLY,—It is our gude freen' Mr Lyell has got me to write you a brief narrateeve of the strange adventures which befell him and the Sergeant—Sergeant MacTavish —when they went doun in the Dunara Castle to testify to the Hielanmen for the pure word against Robinson Smuth. He is lying in bed with his wife's mutch tied round his head, and a tumbler o' water-gruel on the table; for the cauld that took him at Loch Boisdale sattled on his stamack, and he is verra bad indeed, and has not drank wan glass of Farintosh neat since Monday week.

Now, you see, we had been at Machrihanish for twa-three roun's o' the links, and gran' links they are, and the bunkers are jist uncommon. It had been a het afternoon, and the Schoolmaister had been constantly in Hell: so we were takin' a coolin' drink in front of the cozy bit inn at the Pans, kept by that fine woman Mrs Rae, and you know her weel, Mr Drumly. There was an east-country caddy hangin' aboot the door, Ned by name, who had arrived that mornin' by the boat. He had carried for the Captain in the great St Andrews match, whan the Champion Cross had been won by Fasnacloich against heavy odds,—tho', indeed, there is not wan man on the green can beat Fasnacloich whan he is in trim. But it had been a sair fecht, for Gilbert Innes was the last man in, and a better player than Gilbert Innes never handled a club.

"You'll tak' a dram, Ned," says Mr Lyell, pleasantly; "it has been het wark to-day."

"I'm beholden to you, Mr Lyell," says Ned; "but it's only the laste taste in the warld I can be takin' to-night; for the Minister, you see, has garr'd me jine the Ludge. Stop, sir, stop—a thumlefu' disna coont—but—and here's your gude health," he added, drainin' the glass wi'oot farther ceremony. "It's Mrs Rae that keeps the gude speerits, I reckon."

"That she does, Ned, that she does,—an exemplary woman —an exemplary woman. But this single between Fasnacloich and Mr Gilbert—I wish I had seen it, man—the fecht maun hae been truly Humeric. Tell us a' the oots an' inns, Ned; and you may bring ben anither mutchkin, Mrs Rae, whan you are not otherwise occupied."

"Weel, sir, you see they turned a' even—neck an' neck. The first hole hame was halved—the Laird holin' a lang putt. The Captain wan the neist an' the neist—twa holes to the gude, and sax to play,—lang odds. But the Laird was cool and keen, and he pit the heather hole in his pooch—the Captain comin' to grief amang the stiff whuns on the brae. At the hole across baith drove weel aff the tee, weel on to Elysium; but the Captain's second shot gaed slap into Hell, an' that sattled *him*. A' even again, and fowr to play—a teuch fecht,—the Laird as white as death, and the Captain verra douce, but no canny to come across. Weel, the fourth hole was halved—never seed it played better; but the neist finished the match—the Laird hookit his ba' into the Preencipal's Nose, and the Captain lay snug on the green at the like. After that, the Laird never lookit up, an' Fasnacloich wan easy at the burn."

It was a bonny evenin' in August—the boom o' the Atlantic in Machrihanish Bay was nae mair than the saftest lullaby— we could hear the bag-pipes across the water in Jura. Weel, Mr Drumly, just as Ned's story cam' to an en', there was a rummle o' wheels on the road ahint the hoose, and presently a pairty o' gentlefolk descended at the front door,—as far as we could judge in the uncertain light, they were three o' them —twa in black coats and white stocks, the third in a kilt.

"Gude be here!" said Mr Lyell, whan he saw the kilt, "it canna be Plackie, surely. Sergeant," says he in a whisper, turnin' to Mr MacTavish, wha was takin' his drink quietly, like the douce man he is, "it's the Gaelic chair, Sergeant—the Gaelic chair, wi'oot doot. *The appintment is made, and you're the man.* But no—that's the MacGregor tartan; and it's the Royal Stuart (for he is sib, you see, to the auld Kings) that the Professor wears for choice."

They gaed into the hoose, and after a bit Mrs Rae cam' oot to whar we sat. "They're seekin' you, Mr Lyell, you and the Sergeant, and you're to gang ben directly."

Noo, Mr Drumly, what I am aboot to relate is strickly private; on *that* Mr Lyell is positive; and you maun gie your word of honour that you will not divulge it—not even to Mrs Drumly—this side the grave. Dr Wull and Sir Hairy are men aboon suspicion; sae are the Sergeant and Mr Lyell: but there are ill tongues waggin' in the warld, and if it was to get into the irreleegious papers, there would be the deevil to pay—and mair.

"We've come to see you, Mr Lyell," said Dr Wull, oot o' the partial darkness, for the can'les had not been lichted, "aboot that unhappy lad Smuth—Robinson Smuth. We are fairly seek o' him and his warks. It is clean impossible to grup him—wan micht as weel grup the aurora borealis or the ignis fatuus. He has nae respeck for age and infirmity—mental or pheesical. Auld Dr Muddy is fairly worn aff his legs—Shirra Cawmell is in the dead-thraws—there are times, indeed, whan Sir Hairy himsel' is not sure if he's standin' on his head or his heels. And what's waur,—they are beginnin' to say that his laa is better than the liars', and that he has mair deevcenity than a' the dee-dees. The pison o' asps is under his tongue, and the elders o' Aberdeen and the deacons o' Dunfermline are infeckit wi' the pison. There is not wan Presbytery this side Strathbogie through which the deadly venom has not spread. The demon o' rationalistic creeticism, Mr Lyell, is stalkin' thro' the lan'; it waukens up MacHowley in the dead o' nicht, sae that his puir wife canna get a wink o' sleep: there is an end o' Presbyterian simpleecity and domestic feleecity if the evil spirit is not laid. Noo, you maun understan' that we had a bit conference last week,—there was me, and Sir Hairy, and Dr Bagg, and Mac-Howley, and a wheen mair; and we have resolved, Mr Lyell, to bring the business to a feenish. You see, the Commission have appinted a Committee of Inquiry; there are some raw lads upon it—freens o' Smuth—(appinted *per incuriam*,—tho', indeed, we cud not help it); but the majority are discreet and reasonable men, wha ken what belangs to Gospel truth and is becomin' in a meenister o' the Word. The Report is not yet prepared, and it wull not be prented till the Commission meets; for it is onsuitable to expose it to the ignorant creeticism o' the ungodly and malignant. But it wull prove that the articles in the *Cycolpædia* are in fack an' laa a pernicious and detestable assault upon the infallibeelity o' the Scripture narrateeve, inasmuch as thay contain divers passages in which the saintly men o' the Auld Testament are treated wi' unbecomin' fameeliarity, and in which the predictive aspect o' the prophecies (and what is prophecy if it disna predick?) is disowned and discredited. I tell you this in confidence, Mr Lyell, for it is right that *you* should know what the Committee—whan it deleeberates—will do. Noo, the Commission *in hunc effectum* (as Sir Hairy says) is convened to meet on the 27th of October, and this is the 20th of August. It is essential, Mr Lyell, for the peace and prosperity of our Zion, that the Report should be adopted by an overpoorin' majority. But, as I have said, there is a speerit of revolt abroad in the Low country; and the fack is, my freens, wi'oot further prologue, that we maun get the Hielanmen to come and help us. From the bleak hills of Judea the chosen people lookt doun upon the Pheelistines; and amang your hills and bogs, Sergeant MacTavish, the pure flame o' Gospel truth still burns freely, undimmed by the fogs o' German pheelology and the stour o' Oxford rationalism. It is not the first time, Sergeant MacTavish, that the Hielanmen have sweept the plain; it is not the first time, Mr Lyell, that, wi' their Bibles in their han's and their broadswords on their backs, they have testified for Kirk and Covenant! Listen, Mr Lyell—this is what Dr Bagg said at the Conference—his verra words;—Go to that understanding man, Mr Lyell, schoolmaister in Cawmelton. He is weel acquaint wi' the great Gaelic scholar, Sergeant MacTavish, who is a cawndidate for the Gaelic chair. Tell them that they are summoned and commissioned by the Kirk to carry thro' this goodly matter. They maun gird up their loins, and go doun in the Dunara Castle to the Outer Hebrides. Amang the misty islands whar Columbus introduced his papistical superstitions, they wull seek oot the deacons and meenisters o' the true Kirk. The puir bodies will be swear to come a' the road to Edinbro',—for the haerst is late this year in the Lews; but thay maun leave the pleuch and the harrow and the reapin' heuk, and trust that

Providence will keep the winter back a bit.   The Sergeant's
Gaelic is known to be the best in the Hielans ; and if he and
Mr Lyell between them canna persuade the Hielanmen to
atten', it will be fairly impossible for either you or me, Doctor
—I tell you frankly."

Weel, Mr Drumly, the upshot o' the matter was, that the
Sergeant and Mr Lyell agreed to go.   It was a serious re-
sponseebeelity undootedly ; but the gude opeenion o' the
Kirk was verra flatterin', and the weather was fine for the time
o' year, and the eatin' and drinkin' on boord the Dunara
Castle is o' the verra best, and beats the Clydesdale's fairly.

"And ye'll be pleased," says Dr Wull, turning at last to
the man in the kilt, wha was sittin' in an obscure corner wi' the
tail o' his kilt pued between his legs, "to meet the Laird o'
Fer——"

"Whist, Doctor, whist," says Sir Hairy, kickin' his freen's
shins promiscuously under the table.

"The Man in the Mune," says Dr Wull, pu'in himsel' up,
an' winkin' pleesantly on the company.

"Is it possible?" says the Sergeant, gettin' on his legs,
and glowerin' into the darkness ; "him that was taen up for
gatherin' sticks on the Sabbath——"

"The Chancellor o' the Exchequer," the Doctor went on,
wi' a humersome chuckle, disregarding the interruption.

"Ho, ho!" says Mr Lyell, beginnin' to see how the land lay.

"There is a distressin' amount o' destitution in the Hielans
an' Eelands o' the Wast Country, Mr Lyell, especially amang
the elders and deacons and meenisters o' the Kirk——"

"Exackly," says Mr Lyell, noddin' his head.

The Doctor nodded in seempathy ; but Sir Hairy had
turned his back, and was attentively regardin' the prent of the
Dook aboon the lum.

You have heard of the enchantments of the *Arabian Nichts*,
an' have nae doot wutnessed the wicked devices o' the Wuzard
o' the North,—the late Mr Anderson ; but it's the truth I'm
tellin' you, Mr Drumly,—*three wechty bags o' Bank o' Scotland
notes and bullion appeared as if by magic on the table.*

"And the Laird proposes that a decent an' conscederate
man should undertak the deestribution, wi' sic personal remun-

eration for travellin' expenses an' subsistence-money as may be deemed necessary an' reasonable."

"But the laa again' treatin', Doctor?" Mr Lyell inquired dootfully, after a pause.

"Hoots, Mr Lyell!—the State may stick at trifles of that kind; but the Kirk, as you know, is not subject to Cæsar. Whar wud we have been in the '43 if we had permitted oorsels to be hampered by the freevilous technicalities o' the laa? The Ceevil Coorts have nae jurisdiction within a releegious society; for a releegious society is a laa unto itself, and its title-deeds are in the Registry above."

"I was hearin' they were seen to by that glib lad Tyler (an' indeed he is glib wi' the pen, tho' a yammerin' body on his legs)," says the Schoolmaister, who can never resist his bit joke.

Sir Hairy leuch, but the Doctor was not pleased.

" For every idle word, Mr Lyell——"

" Hoots, hoots, Doctor! it was only a bit joke, and a bit joke hurts neither man nor beast. But it's time we were muvin'," says he. " 'The Dunara Castle, they were tellin' me, is to stop at Arran this trip for twa muckle stots the Dook is sendin' to Lochiel; so we wull take the early boat to Loch Ranza, an' meet the steamer at Brodick in the evenin', after dinin' wi' my gude freen Mr Macdonald at the Douglas Arms."

Tho' the early mornin' was thick, the fog lifted wi' the sun. We took a short cut across Ben Noosh,—sendin' the pock-mankey (*which was wechty, as you may believe*) roun' by the Ivanhoe. The Mountain o' the Wun, steeped in thun'er and racked wi' storm, stude up black as ink against the sky; yet at pints there were glints o' sunshine that pented the green on the bracken and the purple on the heather; and from the tap o' Tarsuin we saw a streak o' silver in the west—which betokened fine weather at sea.

" It will be a goot day to-morrow whatever," said the Sergeant on the road doun.

" 'The boat is rather crowded to-night," says that fine man Mister Donald, as he gaed us oor tickets, after seein' the stots hoisted in wi' the landing-tackle. " We have the Grand

International Social, Scientific, and Leeterary Congress (personally conducted) on board, and they occipy every corner o' the cabin. But it's a nice warm evenin' whatever, and you and the Sergeant, with your rugs, and a taste of Talisker to keep the Clyde fog oot o' the stamack, will do fine on deck, Mr Lyell."

"And this is Mr Lyell," says a tall, handsome, middle-aged young man wha was smokin' a sceegarette on the gangway. "What an unlooked-for pleasure! I was afraid I might have to leave Scotland without meeting you and the Sergeant. Sergeant MacTavish, I've written a book on the Gaelic myself, and I'm proud to make your acquaintance."

"I didna jist catch the name," says Mr Lyell, dootfully.

"To be sure—I forgot to introduce myself. I'm Matthew," says he, liftin' his hat, "Matthew, Mark, Luke, and John—all the Apostles rolled into one—the subtler spirit and finer aroma of their rather crude thaumaturgy, you understand,—but you may call me Matt if you like—all my friends do—it's handier. Come along—I've got Mr Donald to put some easy-chairs on deck, and the steward is to bring us a venison pasty and the hot water presently, and we'll make ourselves comfortable for the night. What a balmy night, to be sure!—with just a tonic touch of salt from the sea. Your Scotch stars are highly respectable, Mr Lyell; but it's a thousand pities they couldn't spare you a moon."

The fascination o' that lazy lang-legged English chiel, Mr Drumly, was perfectly incomprehensible. Andrew Lyell is a man o' the warld, and the Sergeant has seen service in ilka quarter o' the globe; but they were hand in glove wi' him before the remains of the pasty had been removed. It was no gude trying to be deefident and deeplomatic;—he had learnt ilka word aboot the Confidential Mission to the Hielanmen before the third jug of punch was brewed.

"I'm a detective, a spiritual detective," says He, lauchin'; "don't you fancy you can keep anything from *me*. By the way, Mr Lyell, that portmanteau which I lifted up the ladder —*it's verra wechty*," says he, lookin' the Schoolmaister stracht in the face, and speakin' suddenly in the purest Scots. "Is it the family plate, Mr Lyell——?"

"O Lord!" said the Schoolmaister, lookin' as white as death.

"Never you mind, Mr Lyell—I'm neither a thief nor a constable—the family silver is safe for me.   But this Smith that you speak of—(I've heard the name before, I think—or was it Brown?)—he's clearly a desperate bad one ; and, were I you, Mr Lyell, I would look well to the spoons.—And so you are bound for the Hebrides like myself, — the farthest Hebrides, as Wordsworth says in one of his forgotten poems—

> "'Breaking the silence of the seas,
> Among the farthest Hebrides.'

I'm not a Wordsworthian myself, mind you—though perhaps the most remarkable and fruitful discovery of my life is connected with the old man of Rydal. You have heard of it, Mr Lyell?   No?   Most people have ; but, to be sure, we are here on the confines of civilisation.   A LITTLE OF WORDSWORTH GOES A LONG WAY,—that's the text, Sergeant, which I have elaborated with astonishing success in my recent selection from his poems. *To be recognised far and wide as a great poet, Wordsworth needs to be relieved of the poetical baggage which now encumbers him ; and until this is done, he has not had a fair chance before the world.*   That's what I said in the Preface ; and I flatter myself that I divided the ore from the baser metal, the wheat from the chaff, the heavy impedimenta from the more portable Gladstone bag, with true critical fidelity.   And by the way, Mr Lyell, can you furnish me with the missing link?   The Gladstone bag!   What is there in common between the copious rhetoric of St Stephen's and this compact and unpretentious article?   You cannot explain it ; nor do I wonder at your inability.   For our popular judgments are incalculable!   To establish an Academy of Taste, to which questions of the higher criticism may be referred, has ever been my ambition.   But the Forty Thieves —the Forty Immortals, I mean,—where are they to be found ? You, and I, and the Sergeant, Mr Lyell——"

They were aff the Mull by this time, and the conversation was temporarily suspended.

"Mr Lyell," says He, whan he had returned from the side o' the ship, "this is my first (and last) experience of a personally-conducted party. The idea was good : it was intended to bring the leaders of Light and Sweetness together in a friendly way ; but it hasn't worked ; we started from Euston three days ago, and to-night not a soul is on speaking terms with his neighbour. Browning has done nothing but tear his hair over *Sordello ;* he has clean forgotten what it meant, and as not another soul ever knew, it is now an unfathomable mystery,—like the Darnley murder or the song that Achilles sang ; and Alfred—but hush—here he comes——"

And a verra big man began to pace up and doun the deck in front o' us, his lang elf-locks streamin' in the nicht-wind. He was muttering uneasily to himsel'.

"Poor old Alfred,—he is worrying himself about little Ally. He can't at all make out, you see, where the dickens the boy came from ? He is at it now, Mr Lyell,—it is really very distressing, and one hasn't a notion what to give him,—we should have brought Dr John,—ay, ay, there he goes again."

And oot o' the darkness o' the star-licht cam these mysterious words,—

> "O dear Spirit, half-lost
> In thine own shadow, and this fleshly sign
> That Thou art Thou—who wailest being born
> And banished into mystery, and the pain
> Of this divisible-indivisible world,
> Among the numerable-innumerable
> Sun, sun, and sun, thro' finite-infinite space,
> Infinite-finite Time—our mortal veil
> And shattered phantom of that infinite One,
> Who made thee inconceivably Thyself
> Out of his whole World-self and all in all."

"Alas! alas!" observed a dreich-lookin' man, wi' his hair pued across his nose, who had joined us unnoticed as we were list'nin' to the geeberish. "It is clear that to Tennyson, as to Carlyle and myself, it has become a quite utterly unspeakable business. Life and death, birth and begetting, the unknown eternity of the past and the unknown eternity of the future—have they not, one and all, become intensely incred-

ible? And we are expected to unravel the tangled skein by
the rule of three and the fardels of political economy! You
fancy, my foolish friends (some of you at least), that two and
two make four; it is not so; that two and two make four has
been to me for many years a proposition not only intrinsically
preposterous, but profoundly immoral. The shallow sophistries
of a servile logic, the degrading formulas of a mercenary
arithmetic——"

He followed the ither into the darkness like a dream; and
then Mr Matthew resumed,—

"Lively company, you will say, very lively company, for a
man rather hipped by London dinners and London fogs.
The fact is, Mr Lyell, that we English are all Puritans by
nature,—the Hebrew element comes out in us, the Hellenic
cheerfulness drops away from us, the moment we are over
sixty. Originally, no doubt, a form of dyspepsia, Puritanism
has by this time entered deeply into our moral nature, tainting
the conscience as well as affecting the stomach. And—but
what a shindy these fellows in the steerage are making!—why
—God bless my soul!—it's Tom Hughes and Froude trying
to pitch Swinburne overboard. Let us trust, Mr Lyell, that
the vile conspiracy will be frustrated: but of course," he
continued placidly, as he resumed his seegarette, "of course
it's no affair of ours; and if the unspeakable Swinburne should
follow the unspeakable Turk' into the darkness, why, between
ourselves, Sergeant, there are one or two choice morsels of
rhyme, by a friend of my own, with the Publisher—— Well,
Mr Lyell, as I was saying, the gloom that hangs over modern
England is due as much to its religion as to its fog. Why,
then, should you and I seek to perpetuate the grotesque illusions of its dismal and illiberal life? That they are illusions
no one doubts; for, except to some half-dozen old gentlemen
in the country, your precious Westminster Confession has become absolutely antiquated. Indeed, Mr Lyell, the whole
of the anthropomorphic and miraculous religion of tradition
is ceasing to be credible even to our women. You may
make-believe for a little longer if you like; but you had
much better bury it decently out of sight without more ado.
Nor is there anything surprising in this,—you are only reaping

332 A SCOTCH PROFESSOR AND AN OXFORD DON.

what you have sown. The Stream of Tendency by which all things seek to fulfil the law of their being, the Eternal which makes for Righteousness—and what more can we say?—the temple of this August Idea has been materialised into an English middle-class Olympus, from which all the joy and grace of the Hellenic is withdrawn. It is only a superficial antagonism, Mr Lyell, that exists between the man of science and myself—a mere juggle on words. For if the promise and potency of every form of life are to be found in matter, where is the difference between us? Call it matter if you like, Mr Professor; I call it spirit. No, Mr Lyell, the men of science are not the materialists. The ideas which science appropriates are intrinsically *im*material—rising above the fogs of sensible phenomena into an ampler ether and a diviner air; and nothing touches the soul to finer issues than the contemplation of the Sovereign Laws of Universal Life. Whereas those grotesque and fantastic figures which middle-class misery and madness and malice have painted upon the darkness—— Ah, Mr Lyell, on a night like this, when innumerable worlds are wheeling noiselessly through the void, can you not for one brief moment divest yourself of a too obtrusive and clamant personality, can you not lose yourself for one moment in the Mellow Stream of Universal Being, content to have it said for you, as your sole title to immortality—He lived in the Eternal Order, and the Eternal Order never dies?"

There was a curious fire in his eyes—veesible in the darkness—as he uttered the last words, and for some minutes no wan spake. Mr Lyell had a creepin' feelin' aboot his back; he looked at the Sergeant, but the Sergeant was fast asleep.

"Weel," says Mr Lyell, at last, "I'm not illeebral or inqueesitorial; but you wull admit, Mr Matthew, that something maun be done wi' heretics, Papists, Sabbath-breakers, sheep-stealers, and siclike? What wud you do wi' a misbeliever, Mr Matthew, if I may tak the leeberty of asking?"

"IT IS MACLEOD'S UNIVERSAL SHEEP-DIP THAT IS GOOT FOR THEM," said a sepoolcral vice. It was the Sergeant speaking in his sleep; but whether he was meanin' heretics or gimmers or tups, we could not tell.

" Ah, well, Mr Lyell, the Sergeant may not be so far wrong.
For removing inconvenient vermin the Highland sheep-dip is
invaluable. Your Robertson Smiths will cease from vexing
the souls of the fathers in Israel when they have had a touch
or two of the tar-brush. But enough of Scotch theology,—
a little of it, like Wordsworth, you know, goes a long way.
Why, that must be Erin-go-bragh over there? The faint
blue line along the horizon, is it indeed the Emerald Isle?
She looks peaceful enough from the outside, to be sure;
but what a legion of evil spirits have taken up their abode in
her, and how they are tearing her to pieces! You are a
Liberal, I presume, Mr Lyell; most Scotchmen are, I am
told."

" At preesent I'm Leebral. You see I was a Tory durin'
the time they were in offisch; but they never did me ony
gude : and what gude they did to Scotland, savin' to mak
Taper a shirra and Tadpole a lord, I canna tell. So, in the
meantime, I'm Leebral."

" Nothing like conscientious convictions, Mr Lyell. For
my own part, I am rather inclined to go over to the Barbarians.
I love light, and sweetness, and reasonableness, and am as
little a lover of superstition as the most advanced Radical in
the Cabinet ; but the passion of the mob is not a weapon
which I care to handle. What communion has light with
darkness? How can the lover of the idea yoke himself with
the blind tumultuary forces of ignorance and fanaticism? We
were told the other day, to be sure, that a stock of prime
political ideas might be laid in for future use by the young
men of Birmingham meeting together at their political clubs,
and airing over their beer the sterile and passionate commonplaces of Radicalism. Not in this way, ye gods!—not at
such Thyestean banquet of clap-trap—is a wise and understanding people formed.—But against the mighty sweep of
the democracy, what avail our faint and feeble protests?
We shy and modest scholars, Mr Lyell, are an old-fashioned
community, and the new beatitude which Birmingham has
invented—Blessed are the cocksure!—is worth any two of
the old."

He was interrupit by a terrific snort from the sleepin'

Sergeant.   The deep guttural soun's followed each other wi'
melodious preceesion, shapin' themselves at last into the
solemn march and rhythmic cadence of Gaelic pottery.   Mr
Lyell explained to Him how it was.

"My dear sir," says He, takin' oot o' his coat-pocket a bit
slate and skeelyvine, "this is a psychological and philological
experience of the deepest interest.   The Sergeant's Gaelic
differs in many respects from the Gaelic we speak at Oxford.
So please oblige me, as he proceeds, with a free or literal
translation, as suits you best."

I am not good at writing the Gaelic; but the English o'
the Sergeant's monologue, by that fine man and gran' scholar,
Mr Skene—and a fine man and a gran' scholar he is—will be
fand in his Hielan book.

The licht by this time was beginnin' to break: we had
entered the Sound o' Jura.   But He was as brisk as ever.

"What I miss in your lakes and mountains, Mr Lyell—
what I particularly miss in them—is Urbanity.   Scottish
scenery is more or less brutal.   Now, if that Peak" (he was
lookin' at wan o' the Paps) "had dipped the other way, or if
the crude blue of this unusually movable water [1] were softened
by a wash of cobalt, how far better it would have been!
But the Something or Other in the world that looks after the
picturesque has very rudimentary notions of form and colour.
Do not suppose that I harbour any prejudice against your
country;—I am ready to admit (though I was born among
them) that even our English lakes are not entirely successful.
You will know what I mean, Sergeant MacTavish, when I say
that the Note of Provinciality is painfully apparent.   The
Lancashire lakes are local and shallow, and want the ineffable
sentiment of the Middle Age.   This, of course, is the reason
why Wordsworth, their chief interpreter, is local and shallow,
and wants the ineffable sentiment of the Middle Age—which
belongs, indeed, to Oxford alone.   O Oxford! Oxford!—
Hullo! here come the rest of the personally-conducted,
looking very gash in the morning air.   Poor devils, it must
have been stuffy down-stairs.—You see that lad on the taffrail,
Mr Lyell?—that's Black or Brown or Green—I forget his

---

[1] It was only a bit jabble after all.

name—the fellow who hails from Styornoway, you know. By Jove! what a lot of body colour the beggar must use!—doesn't he lay it on thick?—And now, Sergeant, just one mouthful before we turn in for a tub,—a rizzared haddie, shall we say, or the ham and eggs of the British Philistine?"

How it cam aboot, Mr Drumly, was never exackly known. It was an instantaneous cat-ass-trophy. The members of the personally-conducted pairty were colleckit roun' the funnel (for the mornin' air was chilly), and, wi'oot a moment's notice, the biler burst. The hail members o' the pairty, including the conductor, were blawn into the air, while the ship hersel' began to sink, as it appeared to us.

But He was equal to the deeficulties o' the position.

"Let us save ourselves, Sergeant," says He. "Jump into the dingy, Mr Lyell, and we'll be clear of the wreck before they know what we are about. There's just room for three. *Salus reipublicæ suprema lex.*"

And in anither minute we were clear o' the sinkin' ship (if it did sink, which we had nae leisure to ascertain), and floatin' wi' the tide to the nearest lan'.

It's an ill wind that blaws naebody gude. Had it not been for the Sergeant's leg we would never have got to the shore; for there was not wan oar in the boat, and the pockmankey was a dead wecht. However, we managed to get the leg unscrewed; and it answered verra weel as a rudder.

Oh, Mr Drumly, it's a bonnie island! The white eider-drakes are jist in thoosan's, and the sealchs are as tame as Robin-redbreasts. And a' nicht lang you hear the pipe o' the plover and the skirl o' the whaup; and you draw the blanket up to your nose, an' dream o' the blessed islands which were veesited by the wise Ulysses. And the grey rock wi' its border o' purple heather (and the heather this year was jist uncommon) rises oot o' the green sod, whar the bog-pimpernel and the loose-strife are bloomin' amang the bracken. And the ferns, Mr Drumly!—there are jist perfect thickets o' the hartstongue, and the hay-scented, and the sea-spleenwort, and the Royal.

"Indeed, Mr Lyell," says He, "we have fallen upon our feet. This is the island valley of Avilion (as you may have heard), to which they brought the wounded Arthur,—

"'Where falls not hail or rain or any snow';

or is it not rather," he continued, "that warm bay among the green Illyrian hills of which a not altogether ignoble poet has sung?

"'And there, they say, two bright and aged snakes
Who once were Cadmus and Harmonia,
Bask in the glens or on the warm sea-shore,
In breathless quiet after all their ills.
Nor do they see their country, nor the place
Where the Sphinx lived among the frowning hills,
Nor the unhappy palace of their race,
Nor Thebes, nor the Ismenus, any more.'

To us, Mr Lyell, has a like felicity been accorded. Sole-sitting by the shores of old romance and religion—unvext by Bishop or Beadle—we shall recover our sanity—we shall cease to be sad."

And the inhabitants were mair than freenly. Donald the inn-keeper is a man o' judgment and discretion (it is a blen' o' Farintosh and Talisker that he keeps); and wha can describe the Laird, Sir Duncan? You see, the Sergeant had been in his company in the Crimea (whar the Sergeant lost his leg, and Sir Duncan his twa fingers); and the moment Sir Duncan heard it was his auld corporal, he had him up to the Castle, and there were fine times for the Sergeant.

It was only the second morning after we landit that Murdoch the keeper (and Murdoch, who is a fine big man, was pentit for the Queen's ain buik, as you know, Mr Drumly) cam doun to tell us that there was to be a sealch-hunt that day. They were takin' the big boat, and there wud be room for the three o' us. Sae by the time the Colonel drove doun, we were ready on the pier.

Weel, Mr Drumly, we had a famous day. Mr Matthew was jist the life and sowl o' the pairty. At wan moment he wud swear that he didna care a bodle for Sir Walter's bastard epicks (as he ca'ed them); at anither he declared that the Lord o' the Isles was jist as fine and breezy a cruise roun' the wast coast as the heart o' man could desire. He wud settle in Scotland himsel', he said, if it wasna that he micht possibly come across a Scotchman——

"But this is grand!" he went on, whan we had run roun' to the lonely rocks whar the great sea-lions dwall. For you maun understand, Mr Drumly, that there are twa kinds o' sealchs—the Raon and the Tapist. It was the great Tapists we were seekin' that day. They live on the ootside reefs, wi' not a rock (except the Dhu Hertsich) between them and Newfundlan'. It is seldom they see the face of man, except whan a big ship in the wild winter weather, after wan cruel scrape amang the breakers, goes stracht to the bottom wi' every sowl on board. We were lying between Cann-riva an' Ellan-na-rhoan, in a braid open channel which the blind rollers dinna reach. The wan rock was covered wi' sealchs o' the smaller sort—grey shinin' objec's lying aboot in coontless numbers on the wrack. (You can tell a sealch, Mr Drumly, by its shimmer on the wrack; for the tangle, you observe, disna refleck the licht.) Black bullet-heads were constantly appearin' aboon the water,—risin' and sinkin' noiselessly, or lookin' aboot wi' an air o' conseederate enquiry for places to lan' canny. Them on the rock were jist obviously in the enjoyment of perfect feeleecity,—lollin' lazily on their backs in the heat, or fannin' themsels' wi' their flappers as a leddy wi' her fan. Only the great Tapists—the sea-lions on Cann-riva—were snappin' and snarlin' and fechtin'.

"Hand me the glass," says Mr Matthew to the under-keeper, whan we had landit Sir Duncan and Murdoch. "I must have a near look at a Tavish. What a row they are making, to be sure! That toothless old villain is an ugly customer when roused, I'll be bound. Look at his back teeth,—or rather at the stumps! I tell you what it is, Mr Lyell—they are holding an *in hunc effectum* meeting of Com-mission, and the Moderator (that's what you call him?) is in the chair! Now, I wonder what the subject under discussion may be? One would like to know what they think about predestination, and free-will, and effectual calling, and the

Y

origin of species, and the punishment of the wicked? Have
they any Darwins or Huxleys among them? Anyway, it's
theological—for they are beginin' to show their teeth. I have
it now, sure enough: keep the boat steady for one moment,
will you? 'Tis a trial for heresy, I declare; the queer, inquisitive, hungry-looking little chap in the centre is the cul-
prit, and the grandfather of all seals—the owner of the tusks
—has been laying down the law and practice of the Kirk.
The young one wishes to put in a word, but they won't listen
—not they. See how their flappers are going, and their tails!

Hear to the worrying and growling! And now there is a
general scrimmage; old Methuselah has got the heretic by
the tail—he holds on like grim death—they'll be off the
rock presently if they don't look sharp — ay, ay — down
they go into the deep water, and the whole Commission
after them."

    It was Sir Duncan's bullet that, in pint o' fack, had dis-
persed the Assembly; and whan we rowed up to the place,
we found that wan of them had been badly shot. The beast,
however, had slipt doun the side of the rock: and tho' the
hail sea was red wi' his blude, it was lang or ever we could

manage to heuk him up. Whan he cam to the surface, Mr
Drumly, it was jist fearsome to look at him,—a' the warst
passions o' his last mument o' controversy were stamped upon
his face. For it was the Moderawtor himsel'. He weighed
exackly 44 stun.

We ran back in the best o' speerits. There was a spankin'
breeze, and the air was jist intoxicatin'. (If it cud only be
bottled and exported like the meeneral water, there wud be
sma' necessity for pheesic.) And the Colonel and oor Oxfurd
freen' gaed aff a' the road hame like Roman can'les or Manby's
rockets—the best o' firewarks. Mr Matthew sang wan o'
Mendelshun's melodies (improved by Sir Herbert Yokeley);
he danced a reel wi' the Sergeant; and whan he was fairly
oot o' breath, he got Murdoch to recite an Eerish psalm that
was brought to the island by Saint Columba. It is in Mr
Skene's new book, and the translation is fine and lecteral,
bein' for the maist part a concise narrateeve by Fin-ma-Coul
himsel' of what was doin' in Kintyre aboot the time o' the
Deluge ;—

> "As to me, I remained a year under the flood.
> There had not been slept, nor will there be slept,
> A sleep better than that which I had——"

"That'll do, Murdoch, that'll do ; he must have been an
uncommon long time under water ;—unless he was one of
your own seals, I don't very well see how he got it out of
him. But I suppose we were all seals about that time ;
and, to be sure, I would rather any day be a seal than
a chimpansee. I'm told they have a fine ear for music.
Gaudebant carmine phocœ. But they'll prefer the Gaelic
tunes, I daresay, in these parts — Ossian, Fingal, Blackie,
and that sort of thing?"

"Well, sir," says Murdoch, "you will know that aal our
shepherds they have two dogs—the one he speaks the English,
the other he will speak the Gaelic. But I do not know
myself what the sealchs will be saying,—tho' the old people
in the Island——"

"Exactly. They have heard the sea-maids sing many a
time : and by the way, Colonel, the Colonsay mermaid who

lost her heart to the Laird must have been a sweet slip of a lass.   How does the old ballad run?—

> " ' On Jura's heath how sweetly swell
>   The murmurs of the mountain bee !
> How softly mourns the writhèd shell
>   Of Jura's shore, its parent sea !
> And softly floating o'er the deep,
>   The Mermaid's sweet sea-soothing lay,
> That charmed the dancing waves to sleep,
>   Before the bark of Colonsay.'

But—seals or mermaids, Murdoch—there's something very human indeed about a phoca, and when one of them sails up to take a look at my tweed wideawake—with that wistful appeal for sympathy in her brown eyes—hang me if I wouldn't miss her on purpose ! "

The neist day was the Sabbath.

It was wan o' the disadvantages of our position that there was nae Free Kirk in the Island.   But the Rev. Peter Mac-Craw,[1] wha ludged at the Inn, spoke on the hillside on Sabbaths during the summer months.   He was gey an' auld, and he cam here for change o' air,—leaving the parish o' Drambogie to the services o' the assistant an' successor that the Presbytery had provided.   "What's the gude o' keepin' a dowg," says he, "if you have to bark yoursel'?"   He was weel acquaint wi' his co-presbyter, Dr Dingweel o' Drumna-drouthy, and he brocht a sermon by the Doctor in his pocket, which he undertook to read us that day.   It was a verra fine discoorse, and was reported in the *Scotsman* paper at the time (wi' nae gude objec', you may be sure), and if I can get a copy o' the paper I wull pit it in a note.   It was upon Robinson Smuth, as you may easily understan',—Dr Dingweel is faithfu' aboon the lave, and disna spare himsel' or his freens.   Wha was Robinson Smuth ?   What call had he to trouble the Kirk ?   What call had he to hamper them wi' the furms o' process ?   A martyr ?   How cud he be a martyr whan he had

---

[1] Peter is wan o' the Parliament Hoose MacCraws,—ye'll mind Angus o' the First Deeveesion ?

keepit every penny o' his steepen'? The Hielanmen kent
weel hoo to answer his rationalcestic deeficulties : yet it was
said that the Hielanmen were behind the age! It micht be
that they had sma' respec' for the unsanctified cleverness o'
the crectic an' the pheclologer ; it micht be that they had sma'
respec' for ony eminence o' learnin' which cud be reached by
scholarship and not by grace ; but they were steadfast an'
immuvable as their ain immuvable mountains, and it was jist
as possible to tie their han's wi' reed tape and the furms o'
process as the wind which sweept the corries o' Cruachan.

"I like that kind of man," said Mr Matthew, as we tramped
hame thro' the heather in the gloamin'—"I like him and his
picturesque irrationality. Yes, Mr Lyell, these old boys retain
what the young ones want ;—they have *character*,—they are
idiomatic as their native proverbs ; and while the insipid,
emasculate, cosmopolitan puppy will be forgotten to-morrow,
the mother wit and the homely saws of these Patriarchal Sages
will be kept in lively remembrance through many a mountain
glen,—for one generation, if not for two. And then they are
part and parcel of a great corporation, and corporations are
cohesive and permanent. The man who cuts himself loose
from the organised prejudices of his contemporaries is a fool
for his pains. For after all, my friends, what and how much
do the wisest of us know? I stand by the immeasurable sea,
and stretch out my hands into the unfathomable darkness ;—
Tendentemque manus ripæ ulterioris amore."

It still wanted a day till the steamer was due. We were
sittin' on the shore near the Red Rocks. The sea at oor
feet was like a sheet o' glass ; phantom islands rose oot o' the
purple mist : on the ither han', the sunset was clear over Newfundlan'. As we sat there we saw a boat comin' stracht from
Jura. We were rather drowsy at the time. There had been
strange soun's heard in the Inn durin' the nicht, which had
broken oor sleep. It seemed as if a' the deevils that passed
into the swine were fechtin' in Gaelic ootside the front door.
"Wan of oor shepherds and wan of the principallest men in
the island had a sort o' misunderstanding," Donald remarked,
whan we saw him in the mornin'. Then there was an auld

bantam-cock an' a young Cheena fule wha began crawin' hours before it was daylicht. Mr Matthew had flung his brushes, and his big boots, and his best breeks, and every article o' furniture in the bedroom, at them oot o' the window; but they crawed as crusely as ever;—it was a competitive competition, and the little wan wud not be beat. Weel, Mr Drumly, the boat cam nearer an' nearer, but the tide was contrar. It got dark an' rayther chilly; so the Sergeant an' Mr Lyell gaed into the hoose. They were jist tellin' the lass to bring the het water ben, whan—

"Mr Robinson Smuth ! ! !" says Donald, openin' the parlour-door.

"Angels and Ministers o' Grace ! ! ! !" says Mr Lyell.

"The Devil ! ! ! ! !" says the Sergeant.

It *was* Himself, Mr Drumly, and he began the conversation wi' perfec' affabeelity in the native tongue. "Αλδ οβορ οντο φοσκο φορν ιο ριγ δυμ φυν ιδος ἠοτον κρο τον θολιγ ος. But, gentlemen, shall I address you in Gaelic or English?" he added, seein' that Mr Lyell did not exackly follow him.

The Sergeant's eyes watered. "It is the goot Gaelic he has. But you will speak the English, sir, if you please—this shentleman has not much of the Gaelic now."

"More's the pity," says he, "for it is the language of skeelful poets and brave men. Gentlemen, I heard you were in the island, and it occurred to me that a few minutes' conversation in private might tend to remove certain misconceptions which——"

"I'm agreeable, Mr Smuth," says the Sergeant, wi' ready politeness. "But you will be takin' your doch-an-dorris before startin'?"

"Not a drop, Sergeant. Wi' sic a keen and wechty controversialist as Mr Lyell——"

The Schoolmaister booed.

Weel, Mr Drumly, they were at it a' nicht. The young lad was maist respectfu', as was only proper and becomin', seein' that the Sergeant and Mr Lyell are men o' age, and wecht in the community. But, Mr Drumly, facks are facks. If Jeeremiah had mair birr than the minor prophets, what's the gude

of sayin' that he had not? If every word o' the Pentateuch
was not written by Moses, whar's the sense of sayin' that it
was? Facks are facks, Mr Drumly.

The sun was risin' over Jura when they shook han's. The
Sergeant and Mr Lyell walked doun wi' him to the pier, whar
the men were lying asleep in their boat. The sail was hoisted;
the oars run oot; and by the time they gat back to the Inn,
only a dim speck was veesible on the water—weel across to
Ardlussa.

They stude at the Inn door for a bit—the mornin' air was
sweet and balmy.

"What do you think, Sergeant?" says Mr Lyell.

"What do you think, Mr Lyell?" says the Sergeant.

"I think we are twa auld fules," says Mr Lyell.

"You will speak for yourself, Andrew Lyell," says the Sergeant, liftin' his leg to munt the stair. "But he is a clever lad
whatever, and it is the goot Gaelic he has."

(*For Mr Lyell.*)
ANGUS GRIERSON,
Probationer in Cawmelton.

* * *

So much for the Sergeant. *R.I.P.* But it is not
the Sergeant alone who has joined the majority; here
is a bundle of pleasant letters addressed to Mr Lyell,
congratulating him on the success of his embassy;
and the writers are all gone,—"fallen upon lasting
silence," as Mr Stevenson says finely. "Doctor John,"
Principal Tulloch, Spencer Baynes, Professor Sellar,
James Brown of Paisley, John Nichol, Patrick Alexander. The ranks of our little army have indeed been
sadly thinned; only a few veterans remain, and round

them the evening shadows are closing in.   Does the horizon widen as we grow old?   Or does the capacity to rise with the lark,—to rise skyward with the lark and share the rapture of her song—belong to the young only?   I fear sometimes that it does.   Yet even the weariest may be permitted to hail and welcome her.   It is our latest poet who writes—

> " My heart is dashed with cares and fears,
>   My song comes fluttering and is gone ;
>   O, high above this home of tears,
>   Eternal joy, sing on."

THE END.

PRINTED BY WILLIAM BLACKWOOD AND SONS.